ESCAPE
through the Pyrenees

E S C A P E
through the Pyrenees

Lisa Fittko   *Translated by David Koblick*

Northwestern University Press   Evanston, Illinois

Northwestern University Press
Evanston, Illinois 60201

First published in German as *Mein Weg über die Pyrenäen* by Carl Hanser
Verlag, Munich. © 1985 by Carl Hanser Verlag. English translation © 1991
by Northwestern University Press. Published 1991 by Northwestern
University Press. All rights reserved.

Printed in the United States of America

This translation was funded with the assistance of the National Endowment
for the Arts.

Library of Congress Cataloging-in-Publication Data

Fittko, Lisa, 1909–
    [Mein Weg über die Pyrenäen. English]
    Escape through the Pyrenees / Lisa Fittko ; translated by David
Koblick.
      p. cm.
    Translation of: Mein Weg über die Pyrenäen.
    ISBN 0-8101-0975-1 (cloth). —ISBN 0-8101-0989-1 (paper)
    1. Fittko, Lisa, 1909–   . 2. World War, 1939–1945—Underground
movements—France. 3. Anti-Nazi movements—France—Biography.
4. World War, 1939-1945—Personal narratives, German. 5. World War,
1939–1945—Refugees. I. Title.
D802.F8F5313 1991
940.53′44—dc20   91-9629
                                                     CIP

Contents

Illustrations

Reproduction of historical documents and original photographs was done by Michael Yonoff.

Acknowledgments

My heartfelt thanks to all those who offered me their support and encouragement to put into this book my memories and my thoughts—to my family, my friends, and especially to Carol T. Williams, who gave me her invaluable help and friendship.

Prologue: Vienna—Berlin

Whenever I rummage through old papers and documents, I come upon something long forgotten. Recently a letter turned up, a letter written in Vienna after World War II. It had been sent to my father in France by Oskar Maurus Fontana: ". . . indeed, when you changed *Die Wage* [The Scales] to *Wage!* [Venture!] after the First World War, we both thought of it as sort of fulfillment for the risks we took. Alas, that happy end has become even more distant—but the fact that you, too, have remained resolute, as I gather from your plans, gives me new courage to carry on. . . ."

Now it all comes back to me.

"Look at the sketch of our new masthead," my father said, "how do you like it?"

I was ten years old. "Now *The Scales* will be called *Venture!?*" I asked, "Why?"

"Do you understand the difference?"

I thought about it. "Is it better to dare and act than to mull things over?"

"One must know when the time comes to be daring," answered my father.

Now and again I recall those words. How does one know when it is time?

There are many things I must reflect upon. I didn't really know what or where Brest Litovsk was, a name often mentioned by my father, Fontana, Egon Erwin Kisch, and the other *Wage!* people; but it didn't take much thinking for me to agree with my father and *Die Wage* that there must never be another war. Why? Well, for one thing, they had had to send me to Holland because of it, and my brother to Denmark, because we were growing so skinny on the soup the Vienna Writers Association doled out to its members and their families.

1

We moved to Berlin, and I liked the Prussian schools even less than I had the Austrian. Especially their teaching of history. The professor named a battle and pointed his finger at a student, who was expected to immediately jump to his feet and state the date; or, for variety, he reversed the order: date—finger—battle. The battle of Teutoburger Woods came up most frequently.

Those history lessons were one of the reasons I joined the Socialist Students League. It had chapters in the Karl Marx School in Neukölln and in other Berlin secondary schools, those attended in the main by students from workers' families. We were an inquisitive lot—we wanted to know everything—not only know, but understand. We went to meetings and demonstrations, to lectures by and discussions with Hermann Duncker, Karl August Wittfogel, August Thalheimer, and Karl Korsch. Once I got involved in a brawl when the Stahlhelm* invaded a Young Socialist Workers meeting.

I was standing by at an election rally when members of the Reichsbanner paramilitary group beat up a handful of Communists with canes, clubs, and brass knuckles because they were interrupting the rally with heckling and shouting. Appalled, I thought, they're just like the Steel Helmets, and felt that I was a coward, that I must do something to stop the brutality—I must take chances, put my life on the line. But how?

I was there on 1 May 1929, "Bloody Mayday," when the Berlin workers held their parade in spite of the prohibition against May Day demonstrations. When the police continued firing into the next day and the workers erected barricades in the Wedding district to protect themselves, I had to go there and see for myself. Suddenly a fat cop started to chase me, but I could run faster, and from a safe distance I shouted at him, "*Mörderer!*" He lifted his carbine, but I was already around the corner. In two days thirty-three young workers were shot to death.

And yet—and yet—it was also a happy Berlin, the Berlin of my memory: the premiere of "The Threepenny Opera" on the Schiffbauerdamm, tickets for which I had gotten from Leo Lania; Friedrich Wolf's "Cyankali"; Brecht's "Kuhle Wampe," in which my friend Martha from Mulakstrasse played a role; the *Bauhaus* and the *Hufeisensiedlung* in Britz, where on Sundays we used to visit the Mühsams and

---

*Right-wing paramilitary organization.

Erich made us laugh with his somewhat indelicate doggerel; the "Blue Angel" and Kurt Tucholsky, Claire Waldoff and Paule Graetz, Walter Mehring, and all the others. Zille and his *Fischerkiez*, where I felt a sense of well-being. And Heinrich Wandt, who—when he wasn't boozed up—opened up to me in the Bülow-Bogen area a secret doorway to the Berlin underworld. It was there that all the former and future jailbirds shook my hand a little too energetically, clapped me on the shoulder, and warned me, *"Wenn de mit unseren Heinrich kommst, Mädchen, biste eene mang uns mang; aber ohne ihn, von wejen . . ."* ["As long as you're with our Heinrich, girl, you're one of our crowd; but without him, you better watch out! . ."].

There were always more and more unemployed in this Berlin, always more hunger. Brown-shirted mobs callously murdered their political opponents and tried to terrorize the city. Still, the Berlin of my memory remains fair and inspiring; we stood ready to defend it from the Nazi menace, and we sang, "Yonder on the horizon stands the Fascist threat, but our day is not far off."

My parents were not very happy with me. My father said: "You are one of those few favored people who can study—you could learn something. Knowledge will be needed most urgently, but you fritter away your time."

"You don't eat regularly, you hardly sleep," my mother said, " because you're always going to meetings and discussions, and because you have to write leaflets. You're ruining your health, and that doesn't help the cause of freedom; you won't be much use in the fight against the Nazis."

"You just don't understand." I answered. "Now everything depends on beating fascism—I can't waste any time with university and pleasant living. You don't know how much I'm learning, often from people who've only gone to elementary school—they understand so much about things which are never mentioned in university seminars. And not in your Romanische Café,* either."

After the burning of the Reichstag on 30 January 1933, when the arrests, tortures, and executions began, I and some friends collected reports that we had received from the torture chambers in Hedemann-strasse and the Columbia House, and from the Oranienburg Camp. Using circuitous routes, we were able to transmit them to presses in

---

*The well-known meeting place of the Berlin intellectual left-wing elite.

London, Paris, and New York. But the world didn't want to listen to us.
We composed leaflets and distributed them. My parents, who had fled,
as many of their friends had done, tried to talk me into following them
to Czechoslovakia. That was out of the question—was this the right
time to give up the fight, to leave my comrades in the lurch?

Three from our little group were arrested while passing out leaflets.
They had assumed, through some misunderstanding, that I had left
Germany. Thus, as was often done in such cases, they put all the blame
on me: they themselves, they testified, were so young and hardly knew
what it was all about. But, the boys asserted, there was this girl named
Lisa, who was so persuasive that they hadn't been able to resist her.
They got off free—but now I really had to disappear at once.

In Prague there were many hundreds of emigrants and dozens of
familiar faces. Bruno Frei of the *Welt am Abend* and Stampfer from
Vorwärts, writers, artists, actors—half of the Romanische Café. Johnny
Heartfield was there, and F. C. Weiskopf, and Kurt Grossmann, who
founded an Emigrants' Committee. Ernst Ottwald ("They know what
they're doing") and his wife, Traute, daughter of a pastor, came to the
evening rounds of discussion. Grete Reiner, who translated Hašek's
The Good Soldier Schweik, always sat with us in the Café Continental,
where one could linger the entire evening over a single cup of coffee.
For meals we bought mostly "Reklami Salami," the cheapest brand of
sausage.

In a former young ladies' boarding school in the Vodičkova, beds
had been set up for homeless emigrés. There I met a Berliner who had
just arrived in Prague. He was a journalist named Hans Fittko who,
due to his "intellectual authorship," had been sentenced to death in
absentia, allegedly for the murder of an SA [*Sturm Abteilung*—Storm
Troopers] man (who in fact had been shot from behind by his own
comrades).

Hans Fittko. Soon we belonged to each other, and we remained
together until his death.

In Prague, too, Hans wrote articles, handbills, and appeals to the
German people. Czech consumer cooperatives helped to produce
them. He went to the border and arranged for the literature to be
transported into Germany. When Masaryk's government expelled him
"for life" for these activities, we both went to Switzerland, where anti-
Fascist literature was already being produced. With the cooperation of

both Social Democrats and Communists, it was possible for us to set up distribution points and to supply all Baden and Württemberg with the literature.

Later, in Holland, on the Frisian border, we worked in a similar fashion. We were in France when war broke out and upon its defeat were caught in the same trap as tens of thousands of German emigrants.

I shall relate that story in greater detail.

1

Paris, May 1940

1

Paris, May 1940

Four days earlier, when the *drôle de guerre* ended and the German onslaught began, big red placards appeared on walls everywhere announcing that all enemy aliens were to be interned in *camps de concentration*. Enemy aliens were *ressortissants allemands*, citizens of Germany. Indeed, although the Nazi regime had stripped us emigrés of our German citizenship, *ressortissant* could also be translated as "coming from Germany." In any case, the French authorities defined us as enemy aliens, and thus we had to be confined in camps. Even the Austrians who had fled to France after the Anschluss had to go to the camps; as Austria was now part of the German Reich, they were also considered *ressortissants*.

Actually, I felt, as did many others, that I belonged in none of these categories, for I had been born under the reign of Emperor Franz Joseph, not in present-day Austria. But the mere mention of this special case had made the police commissioner even more irritable, and he declared, "I decide who is and who isn't German!"

With all other women, I had to present myself at the ice-skating stadium, the Vélodrome d'Hiver. The commissioner had grudgingly added that "everyone will be screened at the entrance by a *commission de criblage*, which will make decisions in borderline cases."

When war broke out in September 1939, the men had been immediately interned in concentration camps. My husband, Hans, and my brother, also named Hans, were among the few who had been released during the winter. Most of those released were either well-known personalities or people with connections. However, there were some among them whose expertise in the arts of survival and escape had enabled them to remain at large—expertise they had gained during the seven years of Nazi rule.

My mother went up the street with me to the bus stop at the end of La Butte Rouge. La Butte Rouge, The Red Hill, was the name of "our" garden city south of Paris. My father and mother were to remain here, as they were exempt from internment because of age.

When the bus came I wanted to say, "Don't worry, Mother, I'll be back soon." But then I thought, no, what's the point of telling Mother such obvious nonsense. So I just gave her a quick kiss and climbed aboard. On the step I turned and waved, and when I saw her standing there alone by the highway, the reddish houses behind her peeking between blossoming trees, I suddenly noticed how small and thin and bowed she was, and that she—all at once I realized that she had grown old. Till then I must have been blind, she had always seemed ageless to me. I swallowed a couple of times, trying to dislodge the lump in my throat.

Paulette and I had arranged to meet in Paris, and some other women friends came with her to accompany us to the Vél' d'Hiv'. As they had children, they weren't to be interned, and some of the others were also exempt—they had been able to prove that they came from nonenemy countries. I was bemused by the fact that they, who were to remain free, seemed to feel more ill-at-ease than we did.

When I thought about it again a few weeks later, during the endless train ride to Gurs, I realized that these women felt isolated, left behind—they had been excluded, that's the word, "excluded" from internment in a concentration camp. Now they were individuals, lone women who belonged nowhere; as war psychosis increased, they were treated more, and more often, as though they were enemies.

We had already seen how French acquaintances suddenly stopped greeting us, just stared at us coldly. Worst of all was being in the air-raid shelters, jammed together with our neighbors during alarms. Our German accent betrayed us; only the children had "unlearned" it. Here, in this country of refuge, should one be treated so shabbily—after all the years of battle against and flight from the Nazis?

Paulette and I wanted to try to stay together. We each had a light suitcase and a haversack rolled up in a blanket. Paulette, practical as always, had made a list of all the things we would need, and we divvied them up between the two of us in order to avoid carrying unnecessary weight. Finally she wrote down what each of us should bring for herself:

Toothbrush
A pot with a handle, a spoon
Lipstick
Razor blades (in case there was no other way out).

We had to show up at the Vél' d'Hiv' between 9 A.M. and 5 P.M. It was still early afternoon, so we didn't have to rush; no pushing and shoving, we said to ourselves. We walked around a bit in the city, sat in a café for awhile, and then took the Métro.

The streets surrounding the Vél' d'Hiv' were packed with standing women; the lines seemed scarcely to move.

"It's going so slow because of the *criblage* [screening]," said a middle-aged woman next to me, and added, "They'll send me back—I've got a doctor's certificate stating that I can't be interned because I have a liver ailment."

"I wish that for you with all my heart," said a woman on the other side of me, "that your liver gives you a way out. As for me, with my kidney trouble—that's much more serious than the liver—surely I'll be sent home immediately."

Everybody was talking all at once.

"I was born on the Polish border, so I'm really not from Germany at all," I heard a faint voice say. It must have belonged to a short woman, for I couldn't see her behind the others.

"My family has the best connections—they'll let me go right away—," a curly-headed blond began.

Another invisible voice broke in, "My husband registered with the Foreign Legion—I don't even belong here."

Several of our acquaintances had slithered in among us, and we were now an entire group of political emigrés. We listened to the talk around us and were astounded at its naïveté, amazed at how each of the speakers believed she was a special case and wouldn't be interned.

"Mine is an especially fortunate case," scoffed my friend Doris. "The police commissioner has given me his word that I'll be set free as soon as the war is over."

We had to laugh at these childish people. And we were angry at them too, because they hadn't learned a thing from seven years of Nazi terror. They couldn't or didn't want to see the connection between their personal destinies and what was happening all over the world; the boundaries of their worlds were limited to themselves. A long time

passed before I realized that the very ones who didn't understand were
the most tragic victims.

Policemen went along the lines giving instructions: "It is forbidden to
bring knives, scissors, or cigarettes with you." Women scrabbled hastily
through their bags and handed over the forbidden articles to whomever
had accompanied them. Paulette had a knife and I had scissors and a
fairly large supply of cigarettes, but we told ourselves that it would be
impossible to search the luggage of thousands of people; at worst,
they'd simply take the things away from us.

Shortly after five o'clock I felt a few raindrops, and a couple of
minutes later it started to pour. Several thousand women were standing
in the driving rain. The policemen ran back and forth ordering:
"Everyone to the entrance and inside! *Vite, vite, dépêchez-vous!* Inspection will take place later." The women tried to run, but in that press of
bodies no one got very far.

Paulette held tight to my arm so that we wouldn't get separated. We
were shoved from behind and I looked for our friends, but they had
disappeared. Why all this panicky jostling? I asked myself. It can't be
that they'd trample each other to death just because of the rain. Perhaps
it was simply that they'd acquired the habit of obeying orders?

"They've really gone crazy!" Paulette yelled in my ear. "Nobody wants
to be the last one in!"

I could scarcely recognize the Vél' d'Hiv'. The last time I'd been
here—it had been some time ago, at a giant rally for the Front Popu-
laire—my ears had rung with the shouts of *"Des Avions—Des Canons—
Pour l'Espagne!"* It was the dress rehearsal for World War II, the Spanish
Civil War. That time the Fascists were victorious.

We wanted to see what was happening in the hall, but it was impossible to do so in that mass of people: a sea of women and a few soldiers
scattered about, observing us in bewilderment. The concrete floor was
covered with straw, allegedly provided by "the Americans," some said
by Quakers; others knew from a more reliable source that the straw had
come from a Jewish aid organization—one woman informed us that she
had firsthand information to that effect. The food would also be
supplied by Americans, as the French authorities had forgotten that we
had to be fed somehow; that last fact was doubted by no one. *Bobards*—
craphouse drivel, but the French word *bobard* sounds a little more

elegant—flew at us from all directions. Our men had already told us about the numerous *bobards* they'd learned in the camps.

Our men. Where were they now?

A few days earlier all of them who were not already in camps had been interned in open stadia, held there in all sorts of weather to await further transport. The luxury of a roof overhead had been reserved for us women, although unfortunately it was a glass cupola. There were antiaircraft batteries all around us; flak fragments would be likely to break through the glass and fall directly on our heads.

In September 1939 we had still been allowed to bring food packets to our men in the Stade Colombe; we handed them over at the gate hoping that they would be passed on. I well remember the long lines of women with their packets. But now we too were locked up. How would we find each other again? And when?

"Many of these men were incapable of coping with primitive conditions," Hans Fittko related later. "How do you protect yourself from the wind and rain, how do you dry your clothes? How do you take hold of a tin bowl of hot coffee without burning your fingers? How do you find the latrine in the dark? Often someone would fall over a bench and break a bone or two.

"After about a week they loaded us on trucks. At that time the German tanks had already broken through. The age-old hatred of the archenemy, *les boches*, weighed heavily on all of us. To the French we emigrés were simply Germans. We came from there, we spoke with the despised *accent boche*. Even during the years of emigration we always remained, in the eyes of many Frenchmen, the *'sales boches.'* And now— we were prisoners, so we must be spies. Probably Nazi parachutists, the ones the newspapers and radio had warned them about.

"Indeed, before the war we had been reviled as warmongers, because France didn't want to hear about Hitler's plans for aggression. But now it was wartime, and the gross distinction between Nazis and anti-Fascists was no longer recognized. We were the enemy.

"We ran to the trucks between the lines of *flics*, and they struck us with their truncheons. I was lucky to get off with just one smack on the back of my head as I jumped up on the truck. I had a headache for days, and it was small consolation to know that the blow was intended for Nazis."

Paulette and I found an unoccupied straw pile big enough for both of us, and tossed our packs onto it. A cloud of dust rose and I had a sneezing-fit. We looked at each other and started to laugh at how we looked standing there with dripping hair, the water running down us and squishing out of our shoes. Paulette's blue linen dress, which I liked so much because it matched her eyes, clung to her body like a turn-of-the-century bathing suit. "This will probably be our last bath for a while," she said, and pointed to the endless lines in front of each toilet.

I can't remember whether food was doled out on that first evening; surely we'd brought some provisions from home. I know that I longed for a cigarette, but there was no thought of smoking with all that straw on the floor. We walked around and were delighted when we saw a familiar face—as one is delighted in a foreign country to meet someone from home.

"Look over there," said Paulette. "No, more to the left; yes, there, up above, it's really Claudia!" Indeed, there sat the "Queen Mother," the famous anti-Fascist journalist, the Potsdam officer's daughter with the Berliners' big mouth. In the midst of dust and dirt, in that noisy, aimlessly milling throng, there she sat high on a pile of straw, slim and blond and bolt upright. She was wearing white gloves.

That scene stayed with us during the following days of pain and peril. Sometimes when we lost heart, one of us would remind the other of those white gloves. We'd laugh over and over again, and the laughter gave us back our courage, courage to do whatever had to be done.

What did they intend to do with us? Were there any plans at all? How long could they hold us here? There were no answers to these questions, we could only guess. In any case, we had to try to keep in contact with those who had remained in Paris. The guards were young soldiers, not as hostile as the policemen outside. We smiled at them, and often one of them could be cajoled into mailing postcards for us.

We heard no more about the promised screening—we knew that it was probably just a bad joke. How could they have examined thousands of cases? It would have been impossible even with the best of intentions, and especially now, when the enemy was breaking through the lines. Our destiny was being decided by bureaucracy and war psychosis.

Most of the women were apolitical Jewish emigrants who had sought asylum in France from persecution at the hands of the Nazis. They were confined along with us, the political refugees of the Nazi opposition, many of whom had fled to escape death and torture.

And then there were the *Reichsdeutschen*, German citizens with valid passports who had for various reasons found themselves on French soil—or in French waters, like the Rhine river boats—when war broke out. Naturally, there were Nazis among these Germans. I think about the scar on my brother's forehead, still visible today; it was put there by Nazis in his camp who beat him up as the German tanks rolled in. But that's another story.

One day a *criblage* was announced after all, and we were told to line up. At the start there was a lot of crowding and shoving; everyone wanted to be among the first. It dragged on for days, and the women gradually became weary and dispirited. Paulette and I wanted to wait until the end, when the lines wouldn't be so long; nothing was going to come out of the *criblage* anyway. We watched the women go past into the doctor's cubicle, often full of confidence, and saw them exit a few minutes later from the other end. A sharp-featured woman from Frankfurt suddenly seemed to be on the verge of collapse, her eyes wandering about without focusing. The doctor had said to her: "Anybody can buy a breast-cancer certificate like this one."

L'enfant infirme, the fourteen-year-old Renée with the long brown pigtails—how did she come to be here? Children under seventeen were not supposed to be interned. She hobbled out of the cubicle on her crutches. In spite of her polio she was found to be *apte*. In the military, *apte* means "fit for duty"—in this case, fit for a concentration camp. "I don't give a royal shit," she laughed, and hobbled away.

Later, Paulette shook me. "Wake up, we have to go."

"Go where?" I'd had a headache all day, and an hour earlier I'd finally fallen asleep on our strawpile.

"To the screening commission. Come on, we have to get in line. Have your papers ready."

I stood up and went with her, still half asleep.

"You look awful," she said. "Your face is all gray. You'll never be able to induce an officer to release you. At least put on a little lipstick."

"That would be a waste. Just look at the way it's going."

We were now in a sort of anteroom to the cubicle where the medical examinations were taking place.

A guard took our papers. The women followed one another into the next room, where two doctors in white smocks were saying: Mouth open—deep breath—*apte*—next! Many of the women tried to hand the doctor a document, others wanted to explain something. The doctors seemed to be deaf, and said only *apte—apte—apte*. The women marched past.

"Doctor, I'm . . . ."

"*Apte*. Next."

"Pardon, may I . . . ?"

"*Apte*. Keep moving."

Now it was Paulette's turn. "Mouth open. *Apte*."

I still had a headache and wasn't yet fully awake. I stepped up to the doctor and opened my mouth.

"*Vous êtes malade, madame?*"

Surely I hadn't heard right.

"Are you ill?" he asked, this time loud and clear.

"*Non, docteur,*" I answered politely. (Paulette, who was still in the room, said later, "You weren't altogether there.")

"Are you really all right?" the doctor went on, "or are you just recovering from an illness?"

Finally I became alert. "Oh yes, I was terribly sick."

He wanted to know what had been wrong with me.

"Peritonitis," I said, and moaned slightly. It was the worst illness that came to mind. It was even true, although it had happened some years back.

"*Exemptée de tout travail,*" the doctor decided, and I was given a voucher stating that I was unable to work.

So many things happened for which there's no explanation.

We'd already been held in the Vél' d'Hiv' for a week. There were air-raid alarms day and night. We didn't have to run to an air-raid shelter for the Vélodrome didn't have one. We didn't pay much attention to whether the sirens sounded an alarm or an all clear, it was all the same to us.

The drone of the bombers. It wasn't shrill like the sirens, but it grated more on our nerves. We didn't look up at the sky to see whose planes they were; the sky wasn't too visible anyway, even through the glass roof. A few times there was a frightful crack as if lightning had struck, and we knew it must be flak fragments falling on our roof. We heard that in a corner of the hall a projectile had fallen through. Were there any injured? Probably—maybe. Rumors, ever rumors.

Sometimes soldiers furtively slipped us a newspaper. It was only a page or two, but topped with scare-headlines and filled with contradictory news items. One thing was clear: the Germans were advancing, breaking through, overrunning northern France.

What were they going to do with us?

After about two weeks the evacuation order arrived: "Get ready, line up, have your papers handy."

Paulette and I waited until the crowd had thinned out. It took hours, and one couldn't see what was happening at the exit. Gradually we moved forward in the line and then saw that there the women were being split into two groups: most of them on the right side, a smaller group on the left.

Paulette stepped up: *à gauche*. To the left.

Then, to me: *à droite*.

Paulette protested. "We belong together, why are we being separated? Why must I go left? What does this all mean?"

An officer explained that we were being transported for our own protection. Wives of French soldiers, however, could not be interned, so they must stay behind. Paulette's papers stated that her husband was in the French army, even though as a *prestataire*, in a unit of foreign volunteers. Paulette was pushed to the left.

Now things started to move faster. My group was directed toward the exit, and I turned to face Paulette. She stood there looking at me, and tears rolled down her face. She's weeping? I thought, surprised. Paulette, who was always ready for anything, who always found a solution. Before I had a chance to call to her, I was hustled away.

"I couldn't rightly understand," I said to her thirty years later, "why you went to pieces that time. Whenever I remembered that moment, I thought, 'If I ever see her again, I'll be sure to ask her.' "

"It was so very important for us to stay together," she answered, "especially right then, when no one knew what was going to happen. Up until then we had been able to share everything, the worry, the uncertainty. Even shared dirt and shared fleas are easier to bear. And together we could turn away fear—we had fun, we were cheerful."

"That's right—we were cheerful indeed."

"Do you remember," she continued, "how even under those terrible circumstances we could always find something to laugh at? How we laughed—we were still young! Remember when the round cheese rolled out of my knapsack, and I chased after it, halfway across the sport palace? And that stammering soldier who had the hots for you, and whose stuttering kept getting worse, and the drunken officer who made a speech? Suddenly it was all over—nothing's half as funny when you're alone. And the thought: What will become of you, and what of me? If that wasn't reason enough to weep. . . ."

The buses waiting for us outside had large signs on their sides: *Réfugiés de la Zone Interdite*, Refugees from the Restricted Zone (northeastern France). I hadn't imagined it would be so grim. Apparently they wanted to avoid our being lynched as strangers or *boches*; indeed, for many Frenchmen there was no difference between the two.

The bus windows were blacked out and we sat on benches, pressed close together. I couldn't see the faces of other women in the dark, but I could feel the fear and anxiety of all around me.

We were unloaded at a freight depot that we guessed must be the Gare d'Austerlitz. Trains for points south left from there. Of course to the south, where else? The Germans were coming from the north.

The trains waiting for us were infinitely long. The cars had probably been shunted here to the freight station so that we wouldn't be seen by the populace. They put ten of us into a compartment meant for six; a soldier slammed and locked the outer door. The door to the corridor, where the toilet was, was also locked. There was only one among us ten whom I'd seen before—Renée, the girl on crutches.

We rode, we rode, we rode on and on, ever farther into the nowhere; I dozed off into fitful sleep overlaid with a stupid dream. How long had we been sitting here in the train? Was this the third night or the second? Once or twice a day a soldier unlocked the door and gave us each a piece of bread, a small can of paté, and water; but it was never enough. I was the only one who had cigarettes, and every hour we lit one and passed it among the smokers; it helped to suppress our hunger. Only morning and evening was the toilet door unlocked.

Once a soldier brought a pot of warm food. "What is it?" a woman asked eagerly, and held out her tin bowl.

The soldier filled it. *"Du singe,"* he said. The woman shuddered, and brown gravy splashed on her dress. The soldier smirked and Renée giggled. Someone explained to us, soldiers call any kind of meat *singe*—monkey-meat.

We tried to read the names of towns, but the train went too fast through the tiny stations. Once it did stop in a city; it was Tours. A great crowd of people milled about on the opposite platform. They shouted curses at us, and many shook their clenched fists; a few stones hit the cars. Then the train gave a jerk and we rolled on.

The ten of us women sat in the compartment half on top of one another, hungry, thirsty, and exhausted. Now and then we vented our fear and anger on each other.

I can still see one of those women in my mind's eye. She was in her forties, a tall and curly-headed blond, with a shrill voice. She talked incessantly and got on everyone's nerves. She spoke only French; perhaps she was here because of a German grandmother. (In public we emigrants had spoken only French since the start of the war—it was unthinkable to speak the enemy's language, for example, in an air-raid shelter during an alarm. Those of us who didn't know enough French just had to keep our mouths shut.)

The big blond had it in for Renée. *"Ah, l'enfant infirme,"* she jeered maliciously. "Look, the poor child has to have the biggest piece of bread."

"Enough of that kind of talk," the others said to her. "Leave the girl in peace." For a while she was silent.

A soldier appeared and unlocked the aisle door. *"Voilà l'enfant infirme,"* she began again, and laughed scornfully. "Poor baby, she must be the first to use the potty."

Renée paid no attention to the woman; she appeared to be deaf to the verbal torment, impervious to harm. Where did she get her strength—did she take courage from her disability? Was she accustomed to such cruelty? During those days and nights in the train she sat in her corner, sometimes chattering away, sometimes sleeping. When she laughed, her brown pigtails danced about her shoulders.

Still the blond didn't let up. "Oh, God," she cried, "the poor crippled child, she needs more room than the others. . . ."

Suddenly a young woman jumped up. She was small and slender; she hadn't said a word until now, and I had mentally dubbed her "the shy one." She stood up in front of the big blond and held a fist before her face. In a surprisingly deep, hoarse voice I heard her say, "You leave the child in peace—one more word, and I'll——!" The locomotive's shriek drowned out the rest. I saw the blond's face twitch; her mouth drooped, and she raised her arms in defense. Then she sank deeper into her seat and began to sob. She'd been silenced, and I'll never really know how. I'll also never know what became of the girl on crutches. Did she survive?

It seemed as if we'd been riding back and forth across the country for days. We asked every soldier who showed himself: Where are we? And where are we going? But all of them only shrugged their shoulders. Perhaps no one really knew where we were being sent.

Then, from afar, I saw a small city. The train slowed down. I went to the window and tried to read the name on the station sign. Oloron-Ste. Marie.

Oloron, I knew the name. During the past year Hans and I had occasionally sent letters and packages to friends there, members of the International Brigades who had fled over the Pyrenees to France after the Fascist victory in Spain. In Oloron they had been rounded up by the French military and placed in an immense concentration camp. The camp was named Gurs and it was in the Basses Pyrénées not far from the town. The notorious "Gurs Inferno." So that's where they had brought us!

The train stopped, doors were unlocked, we got off. There were trains on other tracks as far as one could see, and more arriving. And a sea of women, more and more of them pouring out of the cars. Nowhere a familiar face.

To the women from my compartment I said, "Now I know where they've brought us—to the Gurs Concentration Camp." But I was unprepared for the reaction to my words.

"She's lying!" screamed one woman, and began to cry.

"She wants to scare us!"—"False alarm! They wouldn't do that to us!"—"Don't believe her—it's not true!" There was general hysteria, and I stood in the midst of it, the target of their rage.

At this moment a gendarme approached us. The women fell silent. "Line up! Forward, march! Fast, faster!"

We walked over a narrow bridge. Basque farmwives stood on both sides, their hostile eyes staring at us. Scrawny, malevolent features atop columnar forms, clad in black from chin to ankle. They spat wordlessly and threw stones at us. In a nightmarish dream which recurs from time to time, I see that narrow bridge in Oloron and walk between those walls of hate. In dreams, of course, everything is distorted.

Beyond the bridge the spitting and stone throwing ceased. Trucks were waiting for us. We drove down a long road, and then we saw the endless extent of the camp—the bare, bleak earth and the barracks. We had reached safety, safety behind barbed wire.

2
Gurs, May and June 1940

The women in uniform cried, *"Un-deux, un-deux, un-deux,"* clapping their hands in time, ever faster, *"vite, vite, un-deux,"* and we ran through the opening in the barbed-wire fence. Sobs and complaints had ceased; now one heard only commands, the clapping, and running feet. Fright and running had taken the women's breath away. How can anyone run fast when dead tired—and why did we have to run, anyway? We'd seen the sign over the gate: *Centre d'Accueil,* Reception Center. This was a reception for criminals.

Other uniformed women stood inside the enclosure. They split us into groups and hurried us into barracks. The interiors were long, narrow, and in semidarkness; a cramped aisle ran down the center. On each side were straw pallets laid close together on bare ground, no spaces between them.

Although now no one was rushing us, many women continued to run. In front of me, two women tried to push each other out of the way, and one of them fell, for there wasn't room in the aisle for two persons to pass without stepping on the pallets.

I went to the other end of the barrack. The corner spot was still unoccupied, and I headed for it. I hoped to have more freedom of movement in a corner. As I tossed my bag on the straw sack, someone grabbed me and pulled me back. It was a younger woman, who screamed: "Get away! That's my place!" I felt like taking a swing at her, but suddenly the thought flashed through my mind: What's happening to me—am I going crazy too? I'll not come to blows over a straw mattress! Just the same, as I left I stuck my knees lightly into the hollows of hers, and she fell nose-down onto "her" pallet. I looked for another spot; there were thirty strawsacks on each side of the aisle. It was hard to see, for the only light was from one feeble bulb high in the center of the ceiling. I couldn't even recognize faces familiar to me.

I think that was the 25th of May.

A few days later we'd all found each other again: old acquaintances, several friends. Barracks were changed on the quiet. Political emigrés flocked together—many barracks were completely occupied by a single political group that isolated itself from the others. I thought, Where are the days of the People's Front?

The camp was partitioned into sections—*îlots*—and each section was enclosed by barbed wire. Every *îlot* had twenty-five barracks, each with sixty sleeping-pads. We were in *îlot* "I", and I was now among old friends in Barrack Number 21. Anni, whom I knew from Paris, lay next to me.

"Something in my strawsack is sticking into me," she said, and pulled out a piece of paper on which a few smudged lines had been written. We peered at it together. "Dear girl," it read, "I don't know you, but I've stuffed this straw mattress for you. Sleep well on it. Heinz, a Spanish Freedom Fighter."

The women in uniform who had greeted us with their *un-deux-vite-plus-vite* were actually professional prison guards and had been instructed to treat us as ordinary prisoners. Get up, Line up, *Corvée*, Silence, Lights out. They were forever thinking up special torments for us, mainly in the name of order and cleanliness. Cleanliness. In a camp built on bare clay soil, in which often after a rain one could sink ankle-deep, and where there was scarcely any water. Order. Order where there wasn't a surface to put anything down on, or a nail to hang something on. No place to throw trash—except in the latrines, which weren't deserving of that name and before which endless lines of women stood.

A shallow ditch surrounded each barrack to catch water that ran off the roof. The guards amused themselves by grabbing one of us and making her scramble down into the ditch to pick up a scrap of paper or some other piece of debris with her hands. I amused myself, when I was chosen, by holding under the guard's nose the chit the doctor at Vél' d'Hiv' had given me that read *exemptée de tout travail*—unfit for work.

The overseers appointed fellow prisoners as barrack leaders. At first we wondered who these women were; most of them were young and spoke both languages fluently. Jews they certainly were not, nor could they be classified politically. It seemed that the guards and these young women knew each other, that they were even friends. "Doll," said Maria, who knew her way around, "are you people ever innocent!

They're just whores. Hookers from back home who were working the
Paris streets."

Our new leaders took charge immediately. "Keep walking—Remain
standing—Clear the barracks—Back into the barracks." Many of them
were even harsher than the French prison guards. It soon became clear
that they also served the guards as informers.

It was forbidden to speak through the barbed wire with the women in
the neighboring sections. It was forbidden to have newspapers.
Receiving mail was forbidden, nor could we send mail out. All contact
with the outside world was forbidden. The Nazi hordes were advancing
and we were locked away in the Pyrenees. Europe was falling apart and
we were locked out.

Some of the women spoke up and said that we should try to do something about conditions in the camp. I thought, At last! It's about time. I
said, "If we want to get anywhere, we have to take some action—okay,
how do we start?" But it wasn't that simple, for many had doubts and
others didn't even want to hear about it.

Via a sentry, a couple of women had sent a letter of complaint to the
camp commandant. They'd enclosed a dead bedbug to illustrate the
unhygienic conditions. The next day a soldier handed them a note from
the commandant: "If the French bedbugs don't suit you, ladies, may I
recommend that you try those in a German concentration camp." We
weren't going to get through to him so easily.

Political emigrés in other sections approached us about organizing a
protest. It required patience and care to communicate through the wire
mesh. A sentry walked back and forth between the *îlots,* and when he
was at the far end one could call over to the next one, loud enough to be
understood but not loud enough for the sentry to hear.

We put together a delegation from the various sections. We picked
prominent women, well-known names, leading personalities of the
German emigration: intellectuals, actresses, leaders of emigré organizations. Debates about the duties of the delegation were difficult and often
vehement. Many simply rejected outright any contact with the camp
administration: "They're just henchmen of the French Reaction, to
whom we anti-Nazis are worse enemies than the Nazis."

"True," admitted others, "but if they allow us to protest against the
treatment here, then let's go ahead and do it!"

"Don't you see that you'll be dealing with the very same people who have reviled us emigrés as a fifth column so that they could incite the French public against us? They haven't locked us up here by mistake."

"The delegation should complain about abuses. It's one thing that the government has shut us up in a concentration camp along with Nazis. But the fact that this camp is inadequate for housing ten thousand women, that's another thing entirely."

(Gurs had been built in 1939. When hundreds of thousands of Spanish Republicans fled from the Fascists over the Pyrenees to France, a large area of bare earth near Oloron was enclosed in barbed wire and the fugitives shut inside. Little by little, material was procured with which the Spaniards put up primitive barracks. Among the Republican troops were men of the International Brigades, and among *them*, the German emigrés who'd fought on the Republican side. I can still hear their song:

> Doch wir haben die Heimat nicht verloren
> Unsre Heimat ist heute vor Madrid. . . .

> [For all that we haven't lost the Homeland
> Today our Homeland is here before Madrid. . . .]

During recent months those among them who had registered to work in war-labor gangs had been released from the camp. Those who elected to remain in Gurs were consolidated in the first two *îlots,* at a respectable distance from us women.

A story went around that in mid-May the commandant had received a phone call from Paris: "We're sending you ten thousand women to be interned. Hello, hello?" The official in Paris waited in vain for a response; he heard only a dull thud—the commandant had fainted dead away.)

The delegation should protest above all about the prohibition of mail and newspapers. Nothing could possibly warrant that opponents and victims of persecution of the Third Reich should be cut off from the world. The other demand was: self-government. We had been brought here ostensibly for our own protection, and now we were being treated like convicts. We could keep better order ourselves.

The next day the delegation was escorted to the commandant. After about an hour we saw the guards bringing them back along the dusty street. Soon afterward their report traveled swiftly through the barbed-wire mesh, from section to section, mouth to mouth.

The commandant had stated as the reason for the news blackout and the "strict surveillance" the fact that although some of the women sent to him were emigrés persecuted for political and other reasons, there was also a large number of *Reichsdeutsche,* therefore enemy aliens. Among them were doubtless many Nazis, and very probably a number of spies.

"I'm not responsible for mixing Nazis with their opponents, but I do have responsibility for security measures." He didn't show the slightest trace of understanding.

When one of the women introduced herself as a member of the Human Rights League, he shouted at her, "These pacifists, the antimilitarists, they bear the guilt for this war!"

The women didn't let it go at that; they stuck to their demands, reminding the commandant of France's tradition of sanctuary for the persecuted.

As long as there were enemy aliens among the prisoners, the commandant replied curtly, he couldn't alter the existing regulations. The camp administration had no way of distinguishing them from the anti-Nazis. Did we, the ones persecuted, want to take over the job of separating the Nazis from the emigrants? Under supervision of the *commissaire spécial de police,* he added as a by-the-way. If we would conduct an investigation throughout the whole camp and cull out the *Reichsdeutsche,* then he could give us access to newspapers. "Make a list of political refugees for me, a list of the other emigrants, and one of the enemy aliens."

"We're not French police," the delegates replied, "we're prisoners, we won't make any lists; it's not our job to make decisions about other inmates. But among ourselves we could easily cope with the Nazis—if we had self-government, the camp administration would have no worries on that score."

He would think the situation over, said the commandant, and with that he ended the discussion.

The next day notices hung at the entrances to the *îlots*: "Each barrack is to elect a leader. Guards will restrict themselves to administrative work. Signed: Camp Commandant."

It was a mild evening, and we sat outside in the twilight. Since the posting of the new regulations we had until 10 P.M. to return to barracks. I thought: If you closed your eyes, you could believe you were sitting in a park. Talking and laughter, whispers and snickering. Two women squabbled, and somewhere in the distance someone was singing. It struck me for the first time that even here in Gurs everyday life was going on as usual.

Marianne asked, "See that group over there?"

"The ones sitting in a circle?" I tried to recognize figures and appearances. "Aren't they the Nazis who flocked together in a barrack at the other end of the *îlot?*"

"Right. One of them is rather tall, with coiled blond plaits and a face like a horse. Watch out for her; she's been trying to make up to our people. She doesn't know you—you want to try to hear what they're talking about?"

At first I could only make out isolated words. I heard *"Judenbande"* and *"der Fuehrer."* They didn't notice me and I slunk a bit nearer. The one with the horseface seemed to be giving instructions. I heard, "carefully observed, especially the people in that barrack there . . . make a report. . . ."

From then on, whenever "Horseface" appeared, the word went out: "Caution! Nazi stool-pigeon!" After a while she didn't show up around us any more. The other Nazis were also easy to spot, and we organized our own warning system.

We started talking about barbed wire again. The nonpolitical emigrants found it hardest to bear—the tangle of wire had become a symbol for them. "How can they degrade us so? It makes a person feel like a dirty criminal—the humiliation, that's the part most difficult to tolerate—."

My young Berlin friend Sala stood next to me and asked: "Barbed wire? That humiliates you? Shouldn't I also feel degraded, sent to a German concentration camp because I distributed flyers against the Nazis?"

I couldn't remain silent. "We, degraded? Who locked us up here? France, England, they all courted Hitler's favor while we fought against the Nazis. We hate the barbed wire because it robs us of our freedom. A symbol? It's symbolic of the mentality that imprisoned anti-Fascists behind it."

"Well, it isn't all that bad," shrugged a chubby blond, "the latest notice states that we're interned only *pour la durée de la guerre*."

"Only *pour la durée*? And you're happy about that?" I asked in amazement. "How long do you think *la durée* is going to be?"

"Oh, not much longer; we'll beat the Germans soon." *We,* said the peroxide blond; above all, she was surely worrying about her hair, dreading the embarrassment she'd feel when its natural color had grown out. I still recall Dita Parlo, whose famous golden blond hair slowly revealed itself from top to bottom as dark brown. Remarkable, how one retains the memory of such trivial things—perhaps because it seemed so absurd at the time, to see Dita in a French concentration camp, the German farmwife who had concealed French officers in the film *La Grande Illusion*.

Not only hair color, but general beautification played a major role at the camp. I remember how amused I was when I had visited my husband in the Vernuche Camp during the previous winter in spite of the ban on such visits. The men looked terrible, with their stubble and their hair grown wild, and as I came closer they all ran off. Gradually, one by one, they appeared again, carefully combed and shaven.

But in Gurs, after the initial shock, the women often spent hours on their morning toilette. It was an astounding scene: I entered a dimly lit barrack where women were sitting on straw pallets from which arose clouds of dust; clods of dried mud littered the floor. The women were making up their faces carefully, pencilling eyebrows, rolling up their hair. Many hired a *friseuse,* a hairdresser, another internee who came each day to comb their tresses.

At noon there were always several women standing out in the open, for at twelve o'clock every day a small plane flew low over the camp. First from one end to the other, then back and forth across it. The women laughed and waved; one of them swore that the pilot waved to her in return. They were unanimous in believing that he was young and fabulously handsome. The women got great enjoyment out of this, but only halfway, not entirely. "It's all nonsense," said a young woman standing next to me, "but then, everyone needs to have a good laugh once in a while."

Every morning I took a random ramble through the camp. It had rained and my shoes kept sticking in the mud, so I took them off and continued my walk barefoot. They were my only shoes—I was wearing them when we were interned in Paris. Once they had been beautiful shoes made of red and blue suede, but now they were coated with loam, and the left sole was tied on with a piece of string. The trouble with going barefoot was that there'd be no wash water until the next morning. But then, if I let my feet dry in the sun, the mud would flake off and I could enter the barrack again.

Here and there groups of women sat or squatted together. Now new discussion groups and classes were being formed every day, in which every possible subject was taught and discussed. I stayed with one of the largest groups, some twenty women; it was a course in English. "Most of my students have a sponsor's affidavit, and want to prepare themselves for America," the teacher said to me later. "Will they ever get there? Right now that doesn't matter. They study English because it means that there is a future for them, and if a future exists, one doesn't get so easily demoralized."

I am at a spot in the farthest rear corner of the *îlot,* wanting to take a look at it by daylight. The earth is freshly turned, there's no doubt about it. No, it's not my imagination—but it's also no proof that what's being whispered about is really true. Of course, the Ruhr Epidemic, dysentery, has become disastrous; it's certainly credible that at night dead are being buried here. That is the worst of all: it's no longer possible to differentiate between reality and the most fantastic rumors.

It's time for my rendezvous with the Spaniard at the other end of the *îlot.* I don't know his name; he and one other prisoner come each day to repair leaks in the barrack roofs. It's strictly forbidden for us to speak with the men. We no longer give a thought to all the things which are forbidden—almost everything. For example, the possession of nails. Nails make life a little easier, here you learn to treasure them. You can drive a nail into the wall above your pallet or on a post, and hang things on it.

The first time I chanced to walk by the Spaniard, he was just standing there; his toolbox stood near him. I saw something glitter: nails! I looked at the Spaniard and he looked at me, and I was sure that we understood each other. I took a quick look around—no guard, no soldier. Then I kept on sauntering. One knee-bend as I walked, and I had a handful of nails and screws! The Spaniard was watching a cloud. Every day after that he set his toolbox down at the same time in the same spot, and soon I'd supplied several barracks with my booty. I'd never known that stealing could make a person so exceedingly happy. It seemed to please him, too, and he no longer gazed at the clouds.

A young woman in a white smock with a red cross on the sleeve hurried through the *îlot*. At last and at least they're giving us a medical orderly, I thought. The woman's bony frame and short-cut dark hair seemed somehow familiar, and I followed her; she had stopped to give an ill woman a drink of water. Indeed, it was Ruth! I hadn't seen her since Berlin, where she had been hurrying around just as busily as she was here.

"Have you become a nurse?" I asked, astonished.

"Not at all! A woman from the 'Puff-Barrack'—you know, *those* women—donated the smock. She'd brought it along as a dressing gown. We cut the red cross from a head-scarf and sewed it on. You won't believe what a 'uniform' like this does for one. People pay attention to me, listen to what I say—they've even turned an empty barrack over to me, to house the ill ones. Some women help to bring the weak and sick to the latrine, especially at night. Tomorrow I'm going to try to get an exit pass—maybe I can buy some aspirin and cough-drops somewhere outside. If one could only find some remedy for this cursed Ruhr Epidemic!"

"*Sanitäter!*" someone called from another barrack, and Ruth hurried away.

Sixteen-year-old Gisela was the youngest in our barrack. A week after we had arrived, a transport pulled in full of emigrants and emigrés the police had evacuated from Paris hospitals. Among them were cancer patients in the terminal stages, and Gisela's mother was one of these.

Once I asked Gisela about her family. "My father was beaten to death by the Nazis. I was there, I saw it. My brother fought in Spain with the International Brigades and was killed."

Each morning if the sun was shining, Gisela brought her blanket outside and spread it smooth. Carefully she lifted her mother in her arms and carried her out to the blanket. She neither wanted nor needed help, for she was tall and strong, her mother thin and frail. Gisela sat next to her, stroked her hair, and spoke softly to her. After some ten days of this her mother died.

I knew little more about Gisela, for she seldom spoke. I never saw her laugh or weep.

Back then it was said, and many still say it today, that everything, all that happened, was the fault of bureaucracy.

One lot of women came from the Riviera. In the previous two years, as the flood of Austrian refugees reached France, these emigrants were not allowed to remain in Paris. Many were sent south, where they settled temporarily. Now they'd been brought to Gurs. It seemed to us as if these newcomers were especially distressed at their first sight of the camp.

Then a long bus-caravan arrived. It stopped near our section, and we stood at the barbed wire and watched as the women were unloaded. We recognized someone here and there, and we soon knew that these were women who had been left behind in the Paris Vél' d'Hiv', women who hadn't been interned because they were married to French soldiers.

I saw Paulette and called to her, but she didn't hear me through the engine noise and the buzz of voices. Her group was brought to "K" section, directly across from ours, separated from it by only a narrow sentry path lined on each side by a barbed-wire fence. By the next day we'd made contact and exchanged information through the fence. When the sentry was at the far end we could utter a few quick sentences, just loud enough for us, but not for the sentry, to hear.

Paulette remembers:

"When the train stopped in Oloron and I saw the mountains, the Pyrenees, I knew that they'd brought us to Gurs, where the Spanish fighters had been interned. When we got off, the women were told they'd be put up in hotels. There was an elegantly dressed woman with a daughter, who spoke agitatedly to a guard, asking where she could find a telephone. The soldier said that she must wait here, but he'd be glad to make a call for her. Please reserve a double room with bath in one of the better hotels, she told him. The soldier left and returned a few minutes later. It's all arranged, your room is reserved. Thanks, the woman said, and calmed down. Then they loaded us into buses.

"Do you remember the first time you saw it? That flat, endless, swampy tract, split down the middle by an arrow-straight road. The *îlots* on both sides, each with its rectangular perimeter of high, thick-woven barbed-wire barrier. And in each of these sections geometric rows of wooden barracks. Barracks, barracks to the invisible horizon. Nothing but barracks. How bleak that was, how disheartening!

"The buses stopped in front of various *îlots*. Some of the women screamed hysterically. Many sobbed in despair, many were numb with shock. I looked around for the woman with the hotel reservation; she was bawling like a child.

"Later, you asked me through the barbed wire: 'And you?' Me, I knew about Gurs, but I hadn't imagined it would be like this. Then I thought: If the men could endure it here for fifteen months, I can endure it too. No, I didn't cry.

"By the way, do you know that Oloron is a beautiful old town laid out on a plateau? Of course, I first discovered that fact when I returned there thirty years later. In the interval Gurs had disappeared—not a trace of it was left. Only the memory."

Some of the women from this last Paris transport were now in our compound. We bombarded them with questions, and they told what they knew. That wasn't much, but they'd seen a newspaper occasionally, and had spoken with the guards. There had been no contact with people outside the Vél' d'Hiv'.

"Nobody knows what's happening," they said, "except that the Germans are advancing lightning-fast. There are rumors that they're not far from Paris."

"Do you believe that?" we asked, and looked at them anxiously. They answered by shrugging and shaking their heads.

Said one of the women: "I have a friend in the *préfecture*. He was able to visit me on our last day in the Vél' d'Hiv'. He said only that they were moving us out of Paris in great haste in order to bring us to safety."

The women from Paris also said that there was panic among the emigrés who were still at liberty. They'd heard that from news that had been smuggled in and from single individuals who had arrived later. Reportedly, lines stood daily in front of the Vél' d'Hiv', lines of women who wanted to get in so that they would be transported south.

"Do you believe that?" we asked again, "Those are only rumors, aren't they?"

"No," they answered, "it's surely true. You just can't imagine how the foreigner psychosis has taken hold. We German emigrés are now the enemy; we're spies and Hitler's agents, otherwise they wouldn't be locking us up. We're the fifth column, we're even coming down by parachute. In Paris newspapers there were headlines like: PARACHUTISTS OVER THE OPERA—FIFTH COLUMN IN NUNS' HABITS. Ever since no nun feels safe in Paris."

Paulette and I stood opposite each other, each in her own barbed-wire corner. The sentry walked back and forth, and we waited until he was at the far end. In brief spurts she told me: "When the train stopped enroute, people threw stones at us . . . they yelled *sales boches, métèques, cinquième colonne* [dirty Germans, aliens, fifth column]. . . . "

"Watch it, he's coming!" The sentry passed and turned.

Paulette asked: "Who else is in your section? Martha?"

"Yes, and other political activists. And in yours?"

"In ours, too. The *commissaire* wants to. . . ." There was a voice behind me, and it was hard to understand what Paulette was saying.

"What does he want?"

"A list. He wants us to make a list for him."

"Paulette, don't make any lists."

"Don't worry, not a chance."

Someone behind me kept interjecting: "Which activists? Why does he want lists? Lists of whom?"

The interruptions annoyed me. "Wait a moment," I said, and turned to glare at the woman, "*Hören Sie denn nicht* [Stop eavesdropping]——" My mouth fell open; it was my cousin Ili.

I'd last seen Ili in Paris some two years earlier, after she'd fled to France from Vienna. She'd told us then about the "Anschluss" in Vienna.

There had been shouts and racket in the street and she looked out. The Nazis were dragging Jewish women out of their houses and making them get down and clean the pavement. Ili threw on her mink coat and went out into the street with head held high.

"Give me a broom," she ordered two of the Nazis, who were goading the women with shouts of "Jewish sow!"

The two looked in confusion at her imposing figure. "But not you, gracious lady," one of them stuttered.

"I'm a Jewess," Ili said firmly, "and I insist on sweeping up just as the others are doing. The broom, or I'll lodge a complaint." The Nazis pulled back and left that street for another time.

She couldn't remain in Paris and so she moved down to the south of France. Now, in Gurs, she continued the tale—this time about how it went on the Riviera. There were many emigrants there who'd formerly moved in "better circles," and some of them still had money. Political emigrés, however, were mainly intellectuals—German writers and artists now without a homeland—whose life in exile was especially difficult.

As elsewhere, the men had already been taken away. Now the women were told that for their own safety they would be taken to a lovely mountain village where cottages awaited them. In my opinion they could hardly have believed that, for they already knew about the camps where the men were.

"The intellect refuses to accept the inconceivable," said Ili. "Just imagine, there was a woman in our transport who'd brought along her serving-maid from Nice."

We called them the "Riviera-women." Of course, all who came from there were not Riviera-women. I recall that in Gurs, Ili was exactly the way I'd always known her to be; she had to know and to understand everything. Dirt and hunger couldn't smother her temperament nor dampen her humor. After a few days she took out a painting kit she'd brought with her and sat out in the open with it. That was something new, and the others stood around and gaped at her. The next day she began to teach a drawing class, which soon had greater attendance than the English lessons. Whenever I came into the vicinity of her barrack, something was going on. Women hurried back and forth, busying themselves to make their lives more bearable, more interesting. I still remember that every time I came by, Ili gave me a piece of chocolate from her stores. Only someone who was in Gurs could appreciate the value of such generosity.

The main daily meal was *pois chiches,* chick-peas. Except for one piece of bread per day, they were our sole nourishment. Chick-peas are little stone-hard spheres that must be soaked in water overnight to soften them before cooking them for hours to make them edible. But we had no cooking-pots for that purpose—what pots we had were used in the mornings for the nauseous slop they called *ersatz*-coffee, and how and when could you prepare chick-pea soup for some thousand humans in our section? So, food was a ladleful of warm murky water in which these pebbles floated, pebbles one had to swallow whole. How I hated those chick-peas! Every day I had to force myself to gulp them down.

Paulette remembers:

"The chick-peas were horrible. But we were so hungry that there were never enough. Every day I counted how many were swimming around on my plate. Mostly there were fourteen or fifteen, and once in a great while sixteen. Sometimes there was also a piece of half-spoiled cabbage leaf or a slice of carrot among the chick-peas.

"I was the one who cut the bread, because I had a good eye for measurement. The white bread we got each morning was for six women, and that sixth-of-a-loaf had to last all day. The others stood around, and as soon as I touched knife to bread, from all sides came: 'That's too large!' and 'Now it's too small,' then' 'No—bigger, much bigger!' Each of them was afraid she'd get a skimpy share. That was the most important happening of the day, divvying up the bread."

I remember how every morning I was confronted with the decision: How much bread should I eat right now? If I eat a two-finger-thick slice, will there be enough left for noon and evening? Maybe I can get by with a slice a little thinner—then I'll still have a piece before I go to sleep, when I'm the hungriest.

One had to keep careful watch over the bread during the day. Mine was stolen only once, and the thief was a woman from another barrack. It was my own fault, I'd left it out in plain sight.

Martha believed that it was the chick-peas which caused her so much pain, pain that had to do with her gallbladder. We wanted to help her somehow, but there were no doctors nor any medicine. I still see her lying there in front of the barrack on an old blanket, her slightly graying hair spread smoothly back from her head.

"There's a woman here," she told me, "who goes among the sick ones every day and lays her hands on them. She's convinced that she has healing power. Naturally I don't believe in that hocus-pocus. I can't explain it to myself, but when she puts her hands on my belly, here at this spot, I can feel how the pressure eases."

Martha was somewhat older than we were. She still knew many from the early socialist youth movement. Whenever I think of her, the epithet *The Hell of Gurs* goes through my mind.

One day the nuns arrived. They came in two buses, and they were put in our section. We all stood at the wire-mesh and watched as they got out. The dusty street swarmed with black-clad figures. They were distributed among several barracks, but one of them, probably a Mother Superior, parleyed with the chief wardress, and they were given an empty barrack for themselves. I noticed some unusual activity going on and took a curious peek inside; they were trying to hang curtains up between the strawsacks—bedsheets, coverlets, and rags of all kinds which they hung from the rafters.

"Why are they doing that?" I asked one of my Catholic friends.

"They must not see each other when they undress," she explained. I found that highly amusing.

Later I asked a few nuns why they had been brought here. Did they come from Germany?

"We're from Alsace," they replied. I thought so, I could tell from their accent. But hadn't Alsatians been French since the last war? Why were they being interned? Yes, that's just what they didn't understand. All of them were orphans who had been brought up in the convent; they had still been children when Alsace fell to France after the First World War. Thereafter they remained in the convent and became nuns.

A week earlier the police had come to the cloister and called out their names. When they were all assembled there together, they were told to pack their possessions and come along. They were unable to comprehend it. You're all enemy aliens, *ressortissants allemands,* they were told, so you must go to a camp. The Mother Superior had demanded an explanation and the chief of police was consulted.

The records show, he explained, that the nuns were born in Germany, not in Alsace, and apparently did not become French citizens in 1920. He admitted that this was peculiar. Should it all be due to an error, it would be rectified at the camp. He was only following orders and doing his duty.

The next day the nuns came to my notice again. There was the usual pushing and jostling when food was doled out, the customary arguing, shoving, and verbal abuse. As I walked by I heard someone say, "Please go on ahead, we can wait," and three smiling nuns stepped aside to make room for the women behind them. Such behavior was completely out of place here; the other women looked at the three nuns almost in terror, and the commotion came to a halt.

"Weren't you hungry then?" I asked one of the nuns later.

"It really didn't matter to us. The other women surely hadn't had proper food to eat for a long time."

I had imagined that nuns concerned themselves solely with devout and pious acts, and now it turned out that these at least took the concept of charity seriously. Astounding!

Then I considered our barrack, and how natural it was to me that there was no quarreling over food in Number 21. The solidarity among us anti-Fascists was stronger than hunger—common convictions held us together. We'd also had practice in fending for ourselves. A large pot was "requisitioned," I don't know from where, and food for us sixty women was put inside it and portioned out. If there was any left over, it was given to the gauntest and weakest among us.

I remember that one day I stopped eating. I could no longer stand to see and smell the slop with the hard pellets; perhaps my stomach refused to participate. I just lay on my strawsack when the broth was doled out. I had no interest in food, I felt no hunger. Anni, my pallet-neighbor, brought me my portion. "I don't want any," I said, "you eat my share."

"Nonsense," she said, "don't be silly. The most important thing is for all of us here to pull through."

I knew then that Anni couldn't have had enough. But the solidarity was stronger than hunger. Brecht's words ran through my head:

> . . . und nicht vergessen
> worin unsre Stärke besteht.
> Beim Hungern und beim Essen:
> die Solidarität.

> [". . . and never forget
> our strength lies in this key.
> Through hungering or feasting:
> it's solidarity."]

Incidently, the nuns weren't the only ones by a long shot who didn't know they were German. I particularly remember one of the women in this jumbled multitude of human beings. She understood not a word of German. I asked her how old she'd been when she came to France.

"I'm French," she said, "born here. I've never been out of the country. Certainly never in Germany."

"Then how can you be interned here?" I asked, "and———."

"That's what I asked the police when they picked me up," she broke in, and waved her hand wildly before my face, as if I were a cop, "'Scram,' I told them, *fichez-moi le camp!*' Then they showed me the records. I'd almost forgotten, it was so long ago; I was only eighteen years old and a real innocent—I was so in love with this German and we got married right away. It only lasted a few months, he wasn't worth it, *ce sale boche*. Now they maintain that I have both French and German citizenship. Anyone can do something stupid when she's young, she makes mistakes—but they can't, or shouldn't, lock a person up because she did!"

Out in the open, along the barbed wire on the road side, stood long feeding troughs. Above and parallel to them hung a thick pipe with water spigots, actually only holes, at about one-meter intervals. Those were our washing arrangements. Only in the morning was there water, and sometimes it only flowed in driblets. In these two hours more than a thousand women in our *îlot* had to wash themselves and their belongings.

The cursed soldiers were the worst annoyance. During the washing period they patrolled right in the vicinity of the wash-troughs, back and forth, nearer and nearer.

"It wouldn't pay for them to watch me," said a woman next to me. We looked at her enviously: she had a raincoat, the only garment she wore while washing. There were women who simply couldn't manage to wash themselves under the leering, ogling eyes of the *armée glorieuse*. They tried by grotesquely wriggling and squirming to cover themselves with their towels, above and below, then behind and in front. Others calmly shed their clothes. "Like they don't exist," said a Viennese woman.

There wasn't much left of the soap we'd brought with us, so we used it sparingly, for we couldn't buy more. Actually, there was a black market in soap, but the sole method of payment was work. Those who had none washed the clothes of the soap-owners in exchange for an extra piece of soap with which they could do their own laundry and also the laundry of others, who in turn paid with edibles or other things.

Later there was a canteen run by the wardresses; there one had to pay with money. You could, for example, order an egg, a carrot, or a tomato (especially a tomato, for it would protect you from vitamin deficiency). The wardresses fixed a price, and one had to pay them in advance. Then one waited until they could deliver the order, sometimes for days—and sometimes it didn't come at all. The money was never refunded.

Paulette remembers the latrine:

"It was a wooden platform supported by thick piles about two meters high. Rough wooden stairs without handrails led up to it. There were round holes in the platform, separated by small boards reaching about waist-high. Huge metal containers stood under the holes. When you came up the steps you had an unavoidable view of the women squatting over the holes without anything to hold on to.

"For us these steps weren't worst of all, but there were older women and sick ones. I can't forget the first evening. We were standing in line, and I saw an older woman standing at the foot of the steps and weeping, 'I can't do it, I can't get up the stairs.' I took her arm and led her up the steps and spoke encouragingly to her, but it was so sad that I almost wept myself. How often one saw women standing there helplessly. They had tried to climb the steps but couldn't until someone helped them. Sometimes one fell back down. How many tears were shed at those latrine stairs!

"Often older women had to go at night, and that was always a catastrophe. We weren't allowed to leave the barrack at night, and even when one risked it, she could scarcely find her way in the dark. When it had rained, one sank in mud up to one's ankles. I remember agitated discussions about whether we should allow potties in the barracks for these women, although windows couldn't be opened and the doors must remain closed during the night.

"Latrine containers were collected in the mornings. Outside the camp, right along the wire entanglement, narrow-gauge tracks were laid. Manned by Spaniards, a little train with small flat-bed cars ran from *îlot* to *îlot*. When the train came we called to the women up on the latrine:

'Quickly, make haste, the Gold-Express is coming!' Then the train stopped, the Spaniards jumped off and went to the latrines. Women stood along the barbed-wire fence and the men smiled at them.

"At one end of the fence was a narrow strip of brownish grass and dusty dandelions. Sometimes we went there; you had to hold your nose with one hand because of the stench from the open Gold-Express. With the other hand we plucked dandelions and threw them to the Spaniards. The men laughed and blew us kisses. They hadn't seen a woman for more than a year, and now there were thousands of them."

Loud voices woke me. The barrack doors were open. Women were all talking at once, but no one knew what was happening. I heard whispering nearby: The Germans . . . ? Luftwaffe . . . Stukas. . . . I sprang up and went outside.

Women were standing around outside, soldiers among them. I went up to one of the larger groups. I heard a man's voice and stood on tiptoe to see what was going on. It was the *commissaire spécial,* his cap pushed back from his forehead, speaking quickly and excitedly. I pushed nearer in order to understand what he was saying.

"My lists . . . the Nazis . . . they've stolen the lists."

A woman's voice called: "What kind of lists are they? Whose names are on them?"

"Very important lists," he replied, "strictly confidential material which could be dangerous in the hands of the enemy." For that reason all of us should help him find the lists.

I walked back and thought it over. No one really knew what this *commissaire* had done. We could do nothing about it anyway, we just had to stay alert. Then it occurred to me that on the previous evening at the fence Paulette had wanted to say something; she'd started to speak a couple of times and then broken off. Once she said, "No, right now I can't say anything." Could Paulette have had something to do with this affair?

"When the mail restriction was lifted," recalled Paulette, "there was great joyfulness and hope. Now one could make contact with one's family again, and packages could be sent and received. It sounds nice indeed, I thought, that now we're allowed to send and receive mail—but what good is that permission if the country is overrun by Germans and there are no more transport facilities? Still, when they sought a volunteer to work in the newly set-up post office in our *îlot,* I signed up, for I thought the work would help pass the time. I like to meet new people too, and I'd surely see many things.

"So every day for a few hours I sat at the rickety wooden table they'd placed in the corner of the Administration barrack. Women from the section came with their letters, which had to remain unsealed, and I sold them stamps. I was so certain that the postal service was no longer functioning that I didn't even write to my mother in Paris. And you surely know how worried I was about her.

"There were some better-off women we named 'high society' living together in one barrack we called the 'Puff-Barrack,' because the women had such pretty things, wore elegant lingerie, and were incessantly preoccupied with their own beauty. Many of them also wore expensive perfume, which blended with the stench from the latrines. Now these women were sending one telegram after another to family and friends, asking for help. Nobody received a reply. But every evening, accompanied by a sentry, I went to the central Administration barrack to hand over the letters and telegrams.

"One time I went into our mail barrack to wait for the sentry who had to accompany me. That was when the Germans were getting ever closer, as we already knew. On my table I saw a stack of papers—they were lists, lists of names. Some were names of political emigrés I knew. I had no time to read further, for I heard the soldier coming. I shoved the papers inside my blouse, and we left.

"In the evening there was a big uproar. Do you remember that evening, Lisa? The *commissaire spécial* came to the section looking for his lists. I sweated a little and thought, If only they don't search me! He and the soldiers ran around overturning everything; he obviously couldn't remember where he'd left the lists. I sat on my strawsack and thought up explanations in case I was cross-examined.

"After a while the *commissaire* sent someone to the barrack to fetch me. The lists were still in my blouse, for I didn't want to let them out of my sight. He asked whether I'd seen some papers with names on them. 'Perhaps on your table,' he suggested. I acted greatly surprised, and answered, 'Don't you remember—when you came to the Administration barrack, I was just going out with the sentry. I didn't come back there afterward.' He seemed to believe me, but he was terribly nervous, and made vague insinuations that perhaps 'the Nazis are at the bottom of it.'

"I thought: Now it's high time to make the papers disappear, no matter what kind of lists they are. They could have been names of women regarded as suspect or dangerous—and you know indeed that the police always considered us anti-Nazis suspect. The stuff couldn't be burned because fire would be noticed. So I went with two friends to the latrine. One stayed below as lookout, and we stood up there on the platform in the dark and tore the papers into tiny pieces. Below us we could see the sentries running around looking for the lists we were throwing into the Gold-Express containers."

At the end of the camp was the *îlot des indésirables*—the unwanted ones. These women, who had not come with us from Paris, had been removed from their homes earlier and isolated as "under suspicion," although they hadn't been told what they were suspected of. In this section were held, besides a few Nazis, the most famous women of the anti-Fascist emigration, women of every political shading. The gestapo was not yet in France; it was the *Deuxième Bureau*, the French secret service, that had placed these leaders of the Nazi Opposition in special custody.

The *indésirables* were treated much more brutally than we were. They were kept under strict surveillance and were not permitted to have contact with other prisoners. Their rations were so pitiful that we, who were always hungry ourselves, tried whenever possible to smuggle bread to them through the double barbed-wire barrier. Once when I got a pass for an errand, everyone in our barrack put a piece of their daily bread-ration in a paper bag. Instead of taking the main path toward the Administration barrack I walked in the opposite direction—in case I was stopped I could always say I'd gotten confused.

One could see for quite some distance when anyone came along the straight central path, and so there was a row of familiar faces at the barbed wire as I walked slowly by and then back again. It didn't take much courage to throw the bread over piece by piece when the sentry wasn't looking. One had only to see the emaciated faces and the wide-open eyes, and one's own troubles were forgotten.

Life during those first June days in Gurs was bounded by the daily camp events. News from beyond the barbed wire was nil, it was forbidden to have any. But for the majority of the inmates, what weighed even heavier than that prohibition was the concern about their own existence; it occupied their lives to the exclusion of everything else. Their world had shrunk; it was contained within the Gurs camp, extending only as far as the surrounding fence. Beyond that, the Unknown began, the irrelevant Outside.

But the prohibition was soon surmounted, and news of events in the outside world began to leak through the barbed wire and through the cracks in that self-imposed barrier.

Everything happened so quickly that the mind couldn't keep pace with it. Many details remain buried but still green in my memory, and they surface from time to time.

I still see before me the newspaper that a sentry had smuggled in. Bold headlines covered the entire upper half of the front page: LE ROI FELON—The Traitor King. The Belgian king Leopold had capitulated. That was on May 28th. A report that even kings could be traitors didn't particularly impress me, although Premier Paul Reynaud had stated that this was a first in world history. It wasn't clear whether Leopold had committed treason as king or as commander-in-chief, but it was all the same to us, for the consequence was that nothing now stood between the German army and the French border. And where was the impregnable Maginot Line?

For several days we were cut off from all news. But someone had seen a headline in the Administration barrack: THE ENEMY BREAKS THROUGH. The next day a scrap of newspaper was passed around: L'ARMÉE FRANÇAISE GLORIEUSE EST INTACTE! Then my Spanish Civil War veteran, who should have been repairing the leaks in our barrack roof—I never did learn his name—slipped me this item: THE ENEMY OVERRUNS THE NATION.

It was said shortly afterward that Paris had been declared an open city. No one had read it in black and white, but everyone knew about it. Or was that just another *bobard*, a fantasy? If it were really true—it would mean that Paris wouldn't be defended, that the Nazis would simply march in. Even today I can still feel the sudden constriction in my throat. Paris, where father and mother and all the others had stayed behind, now under Nazi control!—of course, then there would be no bombardment.

June 14th. Newspapers were still forbidden, but now news came through anyway. GERMAN TROOPS MARCH THROUGH PARIS. We knew that the report was in accord with the facts, but we just couldn't comprehend it. Within four weeks!

And it went on. THE BOCHES ADVANCE TOWARD THE SOUTH. Where would they call a halt? If I only knew which camp my husband was in! And what of my parents? Had they remained behind in Paris, or were they among the six million who were clogging French roads?

Always new rumors. The *boches* are near Bordeaux. The military strategists among us explained why that was technically impossible. And if it *were* true? Gurs was close to Bordeaux.

"We have to get out of here."—"Get out? How do you figure to get out of a concentration camp? How do we get through the barbed wire? And where would we go?"—"We have to try and we have to succeed. What do you think we should do? Sit here and wait for the gestapo?"

Camp discipline seemed to fall apart. The sentries, the officers, even the *commissaire spécial de police*—all of them were confused and distraught. They had lost their orientation because there were no guidelines; order broke down, for there were no orders to follow.

It was now possible to slip out of your own *îlot*, a block with nearly a thousand human beings in it, and visit people in another *îlot*. Often the sentries weren't at their posts; they seemed scarcely to see any of us. We started to set up a news network, thin and fragile as it was. Only the *îlot des indésirables* was still under heavy guard; it wasn't clear just why the anti-Hitlerites in this block were especially undesirable. Among these "dangerous ones" were, on the one hand, pacifists, and, on the other hand, those who had warned France of Hitler's preparations for war— those were the "warmongers."

Meanwhile new trucks kept arriving, packed with women. We tried to communicate with them through the barbed wire: "Where do you come from?"—"We're Belgians."—"We come from Holland."

Several women were separated from the others; we wondered who they were. We saw that they'd been escorted to the *îlot des indésirables*.

I must describe the *commissaire spécial de police du Camp de Gurs*. Thickset, erect bearing, perfectly fitted uniform. Wherever he let himself

be seen he exuded authority and power, and everyone knew that he was
the arbiter of Destiny. That was the *commissaire*—up until about a week
ago.

Now all of a sudden he was shuffling about, the jellyfish, the tiny pig
eyes in his pasty face roving restlessly to and fro. Suddenly, as we were
standing around him, he asked *us*, his prisoners: "What can one do?
What if the Germans come this far and take over the camp? Make a list
for me. . . . "

The women looked at him silently. Everyone by now had come to
understand that these eternal lists were not only stupid but also
dangerous—into whose hands would they fall? He stared from one to
the next, and his eyes blinked nervously. "In the end I must follow
orders; if the Germans take command." He held his breath, blood
rushed to his head, and suddenly he roared at the women: "Away from
here! Into the barracks! I give the orders here!"

The next day, a June morning—I do not remember the date—Marianne and I slipped out of our block "I." We looked around carefully,
and went over to block "K," on the other side of the main path. We
wanted to talk to women whom we knew there about possibilities for
escape.

"Goddamn!" Marianne hissed suddenly. I followed her eyes.

"*Merde!*" I said.

The *commissaire* had come around a corner and was walking toward
us. But the way he looked! His uniform—he must have slept in a
manure pile. On his arm hung the young girl who a few days earlier had
been dubbed "*la putain spéciale*," "the special whore." He was
completely drunk, and she, not very sober herself, was trying to hold
him up. They staggered toward us along the dusty path. I don't know
whether she was one of the professional prostitutes they'd put into the
camp with us or a new apprentice. A pretty girl, quite young, perhaps
seventeen or eighteen. It struck me that his nose was almost as red as her
painted mouth and cheeks.

He grabbed me roughly by the arm; a stink of sour wine hit me in the
face. "You two, you speak German," he said. "This—this here is my
secretary—she only knows French." He indicated the girl on his arm,
stuck his short thick finger in her belly, and they both laughed. Then he
tried to straighten up again. "You two will work for me as translators.

Right now—no time to lose. Let's go!" Still holding my arm, he pushed me ahead of him.

What did he want from us? What did he have in mind?

"I have to sort them out, these *indésirables*," he blustered on. "The camp commandant wants to keep only the real dangerous ones there. He's ordered me to quickly make a list, to screen and separate them before the gestapo gets here. So then, who is 'real dangerous'? What does dangerous mean anyway? Dangerous today? Or dangerous tomorrow? He didn't tell me that, the cowardly dog! Simply shoved the responsibility onto me. So get going, you two. You have to translate the interrogations."

He nodded at a small hut off the walkway; his hand still lay heavily on my arm. The smell from his mouth was unbearable. He continued to babble, and his tongue got ever thicker. "I already know how I'll get this done. You two, you make me a list of the fifth columnists among the *indésirables*. That ought to satisfy him, the good Mister Commandant."

That's where you're mistaken, you drunken Mister Commissar, I thought; we'll make no lists. You, the French authorities, put us together in this camp: political and Jewish refugees, odd strangers (Hungarian poets and Alsatian nuns, for instance); and the Nazis together with all of us. No, we'll give you nothing, we won't help you because we don't trust you. We know who the Nazis among us are, we know the enemy. But you, you don't know with whom to side. No, we won't work with your police.

Marianne and I looked at each other. Of course she was thinking just the way I was, as all of us did. She shook her head slightly, and her eyes said, No, we won't cooperate.

It wouldn't be hard to pull out of it. Maybe I could stumble, fall, and cry out in pain. Or better still, faint—I could do that well.

Women from the *indésirable* block were brought to the hut. Hilde was among them; she saw me immediately. How thin she'd become in the few weeks since Paris! Irma was there too, and other familiar faces, and many unfamiliar. And this drunk was now going to decide who should and who shouldn't be handed over to the gestapo! But no, that must not happen—could we—or must we. . . . ?

I didn't fall into a faint. I looked at Marianne again. She nodded her head, bent over to me and said softly in German, "Shall we try it?"

We went into the hut with the *commissaire* and his *putain*. Women in the adjoining *îlots* could see us, and I could feel their eyes on our backs through the barbed wire. And we knew what they were thinking: Those two are working with the police. At that moment it didn't matter, for we had no other choice.

Inside the hut there was a table, a short bench, and a few chairs. The commissar and his "secretary" sat on the bench, Marianne and I on chairs. Soldiers to guard the *indésirables* stood all about. The first women were brought in; one could see by their faces that they knew what was at stake.

The *commissaire* looked at the papers they handed him. They included every sort of identification and a few foreign passports; many women had only a slip saying that they were to be sent to the Gurs camp. The *commissaire* was bored and had trouble keeping his eyes open. He interrogated the women; his authoritarian tone sounded forced, his voice quavered. "How did you come to be here? Why were you arrested? Do you have any prior convictions? Are you a spy?"

We translated the questions into German and the answers into French.

He pulled the girl close to him and said to us, "Now you know what questions to ask, so you question them and simply translate the answers for me."

He leaned against the wall, his belly bulging out over his belt and touching the edge of the table. He put his arm around his *putain* and pressed her body close to his. She laughed and kissed him tipsily as the *indésirables* moved past. Now and then his head fell to the side and he started to snore; then she giggled and tickled him awake. And the women marched by.

The *commissaire* was happy that now we were conducting the interrogation on our own. The requested list of fifth columnists was forgotten.

Our task wasn't difficult—one had only to keep in mind what it was all about: to get the anti-Nazis and the persecuted ones out of the *indésirables* section before the gestapo arrived. Many women were known to us, many at least by name. It was easy to determine with a few brief questions on which side they belonged. The first ones we questioned gaped at us, saw the incredible pair on the bench, looked at us with complete mistrust, and answered evasively—in Gurs one was always alert for a trap. But in a short while word got around among those waiting outside as to what kind of screening ours was.

Among the Dutch and Belgians who had been brought here as "suspected persons" were a number of well-known names: they or their husbands were pacifists, artists, journalists, writers, or union officials. Luckily, the *commissaire*, even when sober, knew none of them. It also didn't occur to him that in Belgium French was more likely to be spoken than German.

And we "translated." *"En règle,"* we said, "papers in order. There is no evidence against this person; not suspect." The commissar hardly listened; occasionally he gave a hand signal to the guard. The woman was let out, and was now an ordinary prisoner like the rest of us, not an "undesirable."

There were mostly *Reichsdeutsche* in the last group. They had kept to themselves here, as they did elsewhere in the camp: German citizens who were suspected of being Nazi agents. It was so easy to distinguish them from the emigrants. Even more positive than their valid German passports was their bearing—how can one describe it? The Third Reich had put a stamp on them, a BDM-stamp (*Bund Deutscher Mädchen*— League of German Girls) that one could hear, see, and feel.

In the few cases where we weren't altogether sure with whom we were dealing, we declared that the woman was not suspect. On no account could we mistakenly send the wrong person back to the *îlot des indésirables*. Among us, a few Nazis more or less were of no importance; they would be quickly recognized and isolated like the others. Without a twinge of conscience we let the clear-cut Nazis go back to their special block; there they could prepare a celebratory reception for the gestapo!

After several hours we were finished with the *criblage*. We had to repeat, "There! That's it!" a couple of times before the *commissaire* grasped that "his" task was ended. He gazed at us glassy-eyed, the little *putain* on his lap. His face was smeared with her lipstick. He looked like a clown. But not a jolly one, not a clown to laugh at. One to turn your stomach.

Marianne and I simply stood up and went out. I must have been under considerable tension, for I suddenly felt my insides relax, and I became pleasantly weary. And I thought: If I ever get the time, I'll have to write all this down: the drunken *commissaire*, the young whore, and the "cross-examination" of the fifth column. But nobody would ever believe it.

Outside, along the central path, the guards were billeting in the ordinary blocks all the women who were no longer classed as *indésirable*. At least they were no longer isolated, whatever might happen to them in the future. Anyhow, the camp commandant had taken pains to see that "only the really dangerous ones" would be held there and all the others released "before the gestapo gets here." Perhaps *l'honneur de la France* stirred him, perhaps he didn't want to stand in the way of our flight from this trap?

Then it struck me that it had all started that morning when we'd been on our way to "K" block to discuss escape plans.

So—it's high time, let's go.

We sat outside around the barrack and looked down the path. Finally we saw tall Lotte returning; you could recognize her from afar by her gangling walk. When she reached our gate we remained calmly seated to avoid attracting notice, although we tried to guess whether it had worked. She squinted at the sun, but we could read nothing in her expression. It seemed like an eternity before she arrived at our barrack at last.

"Have you got them?"

"I sure have."

"How many?"

"Plenty." She put a brown bag down in front of us.

The three of us went into the dark, empty barrack. Tensely we opened the bag; it held a hundred or more blank white forms.

A short while before, Lotte had signed up as a messenger. She'd gotten a pass, and was sent with news and communications between the various sections and the commandant's office. She had made herself useful in the office, helped out a little, and soon knew what there was to find in the various drawers. She'd acquired practice as a "message-runner" in the school of the German Resistance. The forms were release certificates, and at the bottom was: *Le Commandant du Camp de Gurs.* Of course the signature was missing.

We wanted to use the certificates to escape from the camp only if there was no other way to get out. (A certain amount of danger was always attached to false documents, and one used them only when absolutely necessary.) Their main function would be outside the camp; when one entered an occupied area, it was vital to have a document with another name and nationality, especially for women whose names were known to the gestapo. First we had to find out in which other sections the most politically imperiled ones were.

"Anja Pfemfert is stuck somewhere, way at the rear in block 'M.' We must help her, she's not in good shape."

"Frau Feuchtwanger? She's across the way in 'J.' Yes, she wants out— she said she can help us with money."

"Don't forget Hannah Arendt in the next *îlot*. Sure, of course you know her, she's Blücher's wife. She wants to get out with us, but then wants to go her own way. That seems safer to her."

"Do you still remember," Paulette said later, "how we tried to persuade Martha that time? She was my oldest and dearest friend. She wasn't at all well, she was in terrible pain. She was in your section, but she came to the barbed wire every evening so we could talk a little.

"Naturally we wanted to take her out of Gurs with us. With her anti-Fascist past she would've been a goner had the Germans found her. I know that you all tried for a long while to talk her into going. After thinking it over, she said, 'I've decided not to go with you. No one knows what's ahead of us,' she said. 'In my condition I'd only be a hindrance, because I know you'd never leave me in the lurch. An entire group mustn't be sacrificed because of one person.'

"Three days later she came to the fence to say goodbye. She said, 'I wish you luck, my little one.' She always called me 'my little one.' We both knew that it would be the last time we'd ever see each other."

(Shortly afterward, French friends in Limoges helped Martha escape from the camp and hid her with them. When she finally found a doctor, it was too late.)

The next days were so occupied with preparations that we scarcely got any sleep. We wanted to be out of the camp in three days. Nelly had specialized in forging under Hitler, and she'd had so much practice at it that one couldn't tell her commandant's signature from the real one. Now she sat in the barrack all day and worked slowly and professionally while others stood watch. Now and then she called a halt, shook her long reddish blond hair away from her face, and complained: "This shitty paper! It's not at all suitable for forging. . . ."

Ever more hard-to-believe news reports about the German advance. And always the gnawing questions: Where are our families? What has happened to the men? There were rumors that the men's camps had been overrun by the Germans and all of them taken prisoner. I didn't believe it. They wouldn't just sit there calmly and wait for the Nazis, I said to myself: they'd break out. Nonetheless, I got a strange feeling in the vicinity of my stomach whenever I thought about it.

The camp to which my brother, Hans, had meanwhile been sent was called La Braconne. It wasn't far from Bordeaux. "Tell me how it went with you," I asked him years later. He reported in detail as only a scientist can report:

"A group of political emigrés had banded together. No one knew exactly what had been happening, but everyone knew of the German advance, and it was clear that they would soon be in La Braconne. The group wanted to organize an escape from the camp. We assumed that there would be a transition period just before the Germans arrived during which the French guard detail would pull back, or simply flee. We had to seize that moment for our own flight.

"We posted lookouts to observe the withdrawal of the French guards or the arrival of German advance troops. As you know, in La Braconne, as in other camps, there were, besides us Hitler foes, Germans who had been caught in France when war broke out, and of course there were Nazis among them. The Nazis knew what to expect, just as we did, and they planned to detain the Jews and anti-Fascists and hand them over to the German troops. (As it later turned out, combat troops generally took no interest in unarmed civilians.)

"Evenings I stood watch at the barrack window assigned to me. The Nazis knew why I was standing there. A few of them jumped me from behind and tried to drag me away from the window. I resisted, and in the darkness they hurled me violently back into the barrack. When I fell my forehead hit the edge of a bench and blood came gushing out. I was unconscious for a moment, but then I crept back. When the camp doctor saw me he spoke of cerebral concussion and unpredictable consequences, and said that I had to lie quietly for at least a week. He put a huge bandage around my head, but blood still seeped through. I lay down and had an attack of the shakes; I was told that it is to be expected when there has been great blood loss. I suppose I must have lost about a liter.

"The camp guards withdrew the next morning, and the camp stood open. Everything proceeded quite systematically. The commandant announced: *Sauve qui peut*—take flight! Did he speak to us himself? Well, as I remember:

"One inmate had been appointed *chef de camp* by the commandant. The man was a former German officer, a colonel, but he was a Jew and hence an emigré. On that morning this *chef* informed us briefly in the name of the commandant: the Germans are coming nearer—the guard detail will pull back—*débrouillez-vous*—save yourselves, whoever can. Whereupon we simply walked out of the camp. The Nazis didn't try to stop us because the French sentries were still standing around.

"Of course it soon became evident that we had come out of internment into only limited freedom. After a few steps I found myself in an unpleasant situation—namely, right between two tanks, one French and the other German. It seemed as if both of them were aiming their cannons directly at me. In actuality I was in their eyes nothing more than a wretched, limping civilian with a bloody head-bandage.

"So—the area was already surrounded by German tanks. We had to try to succeed in reaching unoccupied ground before the gestapo came in behind the military. One could only guess at the direction—in any case, away from the Germans, so approximately southeasterly. We instinctively traveled alone; a group could easily be mistaken for a military unit. There was no firing, but it was nevertheless an uneasy route with the French on one side and the Germans on the other.

"After a while a French army truck stopped and picked me up. I no doubt appeared heroic with that artistically bloody head-bandage. As I was weary, I was limping worse than usual. The truck was part of a long column of antiaircraft vehicles that were trying to get out of the German encirclement.

"It was a rather gruelling ride, at breakneck speed and to the southeast. We halted suddenly—German tanks were rolling toward us. Our caravan turned and raced back. After we had changed directions several times, we approached a small river—and saw German uniforms at the bridgehead. Stop! then into a side road and full steam in another direction. During the ride they made telephone contact with a command post, and again we halted suddenly and changed direction. It went like that for half a day; it was nerve-racking, this sight-seeing tour through occupied and unoccupied areas, not knowing whether one was already surrounded or about to be captured.

"The column finally succeeded in breaking through the encirclement. We were in an unoccupied area (although at the time it was not known where the Germans would call a halt). I remember that we stopped near a forest, and there was silence all about us. We got out, and the crew began to prepare a real French repast. It was served and I was invited. With my bandage I was, after all, a hero, even though only a civilian one.

"It is impossible to describe how miserable I grew after eating. After weeks of hunger one cannot tolerate a full meal with meat and gravy and sweet things. I still remember what an extraordinary effort it cost me not to throw up, for I didn't want to make a mess in the truck."

Confusion among the camp personnel increased from hour to hour, so we were able to go freely into other sections and hand out the release certificates to our contacts. We planned to make our getaway the next morning. We'd meet about eight o'clock on the left side of the gate and try to get through singly or by twos. Once outside, we'd disappear into various villages and see how far the Germans had advanced.

All of us were still sitting around outside after midnight. That was now possible, for no one troubled herself about regulations any longer.

"I keep thinking it over," someone said to me in the darkness, "I'm no longer so sure that we're doing the right thing." I recognized the voice and turned to the woman.

"What do you mean? What else should we do, then?"

"Maybe it's wrong simply to skip out of here."

I was speechless for a minute. Faltering now, a few hours before the decisive moment? And of all people, she who was known to be calm and deliberate, and who never lost her nerve!

"Really, you can't seriously mean that we should sit here and wait for the gestapo?"

"Look," she said, "each case is different. I'm thinking mainly about Otto; he's among those who are in the greatest danger. He knows that I'm here, so he'll look for me here. If I go away we'll lose contact. Where else should he find me?"

"Contact!" I snorted angrily. "Find you! If anyone ever wants to find someone else again, he must first save himself—he, and you, and all of us. . . ."

She stood up. "You're probably right," she said, "but I can't rid myself of doubt. When one thinks of the dangers—at least here in Gurs I know where I am. Outside is the Unknown. The Nazis will be everywhere. Where are the chances of survival better? Let me go on thinking about it."

Now I couldn't go to sleep. The whole camp seemed to be alert. It was only the end of June, but the night was sultry. Or was it the uneasiness, the fear, which hung in the air and made the night so oppressive?

Suddenly the camp commandant appeared. He had never shown himself before. He seemed to be going from section to section and was surrounded and trailed by a crowd of women; they wanted to know: "What's going to happen? What will be done with us?"

He made an effort to convey military bearing and composure.

"It is true that things are not going well at the front," he began, "but——."

A woman's voice interrupted him; "Where are the Germans?" Others called, "Silence!"

The commandant continued: "——but there is no cause for alarm. France assumes full responsibility for your safety."

Now I heard suppressed laughter. The same voice called out once more, "Where are the Germans now?" And the commandant answered, "They are approaching from several directions."

A woman whom I couldn't see too well called: "Raise an American flag high above the camp. Then Gurs will be thought to be American territory and the Germans won't dare to come in." Someone near me began to laugh hysterically.

The commandant went on to the next section. The women stood around and went on talking. I listened to them and thought: How can they be so passive? They ask *What will happen to us?* instead of *What can we do?*

"The most important thing is to get out of here," I said for the tenth time. "One can easily slip through in this confusion."

"Where to?" asked a woman I'd sometimes conversed with.

"It doesn't matter. The main thing—out of captivity, out of Gurs, before the Nazis get here."

"Without money! One has to eat. . . ."

"You want to stay in Gurs because of the *pois chiches?*"

"But my family—how shall we find each other? The men will surely come here to get us. Don't you want to wait for your own husband?"

"For my husband? I'd have to wait a long time for that. When he learns that one can escape from Gurs, he won't be looking for me here."

(Months later, I said to him, "Hans, didn't it really occur to you to look for me in Gurs? Back then when many men went there to get their wives?"—"No," Hans said, and laughed. "It was obvious that you weren't sitting in Gurs waiting for me. That would have been downright absurd. Once, during the flight from the north, I traveled with some comrades who wanted to go to Gurs. Before we separated they said, 'At least tell us her name in case she's there.' 'Her name is Lisa,' I said, 'but don't strain yourself looking for her, she's no longer there.' ")

Sometimes my own memory puzzles me. It conjures up trivial scenes from that last night. A red blouse hanging up, fluttering in the wind. I also see a woman unknown to me, sitting on a wobbly stool. Then morning comes, and the flight from Gurs. My recollections are blurred; only a colorless chronicle survives. Perhaps I was too tired. Perhaps that was all there was to it.

There were about sixty of us. We'd only show the release certificates if they were asked for. (We'd left the unused certificates behind for others to use.) I remember clearly that everyone was there, even those who'd had qualms at the last moment. We approached the gate, singly and in small groups. In the confusion we attracted no attention.

We saw that Lotte and Nelly, who went through first, had to show their certificates; the sentry studied them. With the next women he gave the papers a cursory glance. After a while Paulette and I went through, and I said, "We're coming right back." I don't remember whether or not my heart was pounding.

Sometime or other, on the highway, a car stopped and an officer picked us up. As soon as I sat down I fell asleep and didn't wake up again until we stopped in a village. It was called Pontacq, and we'd arranged to meet some of the others there.

But first we had to find out where the Germans were now.

3

Searching—Pontacq, Summer 1940

To our horror, the French officer who'd taken us with him stopped his car at the gendarmerie. Two policemen emerged, and our driver got out. He looked quite dashing in his uniform.

"I'm turning these two women over to you," he said. I felt Paulette's hand on mine; it was ice-cold. He continued, in a tone of military command, "I hold the Pontacq gendarmerie liable for the safety of these women. They are Belgian refugees who are being hunted by the gestapo. You are now responsible in this regard; see to it that they do not fall into the hands of the Germans."

They all saluted, he opened the car door, and we got out; he got in again and drove away without even casting a glance in our direction. I was a little light-headed. I looked at Paulette and thought, she's not feeling very well either.

In the office we showed the gendarmes our self-fabricated release certificates: Paulette Perrier and Lise Duchamps, Belgian citizens. The police sergeant said, "We'll see to your safety. Of course you must not leave Pontacq. I hope that you won't give us any trouble."

We stood in the little square at the end of the village and waited our turn. Ahead of us were some twenty refugees from various parts of the country, elderly people and women with children. Underneath the trees in the center of the square a platform had been built. There a municipal official was overseeing the distribution of food and assignments to living quarters.

They gave us a few turnips and some lettuce leaves, a small piece of bacon, some bread and salt. Then we got an alcohol stove and, for each of us, a metal dish. A man guided Paulette and me to a small farmstead. The farmer's wife was clad in black from head to toe, as were all women in the Basque village. She showed us a hut behind the vegetable garden, next to the henhouse. Inside were a large bed and a small table. We asked her where we could get water.

"The village pump is below, at the end of the path," she said. "You can wash yourselves and your things there." As she left, she added: "Don't forget to close the gate behind you, or the hens will get into the vegetable garden. And you don't need to use the outhouse there— manure is good for the vegetables."

"Oh God!" said Paulette. "If my mother knew that, her heart——."

"Paulette," I said, "a bed! A real bed!"

"——her heart would jump out of her body."

We have a bed and something to eat, I thought, and maybe we're safe for the time being. If only the women in Gurs who hadn't had the courage to leave the camp had only known that the fleeing masses were being provided with essentials!

In the village no one knew where the Germans were now, nor whether they were still advancing. Several refugees who had come through Pau thought that one could learn more there, perhaps at the army barracks, which was full of soldiers.

So the next morning we set out for Pau. Meanwhile six more women from our group had arrived and been given accommodations in Pontacq. Others were dispersed throughout several villages. We had to know if there was danger of the Germans coming to this area.

But how were we to get to Pau? There were no buses, no transportation of any kind. "We'll get there and back somehow," we said to the others. We left the village by a roundabout route, so as not to be seen by the gendarmes. There were very few vehicles on the highway, for nobody had gasoline. Drivers were mainly officers, and they whizzed past us.

Maybe it was our own fault? "You're not signaling," I said. "Nobody's going to stop."

"I thought *you* were waving. Haven't you ever stopped a car before?"

"No. And you?"

"Me neither."

We agreed that Paulette would wave her hands around, and if anyone stopped I'd do the talking.

A car came. Paulette murmured, "Oh Falada,* if my mother only knew!" and she waved. The car stopped and picked us up.

_____

*The name "Falada" and the phrase "if my mother knew" are taken from a German fairy tale.

In Pau we went first of all to the army barracks the refugees in Pontacq had spoken of. Soldiers were milling around everywhere, but it struck us that we didn't see any officers. No one could give us any information; nobody knew a thing about the company Paulette's husband was in. The soldiers we spoke with had only stopped to stay overnight in the barracks. "Where are the Germans?" we asked, but we soon quit asking. The soldiers looked at us with vacant eyes. A few laughed, an ugly laugh. Some said, "They're everywhere, *les boches.*" And time and again, "*Nous sommes vendus—*We've been sold out."

We walked around in Pau trying to find out how things stood. The sun blazed; we were weary and truly disheartened. In the City Hall we were able to speak with an official, but he knew no more than the others. He said there were rumors that the Germans would call a halt tomorrow or the next day; there was talk of a cease-fire, an armistice. Rumors. We moved on.

We saw several young men in the street. "They look like German emigrés," said Paulette. The men came over to us. "Do you come from Gurs? What's happening there?" They'd fled from a camp in the north and had just arrived here. They knew only that every place was surrounded by German tanks and that one encountered groups of emigrés everywhere. I wanted to know if everyone had gotten away in time. Or were there camps that had been overrun by the Germans? My husband, Hans, was supposedly in the Tours area. I asked whether they'd met up with anyone from there. No. Although, as far as they knew, most emigrés had fled the camps; in the end, the French commandants had made no trouble and finally had decamped themselves. But then the flight through France, no one knew to where. And, just as one thought, now we've made it, tanks again——.

Several women came by. They'd also escaped from Gurs, and they, too, were on the search.

We wanted to hide ourselves temporarily in Pontacq, remote from the rest of the world. We'd thought of it like that, and that's the way it was—for a few days. Paulette and I often sat on a bench in the village square. There wasn't much to see, but it was pleasant in the cool shade under the trees. The main road cut diagonally across the square; occasionally a refugee or two went by. Sometimes small groups of soldiers in soiled uniforms, trudging aimlessly past. Only seldom did one see a vehicle.

Once we heard engine noise. Two soldiers on motorcycles. Paulette jumped up suddenly and shouted: "Alfred, Alfred!" She flapped her arms and ran after the motorcycles, but they had already disappeared.

"That was young Alfred from Paris," she yelled to me. "You know him too—how can I catch up with him?"

"Now you're starting to go crazy like the others," I said impatiently. "Alfred—he of all people, here in Pontacq!"

We argued about it. Paulette remained obstinate, she hadn't been mistaken.

A horse-drawn wagon came by. Paulette ran up to the farmer slumped on the driver's seat and said breathlessly, "If you see two soldiers on the highway riding motorcycles—one of them, the little blond one, is a friend of ours, but he didn't see us—tell him to come back right away!"

The farmer nodded, and drove slowly on with his little wagon.

"Go ahead and laugh," she said to me. "I'll stay here and wait. One never knows." Once Paulette got a notion into her head, nothing could shake it. And so we went on sitting on our bench, waiting for Alfred.

After a while she said aggrievedly, "It just didn't work out—come on, we have to eat something. But I'm sure that it was him."

Wasn't that the sound of a motorcycle again? It began from far away in the opposite direction. For sure, it was a motorcycle, and on it sat a soldier. He tore through the village, stopped in the square, and looked around. "Someone told me I should come back. . . ?"

Yes, it was Alfred from Paris, sitting on the motorcycle in a bedraggled uniform, exhausted and confused. Alfred, with his blond mop of hair and rosy, boyish face. We went up to him, and he stared at us unbelievingly and rubbed his eyes and forehead. He dismounted and sat down on the grass, and while we talked to him excitedly his eyes closed and he fell asleep. I sat down next to him and whispered softly, thoughtlessly, *"L'armée glorieuse . . . voilà l'armée glorieuse."*

Alfred was a young Pole, barely twenty, who had signed up with the Polish Legion in Paris when war broke out. For the moment, he'd interrupted his flight to the south here in Pontacq, making contact with soldiers scattered about in nearby towns. We sat together in the evening, and he told us about the phony war, the Maginot Line, and the start of the offensive.

"——and when the Germans broke through into Belgium they moved us westward. It must have been the end of May when we went into battle south of the Somme. Our officers repeated General Weygand's words: 'This is the decisive battle of the war.' Our confidence in the generals wasn't very high, but one always wants to believe that those above have some kind of strategy in mind. It was clear that the Somme bridgehead must be recaptured, and we proceeded to attack. But it was futile, we had no support. Three days under continuous fire, without food or sleep. The dead and wounded lay all about and we couldn't even get to them.

"At the beginning of June orders came for a new offensive; the enemy's drive toward Paris had to be stopped. Our attack began in early-morning darkness, and at the same moment the Germans opened fire. Our artillery had mistakenly started its fusillade a few minutes too soon. We thought, 'Where are our airplanes?' They never came.

"Munitions ran out. They told us that supplies were already on the way from arsenals in the south. We waited and waited. The German fire never let up—outside we heard the groans and screams of our wounded. Always more promises: the munitions would be here straightaway. Waiting, cursing—near me someone was sobbing.

"It was well into the third day when we saw two trucks coming. We made a rush for them; I was among the first. One was empty, just empty. The second held a single ammunition chest.

"I don't know any more about the battle of the Somme. From then on there were only rumors. Were we now under French or English command? Were the Germans also at our rear? Had the order to retreat been given? But we could no longer wait for orders."

Alfred remained in our area. Although he had to turn in his army motorcycle, as a soldier he could often help us women in Pontacq. It didn't matter where he holed up, he said, he had no destination. He was one of the countless wandering soldiers, one of the *armée en déroute*, the army put to flight.

Meanwhile the inhabitants of Pontacq had grown accustomed to the sight of us; people looked at us with less mistrust than they had at the beginning. We couldn't understand when they spoke to each other in Basque, but with us they spoke French. We received a small subsidy, paid by the mayor's office to all refugees; we now belonged to that exalted social class. Our farmer's wife wasn't too fond of us, mainly because we often let her hens escape into the vegetable garden. But the ancient farmer, who had taken in three of "our" women, sometimes cooked for all of us. He conjured up thick, fantastically delicious soups in the black iron kettle that hung on chains over the fireplace. Once he sacrificed one of his chickens, and when I marveled at such recklessness, he declared, "It doesn't matter, the hen was as old as I am."

There were still no newspapers, and yet everyone spoke of an armistice. When we went to the town pump at noon with our tin plates, we sometimes met soldiers who had stopped there to wash. They said that they had been bombarded while still in flight. They told of planes spraying machine-gun fire from treetop height.

Paulette and I went farther afield on exploratory trips. Our two-man-strong police force took its duties quite seriously and kept a close eye on us, but we soon found a sure device for getting away: after all, they religiously spent two to three hours on *déjeuner*. We'd learned how to slip out of the village unobserved. *L'auto-stop*, hitchhiking, was now an old habit with us, although motor vehicles were ever fewer and we often walked for long stretches in our tattered shoes. We went to Tarbes and to Lourdes, and to other villages where women who had fled from Gurs with us had hidden themselves. We met up with emigrés still wandering around and searching. Once, when we were standing with other people by the side of a road somewhere, a car with several people in it stopped; a woman stuck her head out and wanted to know where the road led.

"Aren't you Hertha Pauli?" someone asked.

"That's right. Where are we?"

"In the Basses Pyrénées. Where are you coming from?"

"From the west, from the coast. In which direction are we going?"

"Toward the south. Where do you want to go?"

"To Lourdes, maybe . . . ?" The car drove on.

We sat on our bench and discussed what else we could do to find our families. It was hot, even in the shade. Suddenly a crowd gathered—a bus was coming, the bus from Pau was running again for the first time! The whole town watched as some of the passengers alighted. Paulette jumped up and ran straight across the square to the bus stop, crying, "Papa, Papa!" and embraced—I stared at this spritelike figure with the gray mane—it really *was* her father, "der Alte," as we called him. How was it possible that he had found us here in this hideaway?

Very simple, he explained. When he had fled from his camp with several friends shortly before the Germans arrived, they had made their way in the direction of Gurs; he wanted to fetch his daughter. Outside Pau they'd encountered someone who'd met his daughter and other women from Gurs and also knew where they were staying.

"We can't keep him here," Paulette said to me later. He stubbornly refused to let his wild hair, his distinctive feature, be cut. And he didn't speak a word of French. He'd be able to disappear more easily into the crowds of people in Lourdes. So he continued on, and we agreed to follow him soon.

When, a few days later, we saw Bolle's husband, Kaminski, climb down from a hay wagon, it surprised us only slightly. (Bolle was one of the three women housed at the old farmer's.) He too had run into someone who knew where we were. He came from the camp near Tours in which my husband had also been.

In the evening we sat together in the dark in the old man's living room and listened to Kaminski report on his flight from the camp. It was a dramatic narration. He told of a raging river he had to swim across in order to escape from the Germans, who were close on his heels. Then, it slowly came out that he hadn't swum at all, that he'd found a boat to take him across. I asked what he knew about the others. Had all of them escaped? When was the last time he'd seen my husband?

"I ran off with two other men. The others had planned the escape for the next day, but we didn't want to wait. Actually, the Germans did occupy the camp the next day—we heard that no one else got out. We three were the only ones who saved themselves—the others had misjudged the situation entirely."

The room was silent. This jack-in-the-box, I thought, he doesn't know a thing, he's just "heard" and is spreading panic. It's probably only preparation for his next novel. He, of all people, had "judged the situation correctly"—he who didn't know his ass from his elbow. Hans and the others surely must have known what they should do.

And so we searched further and followed every clue, and we met two emigrés on the highway to Lourdes who came from the same camp.

"Hans Fittko?" said one of them. "Sure I know him. In the camp I once pulled a tooth for him. Don't you worry, we all got out of the camp before the Germans arrived. I've already seen Hans outside. I don't know in which direction he went. Give us your address, in case we meet up with someone. . . ."

A truck going in the direction of Lourdes picked us up. We wanted to visit der Alte to see whether everything was all right with him. The driver and co-driver, both of them young men, were talkative and wanted to know everything: what we were doing here, why we wanted to go to Lourdes, where we came from. "We come from Belgium," we said. "Our husbands are prisoners-of-war, and we had to take flight."

"So," said the driver, "from Belgium. Where exactly?"

Paulette remembered the name of a small town.

That turned out to be a mistake. "What a coincidence!" said the driver. It seemed that he didn't quite trust us.

"What did your husband do there?" asked the co-driver.

"We had a gasoline station."

"Which one of them? The one next to the City Hall? Or the one at the intersection?"

Paulette turned to the two men and looked at them with dismay in her big blue eyes. "You're making fun of us," she said, offended. "That's not very nice, to treat wives of prisoners-of-war in such a way." She gave me a slight nudge with her foot.

"Oh, Paulette," I stage-whispered, "we shouldn't have let them take us along. Who knows what they think of us? Let's go on foot, it can't be more than another few hours."

That the two men wouldn't permit. We need no longer fear; they'd ask no more indiscreet questions.

What had they really thought?

Somewhere northeast of Tarbes there was a large transit-point and meeting-place for emigrants who had fled from the camps. Several people had come through there on scouting trips, and they described the route to us. There were hundreds of men from the camps, and even if we found none of our own people, we could surely find out something about them.

It was a long stretch, and we slipped out of our village early in the morning. A truck that was already carrying several farm workers let us get aboard and ride with them. In Tarbes we spoke with an officer standing by his car. It was a beautiful, expensive automobile; the officer was very polite and said he'd be glad to take us along for a way, but then he would have to turn off and leave us midway on the road. That was all right with us.

"He must be a real big gun," whispered Paulette. "Look at his epaulettes."

We got into the rear seat and he drove off. The road out of the city ran across a bridge. As we drew nearer, we saw that armed soldiers were blocking the access. It's good, I thought, that we're with a VIP; otherwise we wouldn't get through.

The officer stopped by the first sentry and spoke to him briefly; from the rear seat we couldn't hear exactly what was said. The soldier shook his head and said, no, he couldn't let the car through. The officer pulled a document from his pocket and the sentry looked at it, then said again: "No, I have my orders. No one may cross the bridge." A rapid exchange of words followed, and we heard the officer say, "Stand back, I'm driving through." The soldier said, "I have orders to shoot," and he leveled his weapon. His hands were right in front of my eyes, and I saw that they were trembling. Suddenly the officer was holding a revolver. The soldier made an involuntary movement backward, the officer tromped on the gas pedal and sped across the bridge. The sentries at the other end jumped out of the way, and the car drove through.

The road led through a summery, peaceful forest, and the officer chattered amiably. He dismissed the incident at the bridge with a cursory remark about "confusion in the present situation."

We walked for a long while after he had let us out and had turned off in another direction. Then another car came along and brought us near to the campground. It was late evening. The night was warm, and we lay down in the open and slept.

We looked all around us the next morning. Large military tents were set up on the field, but there wasn't enough room and most men slept out in the open. They came from camps in all parts of France, from the north to the Mediterranean. But no one knew anything about my husband; nobody knew my brother. Paulette had given up hope of learning anything here about her own husband, for he was assigned to a French military unit. We listened to reports about the exodus: millions of people on the highways—*la pagaille*, the great turmoil. Had my parents been among them? And Paulette's mother?

We also heard about the twenty-two trucks full of emigrés who had driven north during the collapse. They were volunteers who had been attached to the British army as auxiliary troops. They were dispatched to

Dunkirk with the regular troops but could not be embarked anymore. Now the Germans were at their backs. Nothing was known of their eventual fate.

Even those who came directly from the occupied areas did not know what was happening. There was allegedly an armistice, but sporadic firing and bombing continued. Were the German troops still advancing?

"It looks as if," someone said, "they've called a halt, but nobody can be certain."

Nothing was certain.

Most of the men remained just a short while. They exchanged news, rumors, relatives' names, and pushed on—still searching.

We didn't have much luck on the return trip. A car came toward evening, racing past with such speed that we didn't have time to wave. But then brakes squealed and the car reversed, returning to us at the same scorching velocity.

"Take care, it must be a madman!" I said.

It was a man in civilian clothes. He asked whether we could show him the shortest way to the Gurs camp, as we presumably had come from there. "Get in, quickly, I'll take you along. You need have no fear, you're safe with me. Just show me the way—there's no time to lose."

Something in his hurried voice rang true, and we decided to get in. Luckily, the shortest way led through Pontacq. The man became somewhat calmer, but the car still hurtled through the night with a speed that gave us the shivers.

"How much farther is it to Gurs? Can I be there before midnight?" We had to tell him that he still had a rather long way to drive.

After a while he said, "I come straight from Paris. When I learned in my ministry that a gestapo commission is on its way to Gurs, I left immediately. I must get there before they do."

Who was this man? Obviously an official in an important position, one who knew what was what. Could he be trusted? We didn't want to betray our anxiety by questioning him. But after a pause he went on speaking; in his agitated state he doubtless *had* to keep talking.

"I know that Margot is still in Gurs. Margot, my fiancée, is a German emigré just as you are. Now you understand—I must get her out before the gestapo comes."

Yes, we understood.

It was obvious that this unknown person had connections. He was shrewd; he'd certainly get his fiancée out. And what would happen to the others?

We asked him about the armistice.

"Yes," he said, "we've concluded an armistice with the Germans, although apparently there's still fighting going on here and there. No doubt you haven't heard about Article 19?" he asked warily.

No, we knew nothing at all about what was happening.

"It's the reason for my race against the gestapo. Article 19 of the Armistice says: *delivrer sur demande tous les ressortissants allemands désignés par le gouvernement du Reich*—all Germans named by the German government to be surrendered on demand." He shot us a sidelong glance.

I try to remember what impression this news made on us. I don't believe my memory is playing tricks on me. Article 19 of the armistice between Germany and France was only one of many links in the chain of events. It didn't surprise us.

Extradition to Germany (we called it *"Heimat"*) was nothing new to us. Since Hitler's seizure of power, those in every country bordering Germany were threatened by it. For example, in 1936 Switzerland had complied with an extradition request in which an author of anti-Fascist leaflets was charged, although Germany had given only the cover name "Stephan." They didn't know that in actuality it dealt with a certain Johannes Fittko, for whom the gestapo was searching. If I rightly recall, the official justification was that the anonymous man had committed a robbery-murder (or was it a sex crime?). So the Swiss government had issued an arrest warrant and sent off its Special Section of police to look for "Stephan." He wasn't extradited because he couldn't be found, thanks to the help of Swiss friends. The Swiss district attorney who showed me the warrant was named Dr. Gans; with no hesitation, he gave his conscience precedence over his official duty.

For a long time now we had been able to avoid extradition simply by means of undiscoverability.

The man from Paris let us out shortly before Pontacq and raced onward to Gurs. Not until later did we hear from women who were there how the gestapo's first visit went—it was restricted to the *îlot des indésirables*.

That evening we consulted with the other six women and agreed that it was now time to move on, singly or in twos, as we had arrived. This part of the south seemed to be unoccupied for the present, and we needed more freedom of movement. We wanted to be in a larger city— Marseille, perhaps? It was the only overseas port still open.

Paulette and I had to go first to Lourdes, where der Alte was waiting for us. We'd take Anja Pfemfert, who was with us in Pontacq, along with us. It was high time for her to get out of the village. She was unable to adapt, had attacks of anxiety, and was so conspicuous that things couldn't fare well with her much longer. One night she even managed to lose her way in the small village.

On our final "outing" we went to the towns in which other women of our group had been lodged and acquainted them with our plans. On the way we saw Hannah Arendt strolling through a meadow near the town where she'd hidden herself in solitude. She also intended to pull out in a few days. "Do you want to come to Lourdes with us?" we asked.

"I feel safer alone," she replied. "In groups there's less chance of getting through."

On the way back, a friendly, cheerful officer took us with him in his car. We were halted at a police checkpoint en route. That happened more and more often, and as always we crouched lower in our rear seat. It was already dark, and we saw when the car stopped that it was our Pontacq sergeant. The driver handed over his papers; the gendarme examined them and handed them back saying thank you, without looking inside the car. The jolly officer pointed his thumb to the rear and said: "*et ça, c'est l'auto-stop.*" The gendarme bent down and shone his flashlight on us. He stared at us for a long moment, then said curtly, "Report to the gendarmerie tomorrow afternoon."

It never came to that.

The bus to Lourdes was in fact operating, but we would have been immediately noticed upon departure. We had to leave the village unseen.

Alfred, our young friend in uniform, was a first-class finagler; he always knew a way to help, so we conferred with him. Somehow he procured a motorcycle and some gasoline. By a circuitous route, I guided Anja Pfemfert out to the highway where Alfred waited for her, and we loaded her onto the rear seat. I contemplated the picture for a moment: the blond soldier with the rosy, boyish face and, behind him, clinging tightly, the broad female figure with her Kalmuck-eyes under black bangs.

They rode off with a deafening roar.

Again Paulette forgot to close the lattice-gate, and the chickens ran out behind us into the vegetable garden. She returned and chased them, flapping their wings, clucking and squawking, back in. Then we stole around to the rear and out of the village.

4
Lourdes, July 1940

Paulette and I made our entry into Lourdes on the bicycle-crossbars of two soldiers who had seen us slowly plodding along the highway and had invited us to ride with them. That way we easily got through the military checkpoint at the city gate; no one asked to see our papers. As agreed, the others waited on a certain street corner for us.

Lourdes was a city of noise and jostling, teeming with refugees from every part of the country. We walked through a street with dozens of small shops that sold gift articles and religious souvenirs. We stood before the show window of a *pâtisserie*, but it was empty except for a few small sugar Bernadettes. Paulette shuddered and said, "It's incredible—those sweet saints turn my stomach." I said, "They make me sick too; but first things first—we have to find lodgings, someplace where all of us can spend the night."

All of us—just who were "all of us" at that time?

Three women who had fled together from the Gurs camp: Anja, Paulette, and me. Then there was der Alte, Paulette's father, who'd already gone on to Lourdes ahead of us; and last, Alfred, our soldier on the motorcycle.

On the way we'd spoken with several emigrés who had just come from Lourdes. They had warned us about the Centre d'Accueil, the reception center that every city now had. Refugees must first register there upon arrival and quarters would be assigned to them. Make a big detour around these centers, we were told; foreigners and persons without valid papers were seized and put back in camps.

The City of Lourdes had requisitioned part of the largest luxury hotel for the purpose of housing refugees. We wanted to try to find accommodations there. In the multitude of people, we thought, Anja and the old man would be less noticeable. To stay overnight, however, we'd surely need billeting slips.

Anja and der Alte were tired. We dropped them off in a bistro, glad that we didn't have to drag them along with us through the streets. Alfred stayed with them, for they were more secure with a soldier at their table.

Back then Anja must have been about sixty years old. With her wide cheekbones and short-cut, coal-black hair falling in fringes over her forehead, she drew glances everywhere. As she hadn't been able to redye her hair during the time in camp, it now looked as if she had a white skullcap or beanie perched on her head. Her broken French had a Russian twang, the same one heard from Paris taxi drivers. And in the flight from Gurs a slipup had occurred—with her, of all people: in the rush she had been given a release certificate for a twenty-year-old Dutch girl.

Der Alte was also a difficult case. If he'd at least allowed his long gray hair to be cut, hair which stood out wildly around his head and by which he could always be recognized! Even in this jumble of seedy refugees everyone stared at him. He knew not a word of French, and made himself understood by sign language and a few miscellaneous scraps. When he wanted to explain that he was a former delegate to the Reichstag, he said simply, *Député kaputt.*

Alfred in his uniform was a gift from heaven. Of course, his role as guardian angel also had its limits, for his papers showed that he was not French but Polish.

Paulette and I went into the park across from the Bishop's Palace and sat down on a bench to talk and think things over. We'd agreed on a division of labor: Paulette was responsible for "domestic affairs" and my department was jurisdiction over "diplomatic relations with officials."

A young soldier sat down near us. *"Nous somme foutus,"* he said, "We're done for." He stretched out his legs and went on, *"Nous sommes vendus*—They've sold us out." All the soldiers said the same thing. He told us his name was Bernard and his home was in Normandy. He had no *route de marche*, he had no idea where his regiment was, and he also didn't give a damn.

Paulette wanted to know more. On which fronts he'd been, how had it gone when the rout began and later, when the armistice was proclaimed? He told us all about it and seemed glad to have someone listening to him.

After a while Paulette said: "We have to go now. You see, we have a problem; we have to find a place to stay overnight." Through an error, she told him, we had no billeting slip. We had her elderly parents with us and, at the least, had to find a place to put them up. If she only knew where to get a slip! As a soldier, he, Bernard, of course, had no such trouble.

Bernard nodded.

"I have to think it over a bit," said Paulette. "Actually, Bernard could get a *fiche d'hébergement*, a billeting slip, for us; he could say it was for his family. Indeed, that would be a solution."

The youth looked at us mistrustfully. "I have enough to worry about myself—I don't need any more troubles," he said. "Anyway, that whole story, *c'est louche*, it sounds fishy."

"It's the whole mess, everything's coming apart," I said. "We're all sitting here in the same mire; we must all help each other. You're not afraid, are you? You, as a soldier, surely have a sense of honor. . . ."

"Sense of honor! Hahaha!" laughed Bernard, and slapped himself on the thigh. "My honor? Vanished, like everything else."

Paulette grew furious. "Don't you have any sisters?" she burst out.

He stared straight ahead.

"And your girlfriend?" she kept after him. "When she needs help, let's hope she finds someone with more courage!"

He shuffled his feet.

"And your *maman*, your *papa*—okay, you're one of those who doesn't care whether his old parents have a roof over their heads or not. Oh, well."

Bernard got red in the face. "*Vous m'emmerdez* [you bore me]," he said, stood up, and walked away. Without turning his head, he called, "Wait here!"

"Get a billeting slip for the big hotel," Paulette called after him. "My parents have to sleep in a real bed for once!"

I don't remember exactly what happened next. But I do remember waking up the next morning in a hotel room; there were two beds, and several mattresses on the floor. I counted; yes, all five of us were there.

What luxury! Running water, a huge mirror with a gold ornamental frame, clean bed linen, even a bidet behind a curtain. As Paulette and I set out on our first exploratory tour, we felt ourselves neat and clean at last. Now we must learn what was happening here, what information

there was about conditions in the rest of the country, and what one
could venture to do.

We knew that the Germans already occupied a great part of France,
and even then it was clear to us that sometime or other they would
control all of France. We also knew that France was obliged by terms of
the armistice to turn us emigrés over to the Nazis. Therefore we had to
get by without registering at any refugee centers. In the long run,
however, we couldn't go on that way: we were sitting here in a trap and
must find a way out. The trap was France; we had to get out of France.

How could we have seriously believed back then that it was possible?
We were stuck fast here in Lourdes without money, without valid docu-
ments, without connections with anyone who could have helped us.
Still, we set about devising a way—we should try somehow to get to
Marseille, the big seaport.

People fall into a trap; they watch while it slowly closes. Some are
benumbed at the sight of their incomprehensible fate. Others are panic-
stricken and run around in circles. The ones who have objectives search
for a way out. Determination to get out of the trap demands every effort
and suppresses all doubts about its feasibility.

First of all we had to find our families. But how could we find them in
this chaos? Everything had become unpredictable, imponderable,
although the general breakdown itself was not entire; railways and mail
and telegraph services still functioned in the unoccupied zone, even
though curtailed.

Still more important and useful was our own mail service, which had
developed from the first days of the collapse, and by means of which
emigrés usually located each other in a short time, although all were
running in different directions. It is inexplicable how, among the masses
of refugees, German emigrés recognized each other from afar—on the
highways, in cities and villages, in hostels and military posts. Most of
them had a little notebook or only a scrap of paper on which they wrote
the names of people they met and how they could be reached. Only
rarely did anyone have the address of the person sought; but often one
made a contact that could put him on the trail of relatives and friends.

It happened that way with my family. While we were still in Pontacq
we ran into two young emigrants during one of our secret expeditions
who reported to us, "the Austrians are assembling in Montauban." They

gave us the address of Lisl Fischer, a young Viennese. I knew her and at
once wrote her a postcard: "Is anyone of our family in Montauban? You
can reach me through Lise Duchamps, General Delivery, Pontacq,
Basses Pyrénées."

A few days later a card came from my brother in Montauban, short
and pertinent as always: "I escaped from the camp, have just arrived
here, and received your message. Your husband was seen on a bicycle
between Limoges and Montauban. I leave your address for him with
friends here. I just now have learned that Eva and the baby are in a camp
near here and I'm going to fetch them. She'll know what's happened to
our parents. A bientôt, Hans."

I sat down on a bench under the trees across from the post office and
tried to take it all in. I read the card again and thought, he would still
have had room to write: "I'm happy that you're alive." But he'd probably forgotten to do that; he was always forgetting something.

We wandered through the streets on that first morning in Lourdes
and marveled at the number of familiar faces. One stopped and listened
to the latest news and rumors, not knowing whether any of it was true.
Someone had met Paulette's husband, Karl; he was trying to make his
way to Marseille. Various people had seen Hans during the flight and
stated that he'd gotten out of the occupied area and through the
German lines to Limoges; he was in uniform. It was also affirmed that
he and two others had "liberated" bicycles and were riding toward
Montauban. I was given the addresses of several people there, and I
wrote again: "Tell Hans he should write to Lise Duchamps; the address
is now General Delivery, Lourdes."

They let us remain in the hotel room temporarily. In the basement
they had set up a community kitchen for refugees where all could cook
something for themselves—whenever there was any food to buy. We
could also line up for soup at various distribution points, and it was so
much better than the soup in Gurs! Paulette and I received a small *alloca-
tion militaire*, allowance for wives of soldiers. They no longer insisted on
proof; in this confusion that would have been senseless. Also, Alfred
received his pay from some military office or other.

Franz Pfemfert learned from emigrés that Anja was here with us in
Lourdes, and connections were quickly established. He himself had
landed in Perpignan after fleeing from the camp. We thought that this

news would soothe Anja's nerves, but she was still utterly depressed and said continually and thoughtlessly, "I must go to Franz." We assured her, "Yes, of course, as soon as we have permission."

Once Paulette asked her, "Anja, why do you always just sit on the bed and sigh?" Anja looked at her for a long time. "My child, we Jews are an ancient tribe, and we have much to sigh about."

We had to manage to get Anja to Perpignan, and we others had to leave and try to get to Marseille. But how?

In order to take the train to another locality, a permit was now required, a *sauf-conduit*. Many emigrants had been stuck in Lourdes for weeks, unable to get permission to travel. We had to try every possible way—but what documents should we show? The fake release certificates from Gurs? Or the papers we had in Paris from the period before the collapse—papers with our real names, which were possibly on lists of wanted persons? The Paris IDs came in different colors: Mine, for instance, was blue-gray and was a *refus de séjour*, a rejection of residence, and it hadn't been renewed for months. Blue-gray was one of the better colors. Other pastel tints were worse: sky-blue, lilac, pink . . . and white was worst of all. White was the dreaded Expulsion Order.

One must state the reason for the trip, but whatever the reason, the application was more often than not rejected, sometimes even in spite of a summons from the American Consulate, which only a selected few could present. The application must be submitted to the *Commandant Militaire de la Ville de Lourdes*. We were warned about him, because several stateless persons who had applied had been arrested, brought to an assembly point, and from there returned to a concentration camp. Under no circumstances would we go to him.

We tried with other officials. Paulette and I went to both military and civilian authorities, to various commanders and commissioners, always with the greatest caution and always prepared for a speedy retreat. We were turned down everywhere. Sometimes we grew weary and rested on a bench in the park opposite the Bishop's Palace. The voice of the bishop of Lourdes resounded across to us: "Peace on earth. . . ."

"Cold shivers are running down my spine," said Paulette. "That's always an indication that bullshit is present."

Anja's lethargy suddenly turned to aggression. "You want to prevent me from going to Franz!" she snapped at me one morning. We tried to calm her. "You must have a travel permit, and we're trying our best to get them...."

"I'll get one for myself, I don't need you!" She began to sob. "You two are keeping me prisoner here—I'm not going to put up with it any more."

"But, Anja, don't you see that we're trying to help all of us? We attract less attention because of the language."

"No!" she cried. "You want to dominate me—I'm going to the commissioner now, and request my *sauf-conduit*." She grabbed her purse and ran out the door just as she was, uncombed and with her dress only half-buttoned.

"Don't do it, they'll arrest you!" we yelled after her; but in her state we didn't feel able to hold her back. We couldn't follow her either, it would have endangered all of us. So we stayed in our room, waiting. They'd surely arrest her and the police would come here. It was best for der Alte to vanish and not return until later in the evening. The uniformed Alfred remained at the hotel with us. We prepared stories to try to talk Anja and ourselves out of it in case the police came. My name is Lise Duchamps. I'm Paulette Perrier. We're Belgians.

The police arrived, thumping loudly on the stairs. Three policemen, supporting between them the softly sobbing Anja. They comforted her and deposited her gently on the bed. "*Elle est affolée, la pauvre dame*," they explained to us. "She's confused."

She had gone to police headquarters and demanded to speak to the commissioner. The public was not permitted to speak to him directly, but the poor woman was so agitated that she could not be deterred, and she was conducted to him.

"We couldn't understand her—what sort of language does she speak, anyway? She just kept repeating *sauf-conduit, sauf-conduit. Monsieur le commissaire spécial* is a friendly man and tried to placate her, but she broke down completely. When she was able to walk again, we accompanied her here. Perhaps you should give her an aspirin or some valerian drops." He made a gesture of negation. "Don't mention it, *au revoir*."

At last! a telegram at the post office for Lise Duchamps. From Montauban, the first direct news from Hans. So—he had arrived there and had gotten my address. I knew all the time that he'd get through, but as I ripped open the envelope my hand shook a little. I read:

J'ATTENDS LISE À MONTAUBAN. It was signed with an unknown name, General Delivery, Montauban.

I explained my situation in a long letter. Paulette is in Lourdes with me, also der Alte and Anja. We're trying to get *sauf-conduits*. Surely he was also of the opinion that we must try to get to Marseille? As soon as (and if!) we get a travel permit, we could meet at the Toulouse railroad station and go on to Marseille together, for I dare not leave that station. As a soldier he could of course get a permit with no trouble. Soon we'll be together again—.

Someone, I don't recall who it was, told us about a new office. There was now a *capitaine* at the rail station with the title *Commandant Spécial Militaire de la Gare de Lourdes*. It wasn't exactly clear what he was commanding at the station, and my informant knew nothing more about him. But, after all, one could try with due caution to ask him. Maybe he would be willing to give us some kind of ID card or paper with a stamp on it, since his title sounded so impressive. We thought it better if I went to him alone, carrying all our papers; it was certainly not advisable to present him with Anja and der Alte.

No one was waiting, no soldiers or refugees; I was admitted at once. Either the word hadn't gotten around yet about this officer being stationed here, or it had already become known that it was better to stay out of his way.

The commandant's office was a bare, narrow room. He sat at his desk and didn't look up from his work; a wave of his hand invited me to be seated. As he wrote, I observed him closely and thought: He must be about forty years old, and he doesn't look at all unpleasant. Should I address him as *mon capitaine* or *mon commandant*, which is the higher rank? I decided to use *monsieur;* from a woman, *monsieur* is always suitable.

Without quite looking up, he asked what I wanted to see him about. I explained that I must go to Marseille, where my husband was waiting for me. "We're Belgians," I continued, "and I fled to the south with some friends when the Germans invaded. I thought that perhaps you, as station commandant, could help us on our way, me and the three others—."

He raised his hand to cut me off. I was in the wrong place, he said, what I needed was a *sauf-conduit*, and the city commandant was responsible for that, not the station commandant.

"I know," I said.

He looked at me in surprise, and I had the feeling that he was really seeing me for the first time.

"I know," I repeated. "But it's hopeless. The applications wouldn't be approved. I've tried everything, and I wouldn't bother you if it wasn't so urgent. We must get to Marseille. I've come here to beg you for help, Monsieur."

He regarded me silently. He'd evidently become curious. Maybe he was also a little sympathetic? Would he help us? Say something, *capitaine*, or *commandant*, answer me, do.

"You say that you're Belgians?" he asked at last.

I hesitated a moment. "Yes," I said slowly, "that's what I said."

"May I see your papers?" No officer had been that polite to me for a long while.

I handed him the Gurs release certificates; they said that Paulette and I were Belgian, Anja Dutch. Then I gave him der Alte's expired *carte d'identité* from Paris and said, "That is my friend's father."

He looked through the papers and shook his head. He was about to say something, but then just looked at me and remained silent.

"*Pendant la pagaille*, in the confusion of flight," I said, "they sent us to this camp because there was no other housing. When the *boches* halted their advance we were released." That sounded plausible.

He shrugged his shoulders. "You must understand, I *cannot* help you even if I wanted to. My functions here are limited exclusively to military affairs. I am simply not authorized to issue you documents, and if I did they would be of no use to you. You would be arrested at the first train inspection." He spoke calmly and to the point, but I still wasn't completely discouraged—was it something in his eyes? or in the timbre of his voice? I thought I sensed that the matter was not unimportant to him. He was, of course, aware that some parts of my story were rather dubious, yet he was not unfriendly.

"Perhaps it's too much to ask of you," I essayed once more. "And if it were only a normal situation—I mean, if we weren't in this fix—I don't know how to explain it——." I stammered to a dead stop, hoping he'd help me go on, but he was gazing spellbound at a fly on the ceiling, and his hands toyed with a pencil.

I pulled myself together. "I think if you would only stamp and sign our papers—you could just write '*Vu*,' Seen, on them—that surely wouldn't overstep your authority. And if that has no official validity, so what? In the general confusion nowadays regulations are often unclear, and many officials don't even bother to inspect papers closely. I think we could get through to Marseille with them." I'd broken into a sweat. The commandant was also wiping his brow.

"I asked whether you were Belgian citizens," he repeated.

I stared at him without answering.

"What other documents do you have? Passports? Identification cards?"

I was about to answer that we'd lost everything during the flight, but before I could form the words, my instinct took over.

"*Monsieur le Commandant*, I'm not a Belgian. These release certificates were issued to us by the camp administration in order to protect us from the Germans."

The fly still sat on the same spot and he regarded it attentively.

"We're *apatrides*, stateless persons," I continued. "We have no citizenship. We're emigrés from Nazi Germany. We fled to France, the land of political asylum, but now we have to keep moving, moving to somewhere, anywhere. Will you help us?" I tried to read his face. Did he have the red-tapist soul of an official, or had something deep inside of him been stirred?

He pulled open a drawer and brought out a rubber stamp. He took our papers one by one and wrote "*Vu*" on each of them; below he wrote "*Pour Marseille*," then pressed the stamp to them and signed them. He handed them to me and said: "Remember, these are not *sauf-conduits*, and I'm not empowered to issue any kind of permits to you. *Bonne chance!*"

"I don't know how to thank you, Monsieur," I said. "I admire your readiness to help——."

"You embarrass me, Madame," he interrupted me gruffly, and stood up. I looked at him amazed, seeing for the first time how tall he was.

"I don't understand why," I said. "You have probably saved all of us, and——."

He cut me short again. "*Ecoutez bien, Madame*. I am a Frenchman, a French officer. My country signed the article which says that we are obligated to hand people like you over to the Germans. And you want to thank me? We have betrayed you, and you speak of admiration? We stand deeply in your debt." He started to give me his hand, but instead lifted his arm and saluted.

When I am asked today how France treated the Jewish and political emigrés back then, how the French behaved to us, I don't know how to answer. France—which France? "The French"—who are they?

I know that in the eyes of the French authorities we were troublesome strangers who must be kept at arm's length; they held us to be detrimental because we could imperil France's relationship with Nazi Germany. Thousands of emigrés were compelled to scrape along outside the law, somehow to fend for themselves. There were no work permits for us, we had no rights, we could not even marry.

When war broke out the French government declared us to be "enemy aliens" and put us in concentration camps—together with the real enemies, the Nazis. Many emigrés enlisted as volunteers in the French army in order to fight German fascism and instead were impressed into the Foreign Legion and sent to build a trans-Saharan railroad.

The French—Pétain, Weygand, Laval—signed the article of the armistice that handed us emigrés over to the Germans, and the new government made strenuous efforts to outperform even the Nazis.

Yet none of us would have been able to survive without the help of French men and women in every corner of the country—French people whose humaneness gave them the courage to take in these driven strangers, to hide them, to feed them. Men like the commandant of the railroad station in Lourdes, who in the darkest hour of their own defeat assumed the added burden of repudiating that Article of Shame which had robbed their land of the proud name *La France généreuse*.

5

Zigzagging to Marseille

The train arrived in Toulouse promptly at eight o'clock. Right on schedule, I thought; everything else was haphazard, but our train ran without a care about the general turmoil.

I woke Paulette, Anja, der Alte, and our soldier, Alfred. We'd been under way for twelve hours, and after we had finally found seats, I was the only one who couldn't sleep. In spite of my weariness, thoughts kept crisscrossing through my mind. Was Hans already waiting for me at the station? Was he perhaps still in uniform? How long had it been since we'd seen each other?—it was really only three months, was that possible? Certainly he would already be waiting at the depot.

After the rail station commandant in Lourdes had endorsed our papers with "*Vu*," I wrote to Hans at the cover address in Montauban: "We'll surely get through with these papers so prettily stamped, but naturally we won't be permitted to interrupt the journey; we must travel directly to Marseille." I told him the date, that the train would arrive in Toulouse about eight, and that the next train to Marseille would leave at noon. If I didn't hear from him again I would assume that we'd meet at the station and travel on together. That was the only possibility.

The train had left Lourdes after midnight, but because of the war there was an eight-o'clock curfew. For that reason we had had to start our move from the hotel at seven-thirty. Alfred, Paulette, and I carried the few pieces of baggage we still had to the station, so that the two older ones wouldn't have to drag along their sacks and bundles.

"They take us for *clochards* for sure," laughed Paulette. We waited for four hours on the open platform.

The train was overcrowded and we stood for many more hours. Fatigue crept into our legs, our arms; our heads hung ever heavier. Two or three times a military inspector came through and asked for our travel documents. We had folded our papers so that the commandant's stamp was uppermost. It made the intended impression and the papers weren't inspected further.

As said, the train arrived in Toulouse on time. I woke the others, and my heart began to hammer. Hans was surely waiting for me——.

I looked out the window as the train ran slowly along the platform. Several soldiers stood about, but no Hans. We got off and looked around. My husband was not there.

"The train from Montauban surely arrives a little later," I said. "Let me look at the schedule." But Hans's train had arrived twenty minutes earlier, and the next one was due late in the afternoon. "Maybe he's not coming by rail; maybe there's a bus, or else he took a bicycle—we just have to wait a while."

Meanwhile the train for Perpignan arrived, and we put Anja Pfemfert and her bundles aboard. The moment she was in the compartment she became calmer. In a few hours she'd be reunited with Franz, and that was the only important thing.

We continued to wait for Hans. What could have happened to him? No, nothing happens to him, he knows how to get by, how to make it through. Maybe something unexpected turned up; but, then, why hadn't he let me know? He could have telegraphed again, or sent someone else to Toulouse. "*J'attends Lise à Montauban*" was the last thing I'd heard from him—he hadn't replied to either of my two letters. Now it was almost eleven o'clock. Our train for Marseille would leave in an hour.

"I can't go with you," I said to the others. "I must find Hans first, otherwise we'll lose contact again."

"Where will you find him then?"

"Where? I don't know where he could be. Surely in Montauban— but I don't even have an address, only a box number. How could he just——?"

My joy at seeing him again dwindled away. Wasn't that just like him? Still, I couldn't travel on to Marseille without knowing what had happened to him.

"We can't let you go running around in the world alone," the others said. "If you really want to go ahead and try to find Hans—are you sure that's best?—then we'll wait for you here at the station until the next train. It leaves at midnight; you have to be back before then."

"You're all much too tired to do that," I objected, "and aside from that, it would be dangerous for you, you *clochards*, especially for der Alte with his shaggy mane."

"Clear out—get going!" said Paulette impatiently. "But you *must* be back before midnight."

First, to get through the checkpoint without being arrested—Alfred, in uniform, put his arm around me. As we walked through, he kissed me so passionately that I almost tripped over my own feet. I saw the officials smile understandingly—nobody was going to stop a combat soldier and his girl. And then I was outside in the open air, in the station plaza, and Alfred had disappeared. I was a little dazed; I took a deep breath.

"Lisa, what are you doing here? Hans has been waiting in Montauban for you since early this morning."

I turned around, and in front of me, before I'd even taken a step, stood Eva Lewinski. Unbelievable.

"He's waiting? How can he be waiting there for me?"

But she knew nothing more than that, and she didn't know his address either.

"I'll describe to you how you can find my brother Erich, he'll help you find Hans for sure," she said.

"How do I get there without being picked up?"

"Try to go by bus, they check buses less often," Eva said.

The bus didn't leave for two hours, but the driver let me in so I could at least sit and doze. Once a policeman boarded and wanted to know what I was doing there. "I have to wait for someone," I said, "a soldier, a friend." A sympathetic smile. He got out without asking to see my papers. Lucky once again.

It must have been close to four in the afternoon when I arrived in Montauban. I soon found Erich, who was living in a cottage with several friends.

"Lisa! There you are at last."

"How come 'at last?' "

"Hans has been standing in the garden of his villa since morning, waiting for you." He pointed out the way. The street led steeply upward and I was already dead tired.

It was true. Hans stood in the garden on the lookout for me. He saw me, came to me, and held out his arms.

I know that at this point a moving reunion scene should have ensued, but it wasn't like that at all; I still wonder at myself today. "So you're waiting for me in the garden," I snapped at him over the fence. "And I—and the others—what do you imagine——?"

He tried to explain everything, and there really were good reasons. He couldn't get a *sauf-conduit* for another couple of days. And to my surprise he wasn't as certain as we were that going to Marseille was the only right thing to do. Perhaps it was better to go underground somewhere in the countryside. We ought to talk it all over first.

"But why didn't you let me know? Not even a telegram!"

"There wasn't enough time," he answered.

"And how could you have assumed that I'd abandon all our plans, look for you and find you, and do everything without valid papers?" My anger started to rise again.

He looked surprised. "Of course, what else? You certainly wouldn't have gone on to Marseille without me. It's clear that if I wasn't at the station in Toulouse you'd look for me here, so I just waited for you. Right here, since early morning."

Yes, of course it was clear to *him*. What else? How touching that he had waited for me in the garden.

"Let's go in," he said. "Inside we can sit down and talk properly."

The "villa" was really a villa, but it was barely half-finished. Construction had been interrupted by the war, and the owner had put what there was of the building at the disposal of the emigrants from Germany. Most of the outer walls were up, and there was also a roof. There were half-finished stairs inside but no interior walls. Dozens of emigrants sat and lay around; they seemed to be continually moving in and out.

"Here you are at last, Lisa," I heard here and there from voices I recognized. The faces of their owners I can no longer recall; too much time has passed. Yes, there was Boris Goldenberg, whom I knew from the Young Socialist Workers in Wilmersdorf an eternity ago; he immediately started developing an analysis of present conditions, but I wouldn't stop to listen.

We sat on Hans's strawsack; he began to describe his plans to me.

"First you have to understand," I broke in, "that Paulette and her father are waiting for me at the Toulouse railroad station with Alfred, this young soldier. We agreed that I would return as soon as possible; if I don't show, they'll take the midnight train to Marseille."

Hans quickly stood up again. "That won't do," he said, appalled, "they must on no account take that train, we must reach them in time!" Fritz Opel had just relayed the news that all foreigners arriving at the Marseille station recently had been arrested and taken to camps. Paulette would probably get by with uniformed Alfred, but der Alte and his mane—impossible.

Utmost haste was needed. The last train for Toulouse was scheduled to leave at about five P.M. We ran to the station—the train had just left. The bus? The next one wouldn't get to Toulouse until after midnight.

There was nothing else for it, we had to get bicycles. The two bikes that had been "liberated" in Limoges were stored with French acquaintances; we hoped they were still there. We were lucky—a man's and a woman's bicycle. Hans took the woman's bike and I the man's because of its higher gear ratio. We rode off immediately, for it was a good fifty or sixty kilometers, almost all of it hilly country. The road went mostly uphill, hardly ever down; so it seemed to me anyway. We were making ever slower progress and the clock was running ever faster. On steep hills Hans pushed my bike from behind, his hand on the seat column. When we were already near the city, a truck picked us up, bikes and all, and we rode for the last few kilometers. The uniform Hans still wore was a blessing; soldiers need not prove their identity—one helps soldiers.

We got to the station about ten minutes to midnight. The three waiting for us had naturally become fidgety and were about to board the train. When we suddenly appeared, they cried excitedly: "At last! Hurry, get aboard!"

And now we did hurry, but to hold them back. "Wait—you can't take the train—you can't go to Marseille now!" I knew how der Alte was, and that convincing him wouldn't be easy. He stubbornly refused. "If one believed every rumor one heard—I don't care what you do, but *I* am going to take the train—one can't be continually revising one's decisions——!" I don't remember how, but we finally got him out of the station.

Then we walked through the dark, empty streets of Toulouse. In the company of two soldiers we weren't stopped: three civilians with a military escort. Hans led us to a cinema that had been cleared for refugees to use; several hundred of them were sleeping on the bare floor. A few wandered around among the sleepers, searching for friends and family, now and then bending down to examine the face of a sleeper. Hans found a narrow vacant spot for me; the people on either side pulled themselves a little closer together, and I wedged myself in and lay down. My eyes closed, and as I fell asleep I felt someone bending over me saying: "What are you doing here, Lisa? Hans is waiting for you in Montauban. . . ." I wanted to curse, but my tongue was too heavy, and I fell into a deep sleep.

A mess kitchen was set up in the cinema, and in the morning we got a cup of coffee-like brew and a chunk of bread. We sat at a long table and discussed what would be best to do now.

Sirens wailed suddenly, and almost simultaneously came the roar of airplane engines. People jumped up and ran, some crying, *"Alerte!"* others, *"Mais c'est l'armistice!"* Hans bent and pulled me under a table before I could react. Then the sirens fell silent and the engines faded away.

"I've never seen you like that," I said perplexed. "In Paris you didn't want to go to the air-raid shelter, and now, when there's an armistice. . . ."

"An armistice accompanied by cruelty and horror. We've witnessed bombing attacks and machine-gun fire on fleeing civilians. Once three of us were in a farmhouse—that was one week after the signing—and I was going to the pump in the yard; I heard a plane and looked up as I walked. A bomb landed at the same moment, directly on the water-pump. Something like that shakes you to the core."

(The cover-up for Luftwaffe bombing attacks on the French civilian population after the conclusion of the armistice was referred to as "illegal troop movements.")

In Montauban we'd all have a hideout in the "villa." The police didn't trouble themselves about the emigrants there, and up until now nobody had been taken away to a camp. Hans would manage to wangle papers for himself; we must just bide our time and see how things developed in Marseille—and we'd use that time to catch our breath and think things over.

Hans and Alfred rode the bikes back; Paulette, her father, and I took the bus. As I'd already discovered that one could board and sit down early, we avoided the inspection of boarding passengers, which was made this time.

In Montauban we saw acquaintances at every turn, but now their names and faces are blurred in my memory. We met the Hitler biographer Konrad Heiden on the street; I do remember that, because Hans said, "He should also make haste to clear out as soon as possible—what madness, to stroll about openly!"

We discussed our situation and agreed to go ahead and try to get to Marseille as soon as we knew that the strict controls there had been lifted. The idyllic life in Montauban couldn't go on forever. In Marseille there were aid committees and organizations for emigrant support; there one would be in closer contact with the anti-Fascist elements of the emigration.

First of all, Hans needed a travel permit for Marseille. I went with him to the city military authorities. We entered a large waiting room full of soldiers. Many of them were also accompanied by their wives, whom they could very well have just found again. Each of them needed some kind of certificate or document. A few officers sat at a table. When Hans finally reached the head of the line, he presented the military paper he'd received before fleeing from the camp and requested a *route de marche* to Marseille (using very few words—careful with that *boche* accent!). After a while his name was called and his ID handed back to him. He studied the document as he walked back to me through the hall, and I could see his eyebrows lift in surprise. "What does that mean?" he asked, and handed the paper to me. It said, handwritten, "*Route de Marche: Destination Marseille, Dept. Bouches du Rhône,*" with stamp and signature, and beneath it, also handwritten, "*Voie de terre.*"

"What does that mean?" he asked again, "*Voie de terre?*"

A soldier next to us looked over my shoulder. "That means," he said, and then louder, "that means, *mon vieux,* that they're sending you from Montauban to Marseille *on foot.*" Several soldiers stood up, ranged themselves around us, and tried to get a look at the paper.

"On foot, *à pied, mais c'est extraordinaire!*"

The officer at the table explained that, according to regulations, a soldier could travel by train only when he was on his way to his hometown.

"He's shed his blood for France," cried a young soldier furiously, "and now he has to get to Marseille on foot!"

Hans gave me a slight nudge. I said angrily, "We're going to lodge a complaint!" and a few seconds later we were outside. We walked quickly down the street. Hans wiped sweat from his brow. "That's all I needed—if I'd opened my mouth again, with my *accent boche*. . . ."

Back home in the villa, sitting on our straw mattress, we showed the others our historical document. What now? The line couldn't be erased, that was impossible.

"Let me see it a moment," said Paulette, and reached for the paper. "Oh God, oh God!" she exclaimed, as the tin cup of red wine she was holding in her other hand tipped slightly and splashed a few drops directly on the *voie de terre* spot. She examined her work and handed the paper back to Hans; the words were illegible.

"So—now you have a document with a wine stain—that could easily happen. But you don't have to go on foot."

News soon came that the inspections at the Marseille railroad station had become more lax.

Shortly afterward, demobilization orders were promulgated. The men went to Toulouse and received a demobilization paper, a thousand francs, and a raincoat. It also wasn't merely by chance that the door to the warehouse next to the demob office stood wide open and unguarded; a man could simply enter and take one of the sacks of green, unroasted coffee beans. Should one wait until the Germans confiscated everything? Soon the entire villa was redolent with the aroma of roasting coffee—it was being roasted in improvised pans and exchanged for other edibles.

Those are my final memories of Montauban. Then we were sitting in a train again; we arrived in Marseille in the evening and, to attract less attention, passed singly through the checkpoint. I saw Hans go through, then Paulette; her father positioned himself on the other side of the barrier, Alfred behind him. I showed my document with the stamp of the station commandant in Lourdes and got through without further ado. As I walked into the big gray hall, someone seized me by the shoulder and turned me around. I looked into Paulette's wide-open eyes. "They've arrested der Alte!"

"Move yourselves over to the side, otherwise they'll grab all of us," said Hans.

Der Alte didn't glance over at us, he acted as if he were alone. Two officials, one policeman in uniform and one in civilian clothes, were holding and questioning him. Der Alte didn't lose his head; he didn't have to dissemble, he really understood scarcely a word. He shrugged his shoulders helplessly, looked at the officials with an expression of naïveté, and we heard: *"Nix comprend—nix parle."*

"Alfred, you're the only one of us who's not in danger; can you talk to the officials?" Alfred was quickly there.

"This man is stateless," they told him, "and all *apatrides* must be returned to camps."

"But not a man of his age!" protested Alfred.

"Old or young," replied the one in mufti. "He's *apatride*."

"Where will they take him?"

"To Les Milles, all persons are being sent there."

No, nothing could be done. They led him away.

Suddenly Paulette said, "I'm going with him."

Hans held her tightly by the arm. "So that we'll not only have to abduct him out of the camp but you, too?"

It was known that Les Milles was not the worst camp. One could visit the inmates, and now and then they could even get a day-pass to go into Marseille. We'd surely be able to get Der Alte out very soon.

The next problem was: where would we sleep that night? Walking down the broad station stairs we ran into Robert, whom we knew from Paris. We told him our story in a few words.

"It's good that at least you got through—we can surely help out with der Alte."

Robert would find us a place to stay for the night. We went down to the old harbor together, to a shabby hotel, a *maison de passe*, he called it. The landlady greeted him like an old friend; papers were not asked for. There was only one unoccupied room, one with a double bed. That's fine, I thought, we can figure out some way for all of us to sleep.

In the night we heard the blast of a ship's horn. At the same moment the *patronne* banged on the door. "A ship has made port! *Vite, vite,* I need the room! Just throw your things in a corner."

"What does she want of us?" I wondered sleepily.

"Is this a madhouse?" asked Paulette indignantly.

"No," said Hans, "no madhouse, just a whorehouse; or to put it delicately, a love nest—didn't you notice?"

"It's only for an hour," said the woman, "you can all wait downstairs. Nowadays it's a real stroke of luck when a ship pulls in—not like in the good old times."

The next morning we were told about the refugee shelter in the
school at Belle de Mai. It had been set up by the Marseille authorities for
refugees from the north, and no police registration was required. As we
no longer needed the *sauf-conduits*, Paulette and I put away all of our
papers showing false names and used our own identification documents,
even though they had in the meantime become invalid. The ID from
Paris which I now presented at the shelter, my *refus de séjour*, was an ID
(and one of the better ones) well known to the Paris police, but here in
the south it evoked astonishment. I had still another document that I
was never without and that I seldom used. I fished it out now: a certi-
fied French translation of the Deutsches Reichs-Register detailing my
deprivation of citizenship. Two officials read it through attentively,
especially the last sentence: *La fortune de la personne sus-nommée est confis-
quée par les présentes. Signé: Pfundtner.*

"*Ah, ça alors!*" one of them cried. It had achieved the intended effect.
"They took away all your property? *Ces salauds-là!*" The fact that they
had confiscated my "fortune" was more proof that the Germans were
barbarians.

Straw had been laid on the floor in the large school auditorium, and
there were still unoccupied spots. Alfred had found one of his regi-
mental buddies and had gone off to the barracks with him.

It wasn't exactly cozy among that mass of people, but the jumble of
strangers from everywhere, each with a different tale to tell, banished
monotony—among them the ragged emigrés who, often by overcoming
great difficulties, had finally found their way here, and in this confine-
ment were compelled to get along with each other.

In the messroom we were given two meals a day. The food shortage
had already reached Marseille, and our soup grew ever thinner (but it
was so good compared to the pebbly *pois chiches* of Gurs!).

Then came the Ruhr Epidemic, the dysentery that had afflicted us at
the camp. There were three toilets in the school yard and we stood there
in line, in distress and torment. A doctor came every third day, distributed vials with the same medicine to everyone, and departed after a few
minutes, always with the same words: "*et surtout, pas de tomates!* [and
above all, no tomatoes!]" So we were fed tomato soup, tomato salad,
and fried tomatoes.

In the auditorium/sleeping-hall we had a family from the Bretagne, an uncommonly fat woman with five children. All day long she would take one child after another and clean it, as well as she could, with newspaper and old rags. As she worked she sang in a deep, strong voice:

Célina, ma chérie,
Si je t'aime, c'est pour la vie. . . .

Sometimes the others joined in, and the whole hall sang of the eternal love for Célina.

As soon as people were on their feet again, the search went on, the search for family and friends (Paulette's husband, Karl, appeared with a small group of soldiers from his regiment and moved into the school with us), and the search for ID documents (genuine or counterfeit) and bread-ration cards (genuine or counterfeit). People tried to link up with friends who had in the interim succeeded in getting to the States—or to Santo Domingo, or to China. We visited Paulette's father and bent our every effort toward getting him released from Les Milles.

Now that Pétain and Laval ruled with unlimited powers in the "free" zone, it was clear that this was only the beginning. Many of the French refugees—were there six million or was it more?—gradually let themselves be repatriated to their hometowns. Many of our German emigrants let themselves be pulled back and forth between blindness and panic. We had scant sympathy for them, and for that reason very little patience: So wake up at long last, *do* something—you sit there in crap and don't make a move; what are you waiting for?

It was an afternoon in early August—the sun burned down while the mistral blew through one's bones—and, still here in Marseille, we'd been walking for a long time, running into acquaintances now and then. For a while we spoke with Leo Lania and his wife, Lucy; they were sitting on a café terrace. Leo and my brother were involved in some complicated, hush-hush scheme that should help all of us to get out of France. Lucy looked me up and down, shook her head, and said, "I still have another dress with me and I'll bring it to you tomorrow; you really must throw that rag away." Next day she gave me a knitted dress, white with black stripes, real snazzy.

We walked on; I don't recall exactly what we were searching for right then. I said, "Now I have to sit down for a minute." We were standing in front of a broad stairway that led up to a public building. A sign above said *Orphelinat*, Orphanage. I sat on the steps and closed my eyes. I heard a tiny voice say, "Madame——?" Two little girls were standing in front of me. *"Madame, vous êtes une orpheline,* are you an orphan?" They held out a handful of daisies to me.

"For you, Madame Orphan. *Ça porte bonheur——*."

6

The Shoes Won't Fit . . .

Everything, everyone, pressed toward Marseille. The city was crammed with refugees, swarms of German emigrants among them. Maybe there, at the huge port, was a way out of the trap.

My husband, Hans, had scant confidence in all the plans about mysterious ships and ocean voyages; up until now every one of them had fallen through, one after the other. Hans felt more secure on solid land. And these crackpot ideas involving consulates and transit visas, foreign-exchange permits, and choosing between North or South America—they all sounded as if they came from some fantasy-world a man clutches at when he can't cope with the improbable reality. People like us, people without connections, papers, or money, where could we go? All of the neutral countries shunned us like the plague.

Going underground was nothing new for us; we'd been experts at it since 1933. Hans thought it would be possible to continue to do so, to find housing with decent people, probably and preferably in the countryside. While fleeing south during the German advance, he'd been taken in several times by French farmers. Hans, the Berliner in French uniform, felt safer with the French, who had hidden him from the Germans. There must be all kinds of places, he said—for instance, in the Massif Central—where one would be untraceable. One could hibernate there through the winter, as long as this Nazi winter lasts.

It was plausible to me. But shouldn't we also look at exit possibilities? "Sure," said Hans, "look, but don't count on them."

There was a lot of discussion among the refugees about Portugal. Portugal was neutral and would probably remain so. A few emigrés who had American visas were able to obtain Portuguese transit visas. At once a variety of ideas were hatched along the lines of managing to get a transit visa without first having the American visa.

In order to get a transit visa one had, of course, to have an entry visa for some other country. For that, first of all, one needed a passport. The Portuguese required in addition a paid transatlantic fare, to make certain that a person would be off their hands. The fare had to be paid in dollars, which for most emigrés was absurd: they had hardly any money at all, and for sure none of them had a dollar permit.

To travel from France to Portugal one also needed a Spanish transit visa. That, however, one could only apply for when one had the Portuguese document; every country was afraid that the emigrés would settle in with them like bedbugs.

And, then again, one needed money, the money to pay for complying with all these formalities.

Financial help came from an unexpected source: the Demobilization Edict. The men must register, then each received a demobilization certificate with a *route de marche* to his hometown, a train ticket to get him there, and a thousand francs. And, in addition, the aforementioned *imperméable,* the raincoat—apparently the only item the French military had supplied themselves with in abundance *(pour la durée de la guerre).*

In Toulouse demobilization began on a Monday for names beginning with A through E; Tuesday was F through J. My brother, Hans, had to appear on Monday. Hans Fittko, who otherwise was in no haste to register, went with him; it was possible that by the next day there would be no money left, or even that the entire edict would be rescinded. He lined up and was rejected, so he went over to the next window, where he was processed without further ado. He was now an officially demobilized French soldier; and, what's more, he had a thousand francs and a raincoat, which was unfortunately too large for him.

It wasn't altogether clear how one could be, and even must be, demobilized when one had never been mobilized to start with but had merely been a prisoner in a concentration camp. But in this case one didn't ask any stupid questions.

Franz Pfemfert came in from Perpignan, where he and Anja had settled down temporarily. "The Czech consul in Marseille, an old friend, has promised me a passport," he said. "Maybe he can also do something for the two of you." The next morning we went with him to the consulate, where we met some dozen other emigrés; the word had already gotten around.

The passports that the consul gave to German anti-Fascists who had
been recommended to him had a pink cover instead of gray-green like
the official Czech passport. But in Marseille only the consul and people
like us, who had lived in Czechoslovakia as emigrés, knew that these
were "interim" passports, issued to stateless emigrés for identification.
After the consulate was closed, the consul continued to issue passports
through the good offices of the Centre Américain de Secours.

Now the Pfemferts, Hans and I, Paulette and her father, my brother
and his family, all had beautiful new passports bearing beautiful new
names.

There were rumors about honorary consuls who sold "final-destina-
tion" visas. Indeed, at this time it wasn't important whether or not they
were valid; one could at least get to Portugal with them. In the rue St.
Feréol there was a Chinese Bureau that issued Chinese visas for a
hundred francs. Most of the emigrés could afford that amount, and lines
stood in front of the bureau. We, too, got a Chinese stamp in our Czech
passports. Much later, a Chinese friend translated the "visa" for us. It
read something like this: "It is strictly forbidden for the bearer of this
document, under any circumstances and at any time, to set foot on
Chinese soil." That made no difference, for the Portuguese in Marseille
couldn't understand Chinese—or perhaps they didn't *want* to understand it?

It was simple to obtain a paid ship passage, for there was always
someone who knew how to make a profit from human desperation.
Still, it was astounding that even the venerable old English travel agency
Cook sold false transatlantic tickets. Soon every emigré in Marseille
knew about it, and we also went to the big, elegant agency in the city
center. We paid two hundred francs, and the genteel, rather supercilious
official with the British accent sold us the fake tickets without turning a
hair.

"Now it doesn't seem so much like a pipe dream," even Hans said.
"Maybe it really is possible to get out of France." Back then we didn't
think too much about what would happen to us in Portugal; the situation in France was too critical for that.

To procure a transit visa from the Portuguese consulate one had to
line up the evening before. I well remember how cold it was on the
street during the night and how hungry we were, but the next morning

our turn came at last. We actually had Portuguese transit visas. Unbelievable!

The line in front of the Spanish consulate was so long that we had to stand there three evenings in a row before our turn finally came. At first we tried to take turns. Hans held our places while I went home—"home" still being the school auditorium in Belle de Mai that had been cleared for refugees—to get a few hours' sleep on our strawpile. Then, when I came back about four in the morning, there was always a fuss when the people around us got all worked up: "Yeah, anybody could do that --!" "You got a place-card?" "What a nerve!" So we both had to stand and hold our places there for three long nights. Hans had borrowed a friend's jacket and I had the demobilized *imperméable*. The thing hung loosely around me and I dragged a long train, but it kept me somewhat warm. As there was a bread shortage everywhere, we'd bought a bag of dried bananas at a stall in the old port; they had a nauseating, sweetly rancid taste, and I said, "I can't eat them, I'd rather go hungry," but Hans insisted that I choke them down. "Otherwise you're going to topple over on me right here," he said.

Now we and several of our friends had all our papers together, and shortly others would also be that far along. Until then I hadn't even mentioned the *visas de sortie,* the French exit visas one needed to leave the country, because it hadn't even occurred to us to apply for them. Why? Because the visas were issued in Vichy, obviously under German supervision. Therefore we would have to cross the border illegally. More and more emigrés were using this method, and most of them succeeded in getting through; the Spanish border guards didn't usually ask about the French exit visa. But there were cases during this period when it didn't work—from time to time the Spaniards invented harassments. This or that document wasn't accepted, or a new one was required, or the stamp didn't suit them. And then, for example, in accordance with supposed regulations, stateless persons were not allowed to travel through Spain. Several emigrés were arrested or sent back, or even sent to the concentration camp at Figueras. However, as far as we knew up to then, all of them had eventually succeeded in extricating themselves in some way or another. We got the impression that the Spanish authorities didn't want to spoil their relations with either side. But it was disquieting to know that most of those who had trouble at the border were well-known persons traveling under their real names; it appeared that the gestapo had some influence even there.

Those of us who planned to cross the French border illegally discussed how the crossing must be organized. Someone should travel to the border and even remain there a while if possible; we needed to find a safe route, one feasible for those who followed us to use. It must also be possible to establish connections with friendly and helpful border residents, so that we would always have up-to-date information on what was happening at the border.

The "someone" had to be a person with border experience. Women always got by more easily. Paulette perhaps? No, Paulette didn't have all her papers in order yet. Lisa, somebody said. (I'm not sure who said it, but I think it was my husband.)

"We'll raise money for the trip, no sweat. So, Lisa, are you ready and willing?"

"Well, I can give it a try," I answered. "Several friends ended up in the border area during the chaos—maybe they can put me up for a few days." That was vital, because papers were being demanded everywhere.

Just then a letter arrived from Franz Pfemfert in Perpignan, which wasn't far from the border.

"Franz is completely off his rocker," said Hans. "Just read what he's written; I'll bet you can't make head or tail of it!": " . . . and you, Hans, must without fail exchange the shoes you bought, they surely don't fit; you can't use them for mountain-climbing. In any case, the shoes must be *larger* than size *42*. You should also tell this to all our friends—I mean the MEN who wear small shoe sizes. The Spanish know all about it. Lisa can safely keep her small shoes, that doesn't matter."

We worked half the night decoding the letter. The "shoes" were the Czech passports or other documents, which had to be "exchanged," meaning altered. "Size 42" was the age—most of us were under forty-two. Franz was informing us that men under forty-two, those fit for military service, would be nabbed by the Spanish authorities as they crossed the border in order to prevent them from escaping to England and there enlisting in the army. So the Germans had had their way here, too.

A fine predicament. Altering the documents wouldn't have been enough—one could see at a glance that the men were not forty-two

years old, and a falsified birth date would really put them in the soup.
We had to find another way.

At this very time another possibility of obtaining new papers opened
up. A Fort St. Charles sergeant had set up a nice little sideline in his
office: he issued certificates for two hundred francs. They were called
Certificats de Démobilisation et Route de Marche. One gave the sergeant a
name, preferably one with a genuinely French sound, some items of
personal data freely chosen, and stated where in this war one had fought
for France. The certificate confirmed that one was a French citizen with
residence in North Africa. That way one would be repatriated to one's
home at no charge and transported first to Casablanca. For an extra five
francs, the sergeant would even attach a passport photo to the certificate
and validate it with an official stamp. One went with it to the Port
Administration every few days to ask when the next Casablanca-bound
ship would sail, and whether there was a free berth. A number of
emigrés had already arrived in Casablanca.

The decision wasn't easy to make, but it seemed to be the only solution: the women and children would cross the Pyrenees to Spain and
from there proceed to Portugal; the men would go by ship to Casablanca. Then, for the first time, we would all be on neutral ground. And
then? Till we meet again—but where?

There must have been twenty-five or thirty of our friends and
acquaintances waiting for berths, my husband and my brother among
them. There were approximately the same number of women, women
whom we knew and who intended to cross the border to Spain and
travel on to Portugal.

The men went to the Port Office; vacant berths aboard ship "in the
next few days" had been posted. Everything was going according to
plan, and the next morning I would take the early train to the border.
My brother's wife, Eva, with their two-year-old Titi, had found lodgings
in Montpellier; both of them would board my train and we'd ride
together to Port-Vendres, a small seaport just short of the border. If
there was an inspection we could show our Czech passports. As soon as
I found a safe border crossing and everything was organized, we would
advise the others before we ourselves left for Spain and Portugal.

That afternoon we waited in the hotel room of a friend who had likewise gone to the port. He was called "little Leiner," because he had an
older brother—I never did learn his given name. The men had to return

soon, for the Port Office closed at five o'clock. The small room was full of people sitting around on the bed and on the floor, but now the only face I can still see before me is Paulette's.

First my husband and my brother came. I looked at them: "What's the matter with you, what's happened?"

My husband said nothing—when his eyebrows were pulled together like that, it meant he was greatly exasperated.

"We got there too late," said my brother.

"How come? You left hours ago."

"We were stopped on the way. It was ony a few minutes after five when we got to the Port Office, they must have just closed. We'll go again early tomorrow morning; it doesn't make that much difference."

I didn't like that at all. I'd figured on knowing before my train left when the men would sail for Casablanca. Perhaps I should postpone my departure?

We waited for the others. Strange that they should be taking so long when the Port Office was already closed. Not even little Leiner, in whose room we were sitting, showed up. Another hour of waiting and it was clear that something had gone wrong. But how could we find out exactly what had happened?

Then someone came into the room. No, it wasn't any of the Casablanca-bound men, but a young friend—I remember nothing about him except that he was called Erwin and that he was a light blond. He had been sent to us, by whom I also don't know, to give us this report.

The sergeant in Fort St. Charles had been denounced: he'd been picked up that morning with all his stamps and documents. Then the police had gone to the Port Office and arrested everybody who had registered using the counterfeit Casablanca certificates (little Leiner was one of them). No one knew how many there were altogether. The other men must be warned, so that this news would get around quickly. My brother had to vanish; he was one of the few who still held valid documents and thus was legally registered, but the Port Office now had a list of all the "demobilized" ones. His name was on it, and there was danger that he'd also be arrested. The next day, then, he'd move to the strawpile at the school which I'd been occupying.

But should I really leave? Everything was now up in the air. Would the men find another way? Should the women go on to Portugal without knowing whether their men could leave France? Did *I* want to

go? On the other hand, Eva could no longer be contacted and told not
to board the train. . . .

After the others had categorically stated their opinions (my brother:
"You *must* go tomorrow." Paulette: "Now you *must* wait."), my
husband and I thought the situation over. The border crossing had to be
organized in any case, if not for the young men, then at least for the
women, children, and elderly people. The thing with Eva and the child
was really a problem and could have grave consequences. Therefore it
was sensible not to change the plan. I could come back at any time if it
became necessary.

That must have been about mid-September 1940. I sat in the train
but saw nothing of the beautiful autumn in the south of France. I
couldn't shake off my doubts: was this the right decision? I nodded
off—I'd had only a couple of hours' sleep. As we came into Montpellier
I saw Eva and Titi on the platform. I called and waved, and they got
aboard. When Titi saw me, she ran to me along the corridor. After all
this time she recognized me! Then I realized that it had been only a few
months—very long months. With Titi and her excited prattling a piece
of my life came back, a piece that had been separated from us as if by a
fissure in the earth.

"*Tu as des gâteaux? Tu as du chocolat?*" she asked untiringly, as if there
still were any. Now she spoke only French; we were glad that she'd
forgotten her German. Meanwhile our compartment had filled up,
mainly with uniformed soldiers; at that time many of the demobilized
were still in uniform, for they had no other clothes. Titi looked well-
nourished, but she seemed to be constantly hungry. Eva gave her something from a lunch-packet she'd brought along. "*Du pain,*" beamed Titi.
She brandished a piece of bread in the air and then, unexpectedly, in the
midst of silence, said: "*Ça, en allemand, c'est 'Brot.'* " I got goose bumps,
and Eva rolled her eyes in horror. But no one in the compartment
appeared to have heard anything amiss.

When I told Eva the events of the day before, she also had her doubts.
"I wouldn't have gotten on the train if I hadn't seen you," she said. "It's
clear that now we must be extra careful."

"Your husband has decided that you and the child must get out of
France as soon as possible."

"*He* has decided!" she said. "Of course I understand him, but now *I*
have to think things out for myself."

In the evening we arrived in Port-Vendres, the harbor town in the foothills of the eastern Pyrenees. A group of emigrés had settled in there, and compatriots secured lodgings for us: Eva and the child in a basement room with a bed, and me in an attic.

We'd heard about people who in the meantime had gotten across to Spain; in Banyuls, the last town before the border, there was a mayor, Monsieur Azéma. He was a Socialist, and was able and willing to help the emigrés.

So first of all I had to make cautious contact with him and, if possible, with other local residents favorably inclined toward the emigrés. Everything clicked surprisingly fast, although conditions had recently become more difficult; the usual route via the border town Cerbère was now closely watched and must be avoided. But Monsieur Azéma revealed a safe and secret smuggler's route to me; he called it *la route Lister*. General Lister of the Republican army had used it for his troops during the Spanish Civil War.

Maire Azéma insisted that the emigrés themselves should organize the border crossing, thus making sure that the new route would also be known to and used by those who came after. "Perhaps one day I will no longer be here," he said. Also, it was quite imprudent for so many refugees to be reporting to him at the *mairie*. Not until later did I understand just why he'd figured on disappearing some day: he was known to the authorities for his activities during the Civil War. It would be best (he said) if someone could remain here in Banyuls for a time, to help the refugees over the Pyrenees.

"I can provide you with housing and food-ration cards temporarily," he said, and took a few cans of milk and vegetables from a crate under his desk. "*Pour le bébé*," he added.

The cans were heavy, and the path between cliff-walls from Banyuls back to Port-Vendres was long, but what did that matter when one had such treasure! Milk and vegetables, and above all a new, safe border route. I remember returning on that path back then and seeing the region with open eyes for the very first time—the incredibly blue sea and the mountain chain, on its slopes green vineyards with a hint of gold between them, and a sky as blue as the sea. One cannot describe it, one had to have been there to see it.

7

Old Benjamin

It is almost forty years ago today, but I can still recall it precisely, in every detail. Or can it be that I only think I recall it, that I'm just imagining?

I do know that it was the twenty-fifth of September 1940, in a narrow garret in Port-Vendres. I had lain down to sleep a couple of hours earlier, and a knock on the door woke me. I saw gray morning light through the high attic window and thought, "That can only be the little girl of the house from downstairs." The knock came again and I got up drowsily and opened the door. It wasn't the child. I rubbed my eyes— before me stood Walter Benjamin, one of the friends who, like many others, had fled to Marseille as the Germans overran France. "Der alte Benjamin," Old Benjamin, I called him—I really don't know why; he was only forty-eight or so.

"*Gnädige Frau*," he said. "Please forgive the intrusion—I hope this is not an inopportune time."

The world is falling to pieces, I thought, but Benjamin's courtesy is unshakeable.

"*Ihr Herr Gemahl*," he continued, "explained to me how I could find you. He said, 'She will take you over the border to Spain.'"

What had he said, my honored spouse? That was just like him, always taking it for granted that I'd manage. Which was only too true—I'd manage somehow.

Benjamin still stood in the door frame because there wasn't room for a second person between the bed and the wall. I told him to wait for me in the bistro at the marketplace.

We took a little walk away from the bistro so that we could talk without being overheard. In no way could my husband have known about it, I told Benjamin, but since I had arrived here a few days ago I really had scouted a sure route across the border.

First I'd gone down to the harbor and gotten into conversation with several dock workers. One of them took me to the union shop steward. Without asking many questions, he seemed to understand what it was all about. He had advised me to look up the mayor in Banyuls-sur-Mer, Monsieur Azéma. He was the man, as I had already been told in Marseille, who would help me to find a safe route for my family and friends who wanted to cross the border.

"He's a wonderful man, this Mayor Azéma," I continued telling Benjamin. "He spent hours with me working out every detail."

Unfortunately, the way along the Cerbère cemetery wall had become too dangerous. It had been a rather simple route to follow and a succession of refugees had used it for several months, but now it was being closely watched by the *gardes mobiles*. This was apparently on orders from the German Kundt Commission, which was the gestapo agency in that part of still unoccupied France. The only really safe route that still remained, declared the mayor, was *la route Lister*. That meant that we had to cross the Pyrenees farther west, where the mountain crests were higher and thus the climb more strenuous.

"No matter," said Benjamin, "as long as the route is safe. Of course, I have heart trouble and I must walk slowly. And, by the way, two other people who joined me in Marseille also want to cross the border with me, a Frau Gurland and her young son. Would you take the two of them also?"

"Yes, naturally. But are you sure you understand that I'm not an experienced guide in this area? I don't even actually know the way, I myself have never been up there yet. All I have is a piece of paper with a sketch of the route, one the mayor drew from memory. And then he described some details for me, turnoffs we must take and also a hut on our left. Most important is a high plateau with seven pine trees that we must be sure to keep on our right, otherwise we'll turn too far to the north; there's also a vineyard that leads to the right spot to climb over the crest. Do you want to take the risk?"

"Certainly," he said without hesitation. "Not to go, that would be the real risk."

As I looked at him I remembered that this wasn't Benjamin's first attempt to escape from the trap. How could one ever forget his earlier try?

In the apocalyptic atmosphere of 1940 Marseille, there were new stories every day about absurd escape attempts; plans involving fantasy boats and fictitious captains, visas for countries not found on any map, and passports issued by nations that no longer existed. One got used to hearing via the grapevine which sure-fire plan had fallen apart like a house of cards that day.

In spite of everything, we had to laugh time and again at the humorous side of such tragedies. One has to imagine Dr. Fritz Frankel, with his fragile appearance and his gray mane of hair, and his rather awkward friend, Walter Benjamin, with the intellectual scholar's head and the searching gaze behind thick lenses—this pair, dressed as French sailors, had bribed themselves aboard a freighter. Of course, they didn't get very far, but luckily they succeeded in evading capture in the general chaos.

We decided to visit Mayor Azéma once more, this time together, so that details would be impressed on the minds of both of us. First I notified my sister-in-law, Eva—I planned the next week to cross and get to Portugal with her and Titi—and Benjamin and I started off for Banyuls.

But right here my memory fails me. Did we dare to take the train despite the constant inspections in the border areas? Highly improbable. Surely we walked the six or eight kilometers from Port-Vendres to Banyuls on the stony path I had now become familiar with. I do still remember how we found the mayor in his office, how he bolted the door, and how he then repeated his instructions and answered our questions.

Two days earlier, when he'd drawn the sketch of the route for me, we had both stood at the window and he had pointed out the direction— the far-distant plateau with the seven pines and, somewhere high above, the mountain crest we had to climb.

"On paper it looks like an easy stroll," I'd said to him, "but it seems we must climb over those high Pyrenees peaks."

The mayor had laughed. "That's where Spain is, on the other side of the mountains."

Azéma advised us to take a walk in the afternoon and check out the first part of the route to see how well we could find our way.

"Go up as far as this clearing," he said, and pointed to it on the sketch. "When you return, check everything over with me again. Spend the night at the inn, and very early in the morning, shortly after four o'clock, when it's still dark and the vineyard workers are on their way to work, mingle with them and then go the entire route to the Spanish border."

Benjamin asked how far it was to the clearing.

"Scarcely an hour—certainly not more than two hours. A lovely stroll." We shook hands.

"Je vous remercie infiniment, monsieur le maire," I heard Benjamin say. His voice still rings in my ears.

We met Benjamin's acquaintances at the inn, where he had asked them to wait for us, and explained our plan. They assented immediately, and I thought: Luckily, they don't seem to be the sort of people who always find something to gripe about—nor are they the difficult kind I'm always fearful about in such ticklish situations.

So the four of us wandered off leisurely, like tourists enjoying the landscape. I saw that Benjamin carried a briefcase, one he'd surely picked up when we stopped at the inn. It appeared to be heavy, and I asked if I could help him with it.

"It contains my new manuscript," he explained to me.

"But why have you brought it along on this scouting trip?"

"Do you know, this briefcase is most important to me," he said. "I dare not lose it. The manuscript *must* be saved. It is more important than I am, more important than myself."

This won't be an easy crossover, I thought. Walter Benjamin and his strange manner—that's the way he was. Had he had the briefcase with him when he tried to get by dressed as a French sailor in the harbor of Marseille? But now, I said to myself, I really have to observe the route, and I set my mind to interpreting Azéma's sketch.

There was the empty stable the mayor had mentioned; so we hadn't lost our way—up until now. Then we came to the path that bore to the left, and to the huge boulder he'd described. A clearing! We'd made it, in almost three hours.

According to Azéma that was about a third of the way. I don't remember this ramble as being especially difficult. We sat down to rest a while. Benjamin stretched out on the grass and closed his eyes. The walk had doubtless exhausted him, I thought to myself.

We got ready to go back down, but he didn't stand up. "Are you still tired?" I asked.

"I'm all right," he answered. "You three go ahead."

"And you?"

"I'm going to stay here. I'll spend the night here, and you meet me here again early tomorrow morning."

This was even worse than I had imagined. What to do? I had to try to persuade him with reasonable arguments. We were in a wild mountain region—perhaps there were dangerous animals. I actually had been warned that there were savage bulls hereabouts. It was late September and Benjamin had nothing to cover himself with. Smugglers roamed around this area—who knows whether they might do something to him? And he had no provisions whatsoever. No, it was really an impossible idea.

He replied that his decision to spend the night in the clearing was irrevocable, because it was based on simple, logical deliberation. His goal was to cross the border so that he and his manuscript would not fall into the hands of the gestapo. He had attained one-third of this goal. If he now returned to the village only to have to repeat the whole ascent on the next day, his heart would probably give out. It followed that he was going to remain.

I sat myself down again and said, "Then, I'm going to stay here too."

He smiled. "Are you going to protect me from your wild bulls, *gnädige Frau*?"

It would be irrational for me to remain, he explained to me calmly. I had to go over everything with Azéma once more. It was also necessary for me to get some sleep; only then would I be in condition, before sunup, to guide the Gurlands surely and without delay back to this spot and to go on to the border.

All that was, of course, clear to me. Most vital, I had, without ration stamps, to wangle some bread and maybe a few tomatoes and jam-substitute on the black market, so we'd have something to eat while under way. I believe I had only tried to shock him into giving up his plan; but naturally it hadn't worked.

As we descended, I tried to concentrate on the route so I could retrace it again next morning in the dark. But the nagging thought wouldn't leave me: He shouldn't have stayed up there alone, it was completely insane. Had he planned it from the start? Or had the climb so exhausted him that he'd decided to remain once we'd gotten up there? And then there was that heavy briefcase he'd taken with him. . . . Maybe his will to

live was malfunctioning. At a perilous moment, in which direction
would his singular mode of thinking steer him?

Now I remember a story my husband told me. He and Benjamin were
together in the Vernuche camp near Nevers the winter before France's
surrender. Benjamin, a heavy smoker, informed him one day that he had
quit smoking and described the agonies of withdrawal.

"Not the right time," said Hans. It had struck him how incapable
Benjamin was of coping with, as he had once written, the "adversities of
the external world, which, like wolves, appear at times"—and the entire
life in Vernuche was one great adversity. Hans had become used to
helping him find his way in practical matters.

He tried to explain to Benjamin that in order to ride out crises and
not lose one's mind, this basic rule was vital: Always look for the positive side, not at the existing hardships.

Benjamin's rejoinder was: "I can bear the conditions in this camp only
if I'm compelled to concentrate my mental strength on one single effort.
Giving up smoking costs me this effort, and thus will be my deliver-
ance."

The next morning everything seemed to go well. The greatest risk of
being discovered by the police or border officials was upon leaving the
village and at the start of the ascent. Azéma had impressed upon us:
"Leave before sunrise, mingle with the vineyard workers, take nothing
with you except a musette, and don't speak! Then, in the dark, the
sentries won't be able to tell you from the natives." Frau Gurland and
her son kept strictly to the rules I had spelled out for them, and now it
was easy for me to find the way.

The closer we got to the clearing, the more uneasy I became. Was he
still there? What had happened during the night? Was he still alive? My
fantasies began to run away with me.

The clearing at last! And Old Benjamin. Alive. He sat up and looked
at us amiably. But—but what was wrong with him? Those large dark-
red spots around his eyes—were they symptoms of a heart attack,
perhaps?

Possibly he guessed why I was staring at him. He took off his glasses
and rubbed his face with a handkerchief. "Oh, that," he said. "It's the
dew, you know. See, the rims of the spectacle frames. The color rubs off
when they get wet."

My heart stopped pounding in my throat and slipped back to its rightful place in my chest.

Now the ascent became steeper, and we were no longer sure about direction, there being only hills on both sides and cliff walls directly ahead of us. To my surprise, Benjamin quickly found our position on the route-sketch and helped me keep our orientation. Once, after some twenty minutes, it was clear that we'd taken a wrong turn, for the path suddenly led downward and to the right, while the crest was upward to the left. So we hiked back and found the junction where we'd gone wrong.

The term "path" gradually proved to be an exaggeration. Now and then there was a path to be seen, but increasingly it was just a barely recognizable, gravelly track between boulders. Until we came to the steep vineyard, which I can never forget.

But first I must explain why this route was so secure. After the ascent through the green hills that sloped gently down to the sea, our path ran parallel to a well-known "official" road that led along the mountain ridge and was easily negotiable. Our route—*la route Lister* and an ancient smugglers' path—ran below the road and was concealed by the mountain overhang, so that it couldn't be seen by the French border sentries who patrolled above. At some places the road and the path drew very near each other, and there we had to keep silent.

Benjamin traveled slowly and steadily; at regular intervals—I think it was ten minutes—he halted and rested for about a minute. Then he continued on at the same constant pace. As he told me, he had thought it out and calculated it during the night: "I can go all the way to the end using this method. I stop at regular intervals—I must pause *before* I'm exhausted. One must not completely overspend one's strength."

What a remarkable man! I thought. Crystal-clear thinking, an unfaltering inner strength, and at the same time a hopelessly awkward, clumsy fellow.

Walter Benjamin once wrote (in *Agesilaus Santander*) about the essence of his strength: "there is nothing which can overcome my patience." Years later, when I read that, I saw him before me once more, walking slowly along the mountain path at a steady pace. And his contradictory nature now seems less absurd to me.

Frau Gurland's son, José—he was about sixteen—and I took turns carrying the black leather briefcase. I imagined that it was steadily becoming heavier. But I remember that we were all in a good mood, and now and then we talked a little. We spoke mainly about problems of the moment: the slippery path, the warming sun, and how much farther to the border.

Today, when Benjamin is acknowledged to be one of the most important scholars and critics of our century, I am occasionally asked: What did he say about the manuscript? Did he tell you anything at all about the contents? Did he have therein a new system of philosophy?

Heavens above! I had my hands full guiding our little group upward. Philosophy had to wait until we were over the mountain. I was busy rescuing some human beings from the Nazis, and here I was with this odd character, Old Benjamin, who under no circumstances would let himself be parted from his ballast, the black leather briefcase. And so, for better or worse, we had to drag that monstrosity over the mountains.

But to return to the steep vineyard. There was no path at all. We clambered through and between the vines, which were heavy with dark, sweet, near-ripe Banyuls grapes. I think that it was an almost vertical incline, but in the remembering the picture is sometimes distorted. In the vineyard was the first and only time that Benjamin wilted. To put it more accurately, he tried to make the climb, couldn't manage it, and then declared in sober words that it was beyond his powers. José and I took him between us; he placed his arms over our shoulders, and we dragged him, plus his briefcase, up through the vineyard. His breathing was labored, but he didn't complain, did not even emit a sigh, and he continually cast glances at the leather case.

On a narrow ridge above the vineyard we rested for a bit. Meanwhile the sun had risen higher and we felt warm; so we must have been under way for four or five hours. We nibbled at the provisions I'd brought in the musette, but none of us could eat very much. In recent months our stomachs had shrunk—first the concentration camp, then the confused retreat; *la pagaille*, the total chaos.

While we rested, I was thinking that this route over the mountains was much longer and more difficult than we would have supposed from the mayor's description. If one was sure of the way, had nothing to carry, and was young and healthy, one could surely make it much faster. Then, too, Mayor Azéma's data about distances and times were quite elastic, as is often the case with mountain dwellers. How long a time is "a few hours"?

During the following winter months, when we trod the trail across the border two or three times a week, I thought often about Benjamin's self-discipline. It came to mind when in the midst of the mountains Frau R. began to moan: "Haven't you even brought an apple for me?—I want an apple." And also when Senior Councillor Dr. H. placed more value on his fur coat than on his (and our) safety; and when a girl suddenly flew into a tantrum and wanted only to die. But those are other stories.

Now I sat high above in the Pyrenees, ate a piece of bread I'd bought with bogus food stamps, and pushed the tomatoes over to Benjamin, when he asked, "By your leave, *gnädige Frau*, may I serve myself?" That's the way he was indeed, Old Benjamin and his Spanish court etiquette.

Suddenly it struck me that what I'd been sleepily staring at was a sun-bleached skeleton. A goat perhaps? The skull looked like a goat's. Above us in the southern blue sky two large birds circled—they must have been vultures. What were they hoping for? Then I thought, how remarkable! Under normal circumstances skeletons and vultures would make me nervous.

We got up again and pushed on. Although the path now rose only gradually, Benjamin's weariness was giving him trouble; he had been on his feet for seven hours. He walked more slowly and took longer rests, but still according to his watch. He seemed to be concentrating on holding to a constant pace.

Finally we reached the summit. I had gone on ahead, and I stopped to look around. The spectacular scene appeared so unexpectedly that for a moment I thought I was seeing a mirage. Far below, where we had come from, the deep-blue Mediterranean was visible; on the other side, in front of us, steep cliffs fell away to a glass sheet of transparent turquoise—a second ocean? Yes, of course; it was the Spanish coast. Behind us, to the north, the semicircle of Catalonia's Roussillon, with its *Côte Vermeille*, the Vermilion Coast, an autumn landscape with innumerable hues of red and yellow-gold. I gasped for breath—I had never seen such beauty before.

I knew that we were now in Spain, and I also knew that from here the route led directly down to the town below. Now I must turn back. All the others had the necessary papers and visas, but I must not risk being caught on Spanish ground. I looked at my little group and thought, no,

I can't let them go on all by themselves—I'll walk a little farther with them.

We came to a swampy pool. The water was green and slimy, and it stank. Benjamin knelt down to drink.

"You can't drink that," I said. "The water is dirty, and it's surely polluted."

The canteen I'd taken with me was long since empty, but Benjamin had hitherto said nothing about being thirsty.

"Please excuse me," he said, "but I have no other choice. If I don't drink here, perhaps I cannot hold out to the end." He bent his head down to the pool.

"Listen to me," I said. "Won't you just wait a moment and listen? We've almost made it—only a short stretch more and it will all be behind you; I know you can do it. But it's impossible for you to drink that slop. Think about it for a minute, be reasonable. You could catch typhoid fever——."

"Yes, perhaps. But you must understand: the worst thing that could happen is that I might die of typhoid fever—*after* I have crossed the border. The gestapo can no longer arrest me, and the manuscript will have reached safety. You must pardon me, please, *gnädige Frau*."

He drank.

The path descended gradually. It must have been about two in the afternoon when we came to the end of the cliff wall, and I could see the town in the valley below, quite near.

"There below us is Port-Bou! The town has a Spanish border station where you must register. This road leads directly there. A real road!"

Around two o'clock. We had left at four that morning; Benjamin, at about seven. So, some ten hours altogether.

"Now I really must turn back," I went on. "We're in Spain, have been for almost an hour. Descending can't take very long, from here you can already see houses. Go directly to the border post and show them your papers, the travel documents, the Spanish and Portuguese transit visas. As soon as you have your entry stamp, take the first train to Lisbon. But you already know all that. Now I have to go. *Auf wiedersehen*."

I stood for a moment and watched as they started down the bumpy road. It's high time for me to get going, I thought, and started back. As I went I realized with astonishment: Here I am in a familiar area. I'm no longer a stranger, as I still was this morning. What was also remarkable was the fact that I wasn't tired. It had all been so easy—I was light-hearted, and the whole world with me. Meanwhile Benjamin and the others must have made it. How beautiful it was up here!

In two hours I was back in Banyuls. Ten hours up, two hours down.

During the following months, when we could find the route in our sleep, we once made it to the border in two hours, and a few times in three to four hours. It was easy to do when our "cargo" was young and robust and, above all, disciplined. I've never seen these people again, but from time to time a name emerges, and suddenly something clicks into place. Henry Pachter the historian—why that was Heinz and his girl-friend, record time two hours. Or Princeton professor Albert Hirsch-mann—back then he was "young Hermant"—about three hours.

But all of that came later. Then, when I was back in Banyuls after the first trek over *la route Lister*, I thought: Old Benjamin and his manu-script are safe now, safe on the other side of the mountains.

A few days later the news came: Walter Benjamin was dead. The night after his arrival in Port-Bou, he had taken his own life.

The Spanish border authorities had informed the group that they would be returned to France. A new administrative order had just arrived from Madrid: no one could enter Spain without a French exit visa. (There were several different explanations for why Spain closed the border at this time: *apatrides* were not allowed to travel through Spain; Spanish transit visas issued in Marseille were invalid, and so on.) What-ever the new regulation, it was annulled shortly afterward, as were many others. Had the news about border-closing reached us on the French side in time, no one would have crossed illegally, and we would have waited for further developments. Governments of all countries seemed to be involved in this "era of new decrees," issuing commands and instructions, revoking them, first enforcing and then lifting them again. In order to get through, one had to learn to slip through the cracks and loopholes, using every trick and stratagem to slither out of this laby-rinth, which was continually taking on new configurations.

Faut se débrouiller: one must know how to help oneself, to clear a way out of the debacle—that's the way one lived and survived in France back then. *Faut se débrouiller* meant: buy counterfeit food stamps, scrounge milk for the children, obtain some—any—kind of permit—in short, manage to do or obtain what didn't officially exist. For many that also meant to do or obtain such things by means of going along with officialdom, by *collaborating*. But for us, the *apatrides*, everything we did revolved around avoiding the concentration camps, not falling into the hands of the gestapo.

But Benjamin had been no *débrouillard*.

Unworldly as he was, all that mattered to him was that his manuscript and he himself be out of reach of the gestapo. The flight across the border had exhausted him, and he didn't think he was in any condition to repeat it—he'd told me so on the way over. And he'd prepared for that eventuality in advance: he had had enough morphine with him to take his own life with a deadly overdose. Concerned and shocked by his death, the Spanish authorities allowed the Gurlands to continue their journey.

Once, forty years later, I was talking with Chimen Abramsky of the University College in London, and we began to speak about Walter Benjamin and his works. I referred to his last journey and to the manuscript.

Gershom Scholem, Benjamin's closest friend and one of his literary executors, phoned me shortly thereafter. He had heard from Abramsky about our conversation and wanted to know more. I described to him the happenings of that day in late September 1940.

"At least the manuscript that meant so much to him was saved," I said.

"The manuscript doesn't exist," Scholem replied. "To this very day no one has heard anything about it. You must tell me every detail—it must be searched for. . . ."

His voice went on, but I heard only, *The manuscript has vanished*. And all these years I'd assumed it had been rescued!

No manuscript. Nobody knows a thing about the heavy, black case containing the work that was more important to Benjamin than anything else in the world.

Hannah Arendt wrote about that "Bucklicht Männlein," the hunch-backed dwarf, a symbol of the cacodemon whose threat must have been felt by Benjamin throughout his life, and which he strove to overcome by every precautionary means. Benjamin's "System of safety measures . . . in some remarkable and mysterious way, did not so much as touch the real perils," she said.

Yet now it seems to me that Walter Benjamin, during that night in Port-Bou, was aware of the real perils, the actual dangers. It was just that *his* real danger, *his* reality, differed from ours. In Port-Bou he must have met the "hunchbacked dwarf" once more, his own, Benjamin's personal cacodemon; and he must have dealt with him in his own way.

The manuscript could not be found, not in Port-Bou, not in Figueras, nor in Barcelona. Only the black leather briefcase was entered in the death register back then, with the notation: *unos papeles mas de contenido desconicido*—"with papers of unknown content."

Lisa Fittko at sixteen, Berlin, 1925

Lisa Fittko, Berlin, 1928

Lisa Fittko's parents shortly before their flight from Germany, Berlin, 1933

Lisa, passport photo, Paris, 1939. Photograph by Franz Pfemfert

Banyuls. The town has changed little since the 1940s.

The Ventajous' house. The Fittkos' balcony was directly above the Customs Office entrance. Photograph taken 1973

The last houses of Banyuls before the mountains

Walter Benjamin

Lisa and Hans Fittko, passport photographs, Marseille, 1940

Lisa Fittko, Paulette, and friend, Marseille, 1940

Lisa and Hans Fittko on the Canebière, Marseille, 1941

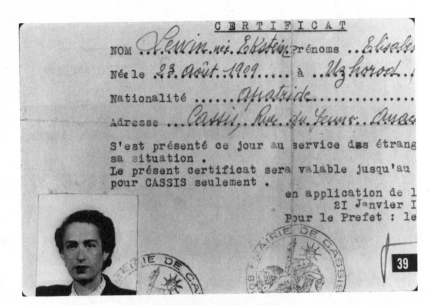

Provisional identity card from the Mayor of Cassis, 1941. For reasons of security, the name Fittko, which was on the Gestapo's lists, was changed to Lewin.

Lisa and Hans Fittko and a group of refugees, Cassis, 1941

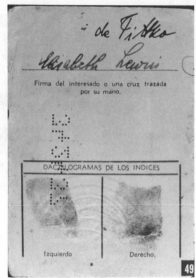

Lisa Fittko's Cuban identity card, 1943

Lisa Fittko at an ORT job retraining center for German Jewish refugees, learning the bookbinding trade, Havana, 1943

Hans Fittko working as a diamond cutter, Cuba, 1945

Lisa Fittko, Havana, 1944

Hans Fittko, Havana, 1945

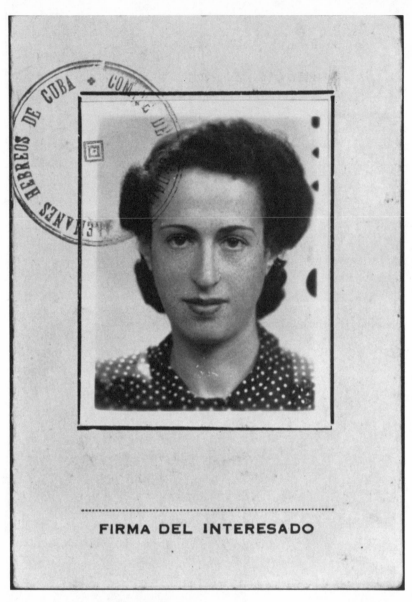

Lisa Fittko's Cuban identity card, 1946

Lisa and Hans Fittko and friend at El Aire Libre, Havana, 1946

Lisa and Hans Fittko, Chicago, 1950

8

"La Route Lister" Is Renamed

We still had not heard about Benjamin's death.

In Port-Vendres, Eva, her child, and I waited for news from our men. Had they found another way to get out?

When we'd still heard nothing from them after several days, we made a mutual decision that neither of us would leave France as long as the men had found no possibility of leaving too. Besides, it would be difficult to get across the border with Titi; we'd have to carry her most of the way. Eva wrote a letter to her husband, a short letter: "Tomorrow Titi and I are taking the train and riding back to Montpellier. There's no question of our going on vacation so long as you have things to do in Marseille. *Je t'embrasse tendrement* ——."

Simultaneously a one-word telegram arrived from my husband in Marseille: "*Rentrez*," Return. Spain had ordered that all valid transit visas must be renewed at once, otherwise they would expire irrevocably.

"Incidentally, those two Americans want to talk to us," Hans said on my return. "They seem to be in a big hurry."

"Which Americans?"

"You know, Bohn and Fry. Bohn, who was sent by the American unions, and Fry from the Emergency Rescue Committee. They are supposed to help their people here."

"I thought that was a big secret."

"All the people from New Beginning have gone abroad by now, so there's no more need for secrecy," said Hans. "Fry has even founded a new committee, Centre Américain de Secours."

Naturally, every political group first attempted to rescue their own people. But nothing should be leaked about that, otherwise everyone would try to crowd into the lifeboat at once, and it would sink.

"What do they want from us?"

"I assume they've heard that you brought Benjamin across. Maybe they want to get a description of the new route, so that others can be helped. They want to meet with us tonight."

It wasn't a very brilliant idea to meet in a small, rather grimy *bistrot* in a side street near the Old Port. The two Americans were completely out of place here, the thought went through my head; they looked so conspicuously neat and nice. Hermant (Albert Hirschmann), who had told us he was working with Fry, came with them.

Fry came right to the point (we learned later that Bohn didn't understand French): Yes, it had to do with the border crossing. They knew that now it was difficult and that I had guided Benjamin over a new route. There were still many emigrés waiting whom the Centre had supplied with papers. Would I help these people, or better, would both of us help them?

"Yes, certainly," I answered. "I can sketch and describe the route to you." Indeed, that was precisely our intention, that the information be passed on to those who came after.

Fry said that he and his friend Bohn had actually thought differently about it. In order to rescue hundreds of the imperiled it was vital to have the border crossing organized, with a take-off point and guides who knew the mountains; someone must be there who had experience in this border project.

Really, it was almost too good to be true. Then the new committee would help us with our border plans? Did they have capable coworkers? Whatever the case, they wanted to come up with the money needed to keep people there for a time.

Fry and Bohn whispered a few words in English. Then Fry cleared his throat like someone who was about to make a speech: "That's exactly what we want to talk to you about. The money is no problem; this all centers around finding the right person with border experience, someone who is prepared to do the job and on whom we can depend." He hawked again. "We've been told that both of you have brought people and anti-Nazi literature across the German border. Would you, for a few months——?"

"We?" said Hans. "No, that's impossible."

"No," I echoed Hans, "we can't afford to do that. Now that we finally have our papers, we must see if we ourselves can get across the mountains and out of France."

"Or, if that's not feasible, we'll hole up somewhere before the rest of the country is occupied." Hans paused. "Oh, maybe for a short time we can break someone in there." He looked at me. "What do you think?"

I nodded. "The best thing would be if a Frenchman could be found. . . ."

"I promise you," Fry said, "that if you remain here during the border project, we will help you get out."

Perhaps he honestly means that, I thought, but in days like these how can one make and keep such a promise? I said, "Maybe you're misjudging the situation."

Hermant entered the conversation for the first time. Meanwhile the *bistrot* had emptied and we were the only guests; the *garçon* had disappeared into the back and Hermant spoke German to us. He said that one could trust these two—they were, of course, not very experienced, but they wanted to learn and to help, and they would provide connections and resources.

Fry understood some German, but perhaps he had trouble following us. And maybe he'd misunderstood Hermant.

"*Combien?*" he asked. "How much?"

"What does he mean?" asked Hans. "*Combien* what?"

"*Combien voulez-vous?*"

Hans turned to Hermant. "Does he think that we would take people across the border for money?"

"Listen a moment," said Hermant. "He doesn't know you, he scarcely knows who you are. You can't expect him to understand people of the German Resistance. He's heard that racketeers are doing a booming business smuggling folks over the border; he doesn't want to deal with them. But he finds it perfectly all right if you want to be paid."

Hans regarded Fry thoughtfully. "Do you know," he said, "that assisting men of military age in illegal border-crossings now rates the death penalty? And you offer us money. We would have to be insane indeed. Do you actually know what an anti-Fascist is? Do you understand the word *Überzeugung*, convictions?"

Fry realized that he'd said something wrong. "I was just thinking of the many human beings who must be brought across—and you can help them. The part about money, that was only a misunderstanding."

"Whoever holes up at the border," Hans said, "needs enough money to live there a while. It doesn't have to be much, but it must be enough so that everything runs smoothly. There should also be a reserve for emergencies, in case something doesn't work out with the refugees."

Fry believed it would be best if the committee let the new border project have a free hand in supplying the refugees with funds for the journey, each according to need. "When you have the new crossing route organized," he said, "what did you call it? *La route*—from now on let's call it *The F-Route*. We can and will come up with financial support."

That all sounds reasonable, I thought, but what does he mean by "F-Route"? He was acting as if we'd already consented.

"My wife and I must think this over thoroughly," said Hans, standing up.

"I give you my word," Fry said again, "that we'll help you obtain your visas."

It was irresponsibly reckless simply to abandon our plans for departure now. All that stuff about the promised visas was rubbish. Where there's nothing . . . then again, maybe they were okay and really would do all they could—but we would never rely on that.

However, we couldn't miss the opportunity to set up a base, a border take-off point. Perhaps we had found the right somebodies, and perhaps it might all come to naught. Yet, if someone had to take the risk, we couldn't say, "Let others do it."

But the gestapo had already been waiting for us too long.

On the other hand, my brother and friends would let us know if new possibilities arose; we wouldn't be cut off altogether.

Should we take a chance?

Just this last time.

9

Banyuls-sur-Mer

Notes from the Diary

12 October 1940

A good omen: There was no inspection in the train from Marseille to Perpignan.

We stopped for a whole day in Perpignan. The Pfemferts were already on their way to Mexico, but other acquaintances and friends were still in the city. Above all, we wanted to see what was going on in the refugee-smuggling trade, and whether we could make any useful connections.

Emigrés sat all over and in every café as they did in Marseille, but here they were more obvious because the city was so small. On the Marseille Canebière only whispers made the rounds, but here all the relevant news was discussed openly. On the café terraces people yelled black-market dollar exchange rates from table to table, who wanted to buy them, and where one could sell them.

"——for hundred-dollar bills they pay triple the rate——."

"Who has hundred-dollar bills?" I asked Hans.

"There are currency speculators everywhere," he answered. "Why not among the emigrés? And even when they're only blowhards talking about imaginary deals, it gives them the illusion that everything is going on as usual."

Even the people-smugglers went nonchalantly about their business. *Fifteen thousand francs—A hundred and fifty dollars—Personal guide—Diplomatic limousine, guaranteed to bring you to Portugal—Seaworthy ship to Gibraltar, with a genuine Navigation Certificate; one can jump overboard and easily swim ashore*—the words twittered through the southern autumn air.

Trude, who had recently married, sat there with her husband—his name was Laufer—knitting a baby jacket. No one would ever have believed that one day she'd be knitting. I found her changed in other ways, too: she no longer giggled, spoke very little, and seemed to be completely absorbed in the pale yellow jacket. Her husband told us how they had gotten all ready for departure, but that now business was going well; therefore they'd remain here until it was time to disappear.

"That could mean until it's too late," said Hans. "The situation can change lightning-fast. No one can predict suddenly issued regulations, or occupation of the south, or God knows what else—whoever has papers and good sense ought to get out of here immediately."

"You don't know me," said the young man. "Everything is ready, there's no way they can catch us."

He had really persuaded himself, he wanted to believe it; there was no help for him. Laufer worked with people who for large sums hired locals to guide refugees across the border. He'd told us of cases where money and their last possessions had been taken from emigrés, who were then abandoned in the mountains. (Some two years later, Trude Laufer and her child were arrested, transported to Auschwitz, and exterminated.)

The day spent in Perpignan was informative. Careful! No contact at all with the bad guys!

Here in Banyuls-sur-Mer we're lodged in an unbelievable house directly on the Mediterranean. Mayor Azéma, Monsieur le Maire, had without hesitation requisitioned the house in the name of the municipality and made it the Centre d'Hébergement de Banyuls pour les Réfugiés. The *réfugiés*—that's us. We can lodge our future "visitors" there quite comfortably.

The house belongs to a doctor who hasn't been here for a long time and who disappeared during the war. It has three floors and an infinite number of rooms with splendid wooden paneling, built-in cupboards, and superb fireplaces, but—there's no water in the house, and no toilets! The woman who had accompanied us here from the *mairie* said, "That surely makes no difference to you—opposite the house on the other side of the street are public *cabinets*."

We've chosen the nicest room on the second floor. The sea is so close to the window that you think you can reach out and touch it with your hand. There was lots of sun in our room but nothing else. Now we've carried in a big bed, a table, and two chairs from other rooms. There are blankets in the wall-cabinets, and even bed linen.

But it still looked too bare to me, so I took off my head-scarf, the colorful one, and spread it out flat on the table. I placed a bowl on it, and now the room looks almost livable. Hans makes fun of me and my tablecloth.

13 October

We had a long conversation with Monsieur Azéma. He's happy that we came and that we'll stay here a while. Most important, he told us about the living habits of the people here, how one should adapt and what one may *not* do. When, in the morning before sunrise, between four and five, we move up and out with the vineyard workers, we should carry no baggage—*et surtout pas de rucksack!* especially no backpack (a rucksack is the proverbial distinguishing feature of Germans)—then no gendarme or customs official will be able to tell us from the natives. We should wear espadrilles, because with ordinary shoes one hasn't enough foothold climbing around in the vineyards and on the stony paths.

14 October

Today we became "legalized," under our real names. The bogus French *cartes d'identité* from the Centre in Marseille, which named us residents of the *zone interdite* in the northeast of France, were to be used only in case of emergency vis-à-vis the Germans. As such, it was forbidden for us to return there. Monsieur Azéma gave us a hand-written statement on the mayor's letterhead certifying that we are residents of Banyuls; that is now our identification. Then he had the secretary enter us in the Banyuls Residents' Register, and we were thereupon issued food-ration cards. Azéma can manage to get extra food stamps for the refugees should they have to wait here for a few days.

Now, for the first time, I've taken a good look at our mayor; a couple of weeks ago I was too busy with other things, mainly Walter Benjamin. He's rather short, but he's broad-shouldered like most of the people in this area, with dark hair and sharply defined lineaments. His most distinctive features are his dark, intelligent eyes. He winks at us roguishly now and then, without detracting a bit from his natural dignity.

15 October

I've shown Hans *la route Lister,* the "F-Route," over which I guided Walter Benjamin and which we'll use for the refugees. Hans has studied everything painstakingly. Our path is indeed concealed by the mountain overhang and can't be seen from the ridge where the customs guards patrol.

I was freezing at the start, around four in the morning, but keeping in motion warmed me up. After one crosses the little silver creek on the outskirts of Banyuls, the path leads through Puig del Mas, a group of houses among towering trees. This was the original town from which present-day Banyuls developed. Azéma had warned us that customs officers were especially vigilant at this spot. We had mingled in the dark with the workers trooping up to the vineyards. The vineyard workers had spades on which hung baskets for carrying earth. As camouflage Hans will acquire such a *cabec,* as they're called here. I've just now noticed that among themselves the people speak Catalan, and now and then we understand a word. With us they speak French, as they do with all *étrangers.* It's a good thing for us that everyone who doesn't belong here is classed as an *étranger,* no matter if he's a Frenchman from another area or an *apatride.*

There's a low, curved stone wall near the first houses of Puig del Mas; the stones are half-overgrown. We saw them at almost the same time, *les douaniers,* the customs guards; both of us have good eyes: behind the wall, between the trees and bushes, two black-caped silhouettes against the dark gray sky. Are they always on the lookout, lying in wait at this spot?

Later, high up on the mountain, I took a wrong turn at the same place I'd erred a few weeks earlier with Walter Benjamin. There's a hill that hides the seven pine trees on the plateau which always indicate the right direction, and the path is barely visible. Hans's good nose soon put us back on the trail. Now it's apparent to me how far into Spain I'd gone with the Benjamin group; that time I hadn't seen the small gray stone which marked the border.

I hadn't told Hans about the mountain peak from which one overlooked both coasts on opposite sides of the cliff wall, because I wanted to surprise him. As we reached there he held out his hand to help me up. Then he looked around and it really must have smitten him, for he let my hand fall and I slipped back. Luckily there was a cliff projection I could hold on to. We sat there for a while and just looked. The picture will remain with me forever.

This time we turned back shortly after the border. We can describe the continuing path to the refugees precisely; we may not expose ourselves to the danger of being caught on Spanish soil.

On the return trip we sat ourselves down for a bit at the same plateau where the Benjamin group had rested. The sun was high and there was dead silence. Suddenly it seemed to me as if I heard a faint rustling. Hans thought I must be mistaken. Then the rustling came again, and this time he heard it too—it came from the side, a steep downhill slope. We stared at the spot—an animal, perhaps? I see something dark and round lift slowly above the edge and then quickly submerge. We keep looking and it slowly appears again, somewhat higher: a cap, and under it two dark eyes. The vision vanishes again, quick as a flash. *"Bonjour, monsieur,"* I say into the silence. It raises up once more: cap, eyes, a very long nose, strong rugged features. Then the rest of him: a lean, muscular man with many parcels tied around his body. We grin at each other. He sizes us up carefully for a minute, then sits down and we have a conversation. He is obviously a smuggler, and he wants to know just who we are and what we're doing here. Naturally, he sees instantly that we're strangers and not professional smugglers. But he's not sure: do we want to cross the border ourselves or are we guiding refugees? Anyway, he informs us, "Nobody knows his way around here like I do," and he watches closely to see whether we'll take the bait. Of course we listen attentively. He tells us he's Greek, "regular occupation" railroad worker. "Maybe together we could make lots of money."

Hans replies evasively, "Money isn't that important to us."

"Voyons!" cries the Greek, astonished. *"Il faut manger, quand même, toi et moi!*—We have to eat, you and I!"

18 October

Yesterday Maurice, our go-between with the Centre Américain de Secours, came to discuss when we could guide the first refugees across the border. Maurice is a Romanian with his papers all in order, so he can travel about freely. Now we know the route in exact detail (we retraced it once more) and everything is ready; the Centre can send us two groups next week. We've decided that we shouldn't be sent more than three people at a time, or the risk is too great. For security we'll be informed in advance who's being sent. We already know the ones coming next week; in all other cases we'll be sent half of a torn sheet of paper and the refugees will bring us the other half. This simple old method is still halfway secure. One of us will pick up the refugees whom we know at the railroad station; others, in Marseille, will be given exact instructions on how to find our house and the names Jean and Lise. Maurice has brought enough money for us to give travel funds to those in need.

People in the village have started greeting us. Many of them are certainly curious, but they're friendly, like to talk, and seem to have nothing against us. Perhaps with our Greek we can find ways to bring elderly and handicapped persons across; first we have to make sure how far we can trust him. Besides that, he wants money, money, money: *Il faut manger.* . . .

Azéma will help us get the refugees' baggage over the border legally. That will make things a lot easier.

1 November

This week we brought people across three times, and twice the week before. Hans wrote to Fry in Marseille: "it's going well with us, our friends have had no trouble . . . we take delight in mountain-climbing but we don't want to overdo it, and possibly go on outings not more than twice weekly . . . the people around here will think we're crazy if we continually go scrambling around in the mountains."

Each evening before, we sit down with the refugees and go over all the details: don't speak until we're in a safe area; carry nothing, don't attract attention; how to talk your way out of it if something goes wrong. We describe the crossover to them in order to allay their fear of the unknown. We repeat with them what they have to do on the Spanish side: descent, customs post, entry stamp (take note: it's called *entrada*), train to Portugal. Some items of clothing must be exchanged; one doesn't go to work in the vineyards wearing an overcoat.

In the morning before sunrise, Hans waits on a corner of the avenue Puig del Mas. When our friends appear and signal that they see him by raising an arm, he walks ahead slowly. There can be no contact here, but he keeps them in sight. (Please, no whispering!) I walk behind them so that I can take action if necessary. We're familiar with the route; time and again I take delight in the view from the mountain to the sea. When one or another of them is nervous (we always must reckon on that), he usually becomes calmer in the mountains. For the younger people we've guided up to now the route isn't arduous; one could almost say it's pleasurable.

In spite of the Centre's warning, the last couple had brought a suitcase. Lotte, the wife, didn't want to be separated from it. "We can't simply leave here without taking a few clothes along," she complained. Max, her husband, declared that he could easily carry the suitcase over the mountains.

"We're not talking about carrying," Hans had said. "It has to do with safety. What's more valuable to you, your life or the rags in there?"

I can understand their fear, to move out into the unknown with nothing, but such compassion could cost us dearly; finally we suggested, as a trial, sending the suitcase by the forwarder Azéma had spoken of. Now we're waiting to hear if it worked.

It's getting colder now. Sometimes the transmontane blows, a wind that goes right through you; it comes over the mountains from the northwest. We have nothing warm to wear and there's hardly anything to buy. It doesn't matter much to Hans, but I freeze easily. We've informed the Centre that the folks must wear warm sweaters or jackets. Mostly on the return, we gather wood and Hans carries it home on his back. We really need it to make a fire in the fireplace; not only for heating, we cook there too. Just as in other houses, a big pot hangs on a hook over the fire. Above all, wood-gathering is a good alibi. Hans makes like a chameleon; at a distance, with his Basque cap and espadrilles, I can't tell him from the locals.

On the days we don't go into the mountains Hans sits for hours on a cliff projecting into the sea. He says that the waves carry away his inner tension, their soft susurrus fills him with peace.

In truth, he no longer makes long speeches in his sleep as he once used to do.

4 November

The luggage forwarding works! We got the delivery receipt for the suitcase, signed by Max. So, the simplest methods are usually the safest; one must just make the right connections.

The mayor of Cerbère (the French border town), Monsieur Cruzet, is a Socialist and ready to help; besides, he owns a transport firm. His business partner is the mayor of Port-Bou, the Spanish border town. We check the baggage (not too much!) here, to go by rail to the transport firm Cruzet in Cerbère; from there it's sent directly to the branch office in Port-Bou, goes through customs, and waits for our people at the Port-Bou railway station. Naturally, this all depends on the "cooperation" of the customs officials on both sides; nowadays they'd rather have cigarettes than money.

Hans has ridden to Cerbère to work things out with Cruzet. He really shouldn't do it without valid papers, for there's a train inspection between Banyuls and Cerbère, and sometimes the Armistice Commission comes sniffing around. But, plainly, one of us must go, so Hans is off with the new assistant he's meanwhile annexed, young Meyerhof, the eighteen-year-old son of the physiologist. His parents crossed the border some time ago but he's lacking some papers, so he sits around here looking lonesome and forlorn. Monsieur Azéma relates the story with great relish, how he, *Monsieur le Maire de Banyuls,* carried the youngster's mother, the wife of the Nobel Prize–winner Meyerhof, from France to Spain piggyback because the path along the cemetery wall was too difficult for her.

The youth is enthusiastic about our project and wants to work with us, and we can use any help. He has a *carte d'identité,* and what papers he does have are in order; and that alone makes him valuable. When the customs and border officials entered the train compartment just before Cerbère, Meyerhof presented his papers. The gendarme whom we often ate lunch with in the pier restaurant was there. Hans wanted to show the slip identifying him as a resident of Banyuls, but it wasn't necessary—the gendarme held up his palm in refusal, "Mais non, monsieur, pas vous!" One must be lucky. Is it really only luck?

7 November

It would be impossible for the couple they sent us today to manage the mountain route—they're too old and unwell, and they both have bad eyesight.

Three possibilities: by train, by ship around the cape, or over the mountains on muleback. We began by crossing off the mules; first, because they were suggested by a man who is always sidling up to us on the beach and who is obviously in cahoots with the people-smuggling racketeers in Perpignan; second, they'd surely fall off the mules; and third, there were no mules to be had for miles around.

Conveyance by small boat turns out to be too complicated; besides, there are too many people involved. We have the connection through the longshoremen in Port-Vendres; a harbor pilot is even in on it. They seem to be good people, and perhaps we can work out something safe and simple—later, not now.

So, the train remains.

10 November

"Our Greek" (his name is Gratacos or something similar) is a locomotive engineer. We've beaten down his prices a little, but he still demands shamelessly high amounts (*Il faut manger*). However, he's proven to be dependable and is uncommonly sly—and he's risking a lot.

We've lodged our problem couple in the inn on the town square, diagonally opposite the *mairie*; we've become friendly with the innkeeper, and he closes both eyes when we bring him someone, meaning that he doesn't ask for papers. For certain people our house is too primitive.

The train to Spain runs through an international tunnel; the Spanish-French border is a few hundred meters before the end of it. Gratacos can drive his locomotive that far, but he has to have some pretext for it.

This morning he sent his young son to tell us: in the evening at ten past eight. Earlier, we described to our refugee couple how it should go, and they assented. When they get off the locomotive they'll see the light at the tunnel exit. They must go that short distance on foot, staying close to the right-hand wall in case a train is coming from the other direction (improbable, according to the train schedule). Then they will be on Spanish soil and should report to the border post.

Naturally the two of them were nervous (so were we), but they weren't difficult. In the afternoon we sat with them on a bench at the beach under palm trees and talked about all sorts of things, just to distract their attention. The woman held fast to her husband's hand the whole time, and the thought went through my head: which one's propping up the other?

Evening. We had watched our Greek help the two aboard the locomotive and then gone home; he'd made us promise that we wouldn't hang around the station. And now we're waiting.

Gratacos will inform us how it went as soon as he returns. We'd also given the fugitives a letter addressed to us for them to pass on to him at the end as a sign that everything had gone well. The Greek, of course, knew nothing about that.

Hans had put his watch down in front of him and looked at it every minute or so. We must assume that, all in all, it would be at least an hour before we heard anything.

"They must have arrived at the border at least five minutes ago," Hans said, more to himself than to me. "He promised to wait until they found the tunnel wall; they can feel their way along it even if they can't see much." Then, to me, "How long do you think it will take them from there to the exit?"

Hans always does that; whenever he dispatches someone on a dangerous operation, he "goes along" too.

"Surely they're at the tunnel exit now. The station's only a minute or two away."

Later. After a long forty minutes we heard footsteps on the stairs. It was the Greek's son, bringing back our letter.

That beats muleback by far.

14 November

We brought the Groetzsches from *Sopade* across okay, it just went rather slowly; they're not so young anymore. They relayed greetings from Fritz Heine—a succession of his friends are now arriving with United States visas.

Yesterday we were still sitting together talking—how now it depends on us to hold out until the end of the Thousand-Year Reich, and then go home and put everything back in order again, ". . . but this time thoroughly, for all time, not like in 1918," Hans added. "We're refugees, not emigrants, don't you forget that over there——!"

It's the Biebers' turn tomorrow. Hans believes he can now go over and back without me. It's true that I always freeze when the transmontane blows, and I think that's because there's so little to eat. Besides. The fewer people endangered, the better. Hans now knows the way as well as any local smuggler. The vineyard *vignerons* on their way to work know us too, and sometimes in conversation one will mention *en passant* what the best way to the border is, and where one shouldn't go.

There are always fewer and fewer edibles to buy. As we're now halfway accepted as natives, we're helped out now and then. Each morning I go to the few shops like the others to buy whatever is available. When I can't get anything at all, we try the pier restaurant, where the gendarmes and sometimes the customs officers eat; the *patron* takes no food stamps from us. At times we sit around for a bit with the gendarmes, drinking the sweet Banyuls wine.

About six P.M. I go to my evening performance in the creamery around the corner. With my little pitcher, but without stamps, I step down the few stairs, and before I'm well inside the shop the little round woman in the white apron calls out in her dulcet southern dialect: *"Pas une goutte, pas une goutte*—I don't have even a single drop!" *"Tant pis,"* I say, "Never mind," and turn slowly away. *"Attendez!"* she cries, "where are you running off to?" I half turn back, she takes the pitcher out of my hand and growls, "You're always running away, *comme une folle!*" Then she goes into the back room and returns with my pitcher, filled with milk. I'm lost in amazement, can hardly believe my good fortune. I thank her, I pay her, and then we both say: *"Bon soir, madame, à demain"*—till tomorrow.

26 November

Everything went so well last week. First Heinz Pächter and his lady friend came. Hans went alone with them and returned quite soon. Fantastic, he said—just imagine, we were on top in two hours! You can only do that with strong young people, and even then, only if they behave with discipline.

Next was a rather young couple and their twelve-year-old daughter, confident and happy to be getting out of the trap. I went along too this time, thinking, Hans feels more secure if he has rear cover. The path wasn't difficult for the girl; she was quite proud of the red espadrilles embroidered with gold flowers which she'd gotten for climbing the Pyrenees. Another few persons brought to safety.

But yesterday! Two young women, apparently healthy and alert. Fräulein Schulz and Fräulein Lehmann, both former secretaries to the SPD *(Sozialdemokratische Partei Deutschlands)* Executive Committee. (The wife of Otto Wels came with them, but she must first recover from a serious case of jaundice and then be sent on an easier route. We lodged her with friends.)

Hans thought he didn't really need me and departed with the two of them before sunrise as usual, walking a few steps ahead of them. They were already quite high up in the mountains and all seemed to be in order; the sun was up, and they were talking. At the place where our path nears the patrolled way, Hans said, as always, "Now we must be quiet." And precisely then Fräulein Lehmann suddenly broke into sobs, then threw herself down on the ground and screamed.

"We tried to calm her down," Hans told me later, "but she wouldn't stop blubbering: 'I'm not going farther, I want to die right here!' I said to the other one, 'Loosen her brassiere and girdle and whatever else she has on so she'll get some air; this is surely altitude-hysteria,' but it didn't work. I tried persuasion, but she cried all the more. Just think—if the customs patrolman up above had heard her, and then found in the middle of the mountains a man with two young women, one with open blouse crying and throwing herself about. . . !

"'Please calm yourself and stand up,' I said to her. 'I'm going no farther, I'll die here,' she howled. Then I thought: she's a good German after all, this Fräulein Lehmann from the SPD—so I pulled her up by the neck, shook her, and bellowed like a drill sergeant: NOBODY DIES HERE! LET'S GO! MARCH!"

I had to laugh. "Well, what happened then?"

"Then she didn't die, she stopped crying, and we simply continued on our way. Orders are orders."

27 November

Now there's something new at our house, our *centre d'hébergement*. Young men arrive now and then, singly or by twos, many of them speaking only Spanish; they vanish again after a few days. We'd like to know more about them, but they appear to be shy of contact. They surely have no papers.

They have no aesthetic sense either; if they're cold, they just break up the beautiful oak doors and bookcases and burn them in one of the fireplaces. We just noticed that the two who disappeared today had burned a hole in the ceiling above the fireplace. And last week one of them asked me for a basin; when he returned it, it smelled funny, a reek which soon filled the whole house.

"Borax," Hans said, "for delousing. Crabs, body lice." My only basin! Helpfulness must have limits.

28 November

A while ago we walked along the pier to see whether there was anything to eat in our restaurant, for there was nothing in the shops. The sun shines. The *boulomanes*, the bowling nuts, are in the town square as usual, engrossed in playing with the little metal balls. They get all excited, they laugh, and rail at each other in Catalan. Suddenly a car is heard—a rare sound nowadays, there's hardly any gasoline. A black limousine appears and stops. Black uniforms, black boots get out. It's the Armistice Commission, *la gestapo* of the "free" zone, who hang around the border a lot, easily recognizable. Maybe they want to have lunch here. They smile at the players, the one with epaulettes greets them condescendingly; they stand around watching the game. The players' eyes follow the balls intently; not one of them looks up. The shouting and laughing has ceased. Then, one after another turns round mutely; none of them casts a glance at the *boches*—they don't exist. It's totally still. Each man looks straight ahead and walks slowly away. In the square, among the black boots, a single small ball remains. It sparkles in the sun and the rays dart to all points of the sky.

"Climb in and drive on!"

30 November

Monsieur Azéma, our elected mayor, has been quietly removed from office and replaced by a man from the Pétain government. The new mayor is some collaborationist official who isn't even from this region. They're being replaced everywhere, Socialist mayors especially, not to mention Communist ones.

Azéma hasn't been seen since. He's no longer on the beach nor at the harbor as before, where he used to greet and converse with people now and then like an ordinary citizen.

Now I remember how he'd said at the beginning: "Perhaps one day I'll no longer be here."

2 December

Maurice shows up every couple of weeks. We've learned from him that thus far all our refugees have gotten through. The Spanish border authorities have made no more trouble, and no one has been arrested during transit. Some of the refugees are still in Portugal; most of those with the U.S. "emergency" visas are already in New York.

We try with Maurice to schedule the weekly contingent of emigrants—not too many at a time, but the most-endangered as soon as possible. It is well known that sometimes political and personal motives influence the selection. "If one belongs to the right group or party, then rescuing even his most distant great-aunt must take precedence," Hans told Maurice. We made it clear to him that we won't let ourselves be misused for political unscrupulousness. He seems to be terribly naïve in that respect; he's not a German and isn't aware of all the intrigues and schisms within the political emigration.

We also spoke about how much longer we're going to remain here. The Centre is still caring for several hundred of the most highly imperiled ones (among them folks on the Extradition List), for whom exit documents are being obtained. That might take months—if so much time still remains.

Maurice brought a letter from my brother, Hans. Our friend Edmund was in Paris and had visited Father and Mother. Mother has started to take in sewing and Father is giving German lessons. Many people want to learn German now. Our parents still refuse to move to the unoccupied zone. The rest of France will soon be occupied, Father says, and what will we live on when none of us has an income?

I can't grasp it at all. In Berlin, back in the spring of 1933, they had decided so quickly to leave everything behind. But that was seven years ago, a difficult seven years. Later in life people become less flexible.

4 December

The mayor's secretary came by to tell me that the new mayor wants to speak with me; I should stop by in an hour and bring my papers with me. He said nothing about Hans, who left early this morning with two refugees. Perhaps they've been nabbed? No, surely not. This mayor probably just wants to give me a bad time. He's stared at me so strangely a couple of times on the street.

Afternoon. I have to write this down right now so I won't forget it. At first he stares again, then smiles charmingly. For a while we hold a light conversation and he asks me every possible question: where did I live before? (Paris); why did I ever come to Banyuls? (beautiful area); what do I do here, then? (stroll along the beach, go mountain climbing).

Then suddenly he says, "I know more about you, Madame, than you think."

Careful! flashes through my head. I can be charming too, if I have to. "*Vous êtes flatteur, monsieur le maire*—You flatter me. Whatever is there to know about someone like me?"

He ogles me seductively but then thinks better of it and asks, with official dignity, "May I see your papers?"

I pass him the document from Azéma stating that we are residents of Banyuls.

"I mean your ID papers *before* you came here to Banyuls."

I hand him the paper from the Paris prefecture, which I'd brought along just in case, and murmur that I hadn't been able to renew it because of the war.

"Just as I thought," he says. "Madame, I've asked you to come here because I want us to understand each other; I know in actual fact who you are."

I think: He can't know, he can only suspect us—he's trying to bait me. Just don't bite. I say banteringly, "That sounds mysterious indeed— *Vous avez l'air mystérieux.*"

"You're a British spy."

"*Pardon?*"

"You're English, and you're here to spy for your country."

I start to laugh. "*Excusez-moi, monsieur le maire.* But how come English, of all things?"

"You needn't think that I'm stupid. It's obvious: here you let yourself be known as Madame Lise, but that's not your right name at all; it's not even Elise, but rather Elisabeth, a typical English name, as everyone knows. And your paper from the Paris prefecture is a *refus de séjour*. You were, of course, to be expelled as a spy."

So he hasn't a clue what we're really doing here. I take great pains to keep a straight face. I explain to him that a *refus de séjour* is far from being an expulsion order, and that the Paris prefecture issued them in great quantities, but he doesn't let me finish.

"Don't take the trouble. I know my way around and I've seen right through you. Of course—," and now he puts on his silly smile again, "I can also keep silent. So, you needn't fear me as long as you don't give me any trouble—*il faut être sage.*"

I didn't ask him what he meant by that. I stood up and politely took my leave.

Well, I never! What does he really want, to blackmail me? Or maybe he wants to be able to prove later that secretly he was not a *collabo*.

7 December

"Three people" we've been casually informed. There were two men we didn't know, and the third person—yes, she's known to us, it's really Frau R. from la Butte Rouge; I think she lived in the same building as the Stampfers.

No one could forget Frau R. She'd had sleeping sickness years ago, and from it a certain nervous disorder remains. In Paris when I saw her on the street, I always thought: that must be awful, when one suddenly jumps backward while walking. But now the question was: how to bring such a person over the mountains, one who walks forward a few steps, then hops back again?

She didn't want to ride the locomotive because she had more fear of walking in the dark tunnel than she had of the mountains; I could well understand that. She was sure she could manage it over the Pyrenees, and both men promised to help.

I went along with Hans in case it got to be too difficult for him alone. She hopped around a bit in front of the last village houses, and for the first time I was fearful, thinking simultaneously, the woman has courage. Then all together we actually brought her up the steep vineyard and over the stony path—it's a miracle. If we held fast to her arm or pushed her from behind, it went better. She complained constantly ("How much higher do we still have to go? Couldn't you find an easier route?"), but that's the way she is. We had the worst of it behind us when she began, "Now I want an apple."

Hans held out the canteen to her. "Drink some water if you're thirsty—no apples grow here in the mountains." She kept whining: "How come you didn't bring an apple for me? I want an apple!" All of us were tired and irritable; one of the men said, "If you don't stop nagging, we'll go on without you."

It was a long day, but the three of them made it across okay.

I thought about Walter Benjamin, of his composure and self-discipline on this route that was so difficult for him.

11 December

Such tough luck, to have to get sick here! Maybe I shouldn't have washed my hair in this cold, when there's not any good soap anyhow. Hans has sent young Meyerhof to fetch a doctor.

12 December

Just now I looked at my eyes in the mirror. Jaundice. The doctor won't come because the boy had told him that we're *réfugiés provenant d'Allemagne*. My fever's over 40 (104°F). Hans said something about the hospital in Perpignan. But without papers?

15 January 1941

Yesterday I finally came home from the hospital.

Home is no longer our house on the beach. While I was ill Hans found another, less primitive dwelling for us, the upper floor in the house of the family Ventajou. It's a room with a sleeping-alcove and a small kitchen (with running water!). A toilet is on the ground floor—not a modern flush toilet, but at least it's inside. Our tiny balcony projects out directly above the customs office. When we came to this town in the fall we thought it wouldn't be easy to fit ourselves in somewhere. Yet now we belong here: we live between winegrowers, door-to-door with customs officials.

16 January

Now I'll see what I can remember since my last diary entry in December. My fever kept climbing and I started to bleed. The doctor still refused to come. Someone fetched the doctor from Port-Vendres; he gave me camphor injections and said, "She must be brought to the Perpignan hospital at once." But he was unable to offer further help. Hans obtained a rental car and some gas, and tried to find someone to drive me—he himself couldn't risk being nabbed on the way, for then what would have become of me?

At this very moment Hermant arrived from Marseille, to be taken by us across the border. What took place then is vague, and I only dimly recall the ride to Perpignan with Hermant. I do remember that I lay alone in the car for what seemed an endless time directly in front of the hospital entrance, and that everything was sticky with blood. Once Hermant came out and told me they were making trouble because there was no one with me who would guarantee payment; he'd straighten it all out shortly. Later I lay in bed in a huge ward while the *soeur supérieure* swabbed me with violet tincture. "The doctor will come in three days at most," she reassured me. For it was Saturday, and he came every second weekday. I was very sick, and in my fever the thought kept going round and round in my head: I must remember everything so I can write it down in my diary. At the same time I was thinking: How can I describe the pain? I tried to form the words; it was important to me to hold fast to every detail.

When the doctor appeared a few days later (meanwhile I'd been painted violet again), he said, "*Cela a tout à fait l'air de scorbut.*" "Isn't it jaundice?" I asked. "Look at my eyes and the color of my skin." But he believed my case looked more like scurvy. "Then shouldn't I be taking vitamins?" I asked. "That is correct," said the doctor. "But there aren't any." I shouldn't complain, I thought, he's spent more time with me than with all the others in the ward combined.

That ward. I gradually came to realize that they'd placed me in the death ward, probably because I looked like I was near the end. Thirty beds in two rows; in many lay patients whose families had brought them to the hospital in the final phases, so that they could die there. Between them lay women with incurable illnesses; many of these had already lived a long time that way, bed to bed with dying persons, continually changing. It was most pathetic to look at Madeleine. For three years, since she was stricken with polio, she had lain in this bed. Now she was fourteen, but she didn't grow or get older, only more transparent.

I couldn't get over my astonishment at the nursing care. I observed the nurses each morning as they applied to various patients small bulbs in each of which a blue flame flickered, some on the patients' arms, others on the chest. I wanted to know the reason for the bulbs. They're *ventouses*, I was told, now used instead of leeches. "Why are they needed?" I asked my bed-neighbor; she explained that they drew poison out of the blood and sickness out of the body. I learned a bit more Catalan, for I was curious about what the women were saying to each other.

Three times a day the nurses went through the ward with bed pans and called out in French, so that we *étrangères* could also understand: "*Faites pipi, mesdames, faites pipi, s'il vous plaît!*—make peepee, my ladies!"

Besides myself there was another *étrangère*, a tall blond woman from Lorraine; the two Spanish refugees, Rosita and Esperanza, understood Catalan. Later a Frau Goldwasser was brought from the nearby camp Rivesaltes (in 1942 the large refugee assembly center for transport to the east). She came from Poland and spoke only Yiddish; the woman from Lorraine and I were the only ones who could communicate with her a little. She'd contracted a pelvic inflammation from the camp's concrete floors. She spoke incessantly about her husband and children back in Rivesaltes. Would they return her to the camp in the event she got well again?

Every second or third day I got a letter from Hans; naturally he couldn't visit me. Twice on his way back to Marseille Maurice stopped by and told me about Hans and Banyuls and about my brother, who now had jaundice too.

It was in the third week, I think, and I was slowly getting better, that I realized the dying around me didn't terrify me anymore. Could it be that one becomes used to it? At first I couldn't admit it to myself, but it was clear that all of us in the ward breathed easier when the prolonged death-rattle from one of the beds finally ceased. Once I called the nurse: "The one in the bed opposite. . . ." The nurse took the woman's hand, felt for a pulse, and let it fall again. *"Pas encore*—not yet," she said, and hurried back to the kitchen.

One of the two patients whom I liked the most was called Rosita, a girl with big dark eyes. Rosita was actually not a patient; she'd told me her story. Some years earlier, when Franco took Catalonia with the help of Hitler and Mussolini, the fifteen-year-old and her family were among the hundred thousand who fled from the Fascists over the Pyrenees. Her father was killed in the Civil War, her mother died during the flight. Rosita reached France; she was ill, and was brought here to the Perpignan hospital. When she was well again she didn't know where to go. She was allowed to occupy a bed in the death ward, in return for which she worked in the kitchen and helped with the sick ones.

When I was able to sit up in bed, Rosita came one morning and tried to comb my hair; it was the first time since my illness. My curly hair had meanwhile grown long; it was sticky with sweat and blood and had become so matted that no comb could pass through it. In every free minute for days on end Rosita sat by me and with infinite patience combed through it strand by strand. "Just simply cut it off," I begged her over and over again, to bring the torment to an end, but she only shook her head: "That would be a sin."

One day there was a big commotion outside and then a small figure was brought in, swaddled in a white cloth from head to toe. It was a seventy-year old *clocharde*, a female hobo; she had been thrust into the bathtub and deloused. "*L'ignominie!*—the disgrace!" she cried, as three nurses attempted to insert her into the freshly made bed, "I warn you, you're violating my principles!" She had made the mistake, she told me later, of coming to the hospital to get some medicine for a stomachache, and there they'd simply taken her and "locked her up." She gradually quieted down and began to read a book she'd brought with her. I'm always curious to know what people are reading; it was a volume of Baudelaire.

However, she never did resign herself to being detained in that clean white bed. Every other day when the doctor arrived, she began to sing the third verse of the Marseillaise, and when he got to her bed she brayed, "*Liberté, li-ber-té chérie. . . .*"

I was recovering, and I often sat by her bed and listened to her as she told me about things that she'd experienced. I was never sure which was experience and which fantasy, but it really made no difference to me. She didn't explain how she had become a *clocharde*, and I didn't ask her, afraid she might be insulted. She didn't get better but she wanted out, "so I'll be well again." But she wasn't released. One day she begged me to do something for her; but first I must swear secrecy. Could I and would I, when I was discharged, smuggle out and mail a letter to her brother? "*Mon frère*," she said, "*il est clochard à Narbonne.*" It sounded like "My brother, the Count of Narbonne." In the letter she wanted to ask him to come with some of his buddies and free her; she'd work out a detailed plan and enclose it.

(I mailed the letter. Again and again, stories whose next installments are missing. Did her brother ever come?)

When I was finally steady enough on my feet to be released, all of them wished me a touching "good luck." They were happy that I'd received such excellent medical treatment. "Treatment?" I asked, astounded. Sure, otherwise I wouldn't have gotten well. It occurred to me that I was the first for a long time to leave the death ward alive.

I was given a couple of safety pins on departure, so that I could wind my skirt around my waist and fasten it, I'd grown so thin. It must have

looked funny, and we all laughed. Then the woman Hans had sent for
me drove me back to Banyuls.

20 January

Today two young Austrians whom we knew from Marseille came, and
for the first time I went to the railway station to meet them. These are
refugees who give us no trouble: people who have gone through the
"School of the Resistance" make adjustments with no difficulty.

"The route isn't easy."

"No matter, we haven't had it easy for a long time."

During my illness Hans had guided a number of persons over the
Pyrenees without particular incident. Only once did an elderly man have
to be brought through the tunnel by our Greek.

The day after Hermant brought me to Perpignan, Hans had gone
over the mountains with him. When it goes so easily, said Hans later, so
trouble-free, one can sometimes forget about the goal and purpose; one
is joyful about everything, as if one were on an outing, a normal
everyday excursion.

(Incidentally, now I know why I'd been left so long outside in the car;
they'd refused to admit me to the hospital until Hermant had paid for
four weeks in advance—luckily he had enough money with him.)

Since we've been living in the house of the Ventajous, the starting-
point for refugees is elsewhere. They can no longer come to us at
home—that would indeed be carrying things too far with the customs
people below us. Persons whom we don't know and so cannot pick up
at the station go directly to the inn on the city square; the *patron* is now
working with us. When we notify him that someone's coming, he
doesn't ask for papers or demand food stamps. Then we meet, most
often in the café of the Grand Hotel at the other end of the harbor. The
townspeople don't come by there often, and we've become friends with
the *garçon*. (He always wants to hear that *notre Aristide*, the sculptor
Maillol, really is famous outside of Banyuls.) The place is ideal; now, in
winter, we're often the only guests and can talk undisturbed. We sit
together, the sea and the green-gold mountains around us, and discuss
how we're going to climb over those mountains the next day, "and then
you're in Spain, and then you'll soon reach safety."

Once a car whizzed past going toward the border, and for a moment
we saw Valeriu Marcu in the rear seat. How was he going to get across?

Maurice was with us, and said, "and he promised to leave a suit here for me—well, we Romanians——."

Fry let us know that many English pilots were hiding out in France. What would we say to helping them get out too? I thought of our mayor: "You're a British spy!"

23 January

I don't exactly look like I'm in radiant health yet, perhaps even a little pitiful. It's astounding nonetheless how helpful the people here are. Today the butcher had pork. I held out my food stamps. He looked at them, asked, "How much do you want?"

"These are all the stamps I have."

The butcher: "I asked how much meat you want, not how many stamps you have." Then he gave me a whole pound; the ration is 100 grams per week when there is any meat at all. The shop next door had knitting wool, and the woman said, "Take as much as you need, just don't tell anyone about it—you look chilled through, *ma pauvre dame*." So I immediately bought oodles of it. Mademoiselle Rosa, the Ventajous's daughter, thinks there's enough for a whole suit. A suit of real, not substitute, wool, that would be wonderful! I could maybe knit a skirt, but how does one make a jacket?

"Give it here," said Mademoiselle Rosa, and took the whole lot out of my hands, "I'm going to help you." Rosa is somewhat stunted and her arms are too short, more like stubs with hands, but she can knit with them, so fast it makes you dizzy. When we're alone she tells me of her secret lover; they meet at night in the garden behind the house, beneath the cypresses. He adores her, he calls her his queen. Mademoiselle Rosa's coal-black eyes sparkle. I know she must have read all this stuff in novels, but I'm fascinated when she tells about it. In the beginning I even believed her.

27 January

The Hirschfeld family who came a few days ago are among Fritz Heine's charges; the man was formerly a big shot in the Prussian administration. They have two children, a girl and a boy about ten and twelve years old. We've impressed the usual precautionary measures upon them and had their luggage transported to Spain via our "special forwarding" system. Dr. Hirschfeld has a fur-lined overcoat which he absolutely will not give up but wants to carry over the mountains. "It's a valuable item, I brought it with me from Germany," he declared. We explained at great length how conspicuous it would be if he carried such a bulky thing with him, and that he couldn't wear it either. No coat is that valuable, and he'd get it back in Spain anyway, in all its splendor. Finally he promised, with a heavy heart, to part with his coat for a short time.

Hans wanted me to rest up for a while longer, so he went with the family alone. He'd soon be done with them (although it's sometimes a bit difficult with children). He was on his corner at a quarter to five; the Hirschfelds arrived promptly, and at the agreed sign Hans pushed off, the others behind him. Across the bridge, then up the path between the Puig del Mas houses. Where the ascent began, Hans stopped, as always, to turn and look at his group. Then he saw for the first time that Dr. Hirschfeld was lugging something with him, a large bundle. At the same time he saw the caped silhouettes of the two customs officers in the first dark gray of day; they were unhurriedly following the family. They apparently hadn't noticed Hans; at any rate they weren't looking in his direction. He stood for a moment to observe what was happening, and as the silhouettes neared the group he walked slowly back along the path toward the family. "Now just stay calm," he said. "The customs men are behind you. Say as little as possible, I'll talk us out of it. No, you must not run away now, nor the children. Remember: We're on an outing, we have nothing to hide—leave the rest to me."

One of the two customs officers was Monsieur Henri, with whom we often ate at the restaurant. He turned to Hans: "Do you know these people? Are they your friends? What are they doing here, where do they want to go? Oh, of course, they're going for a walk up here in the dark, with the children."

"Yes," said Hans, "our acquaintances want to look at the area—they'd like to see sunrise in the mountains. As they don't know their way around here, I've accompanied them. It's a family outing. My wife wanted to come too, but as you know, Monsieur Henri, she's still too weak."

"*Eh oui*," said the customs officer, "*la pauvre dame*. But we still must ask a few questions: Do the people have anything to declare?"

"To declare, no, I can't imagine what——," answered Hans. "We're not running contraband, after all. You mean what my friend there is

carrying?" He turned to Dr. Hirschfeld and looked at the bundle. It was
the valuable fur-lined overcoat.

"Oh, that's his coat," he said. "He surely thought it would be cold up
here. What, Spain? *Mais non, pas du tout* . . . no, I don't rightly know
where the border is."

The Hirschfelds had caught on. The children, who at first were intimidated, now decided that this adventure was lots of fun. They giggled
and ran around in circles.

"The people have no exit visas, without a doubt," Monsieur Henri
began again.

"Exit visas for an outing?" marveled Hans. "I never dreamed that we'd
have trouble here." Now he was annoyed. (As inside he was boiling
with rage, it wasn't hard to show irritation.) "A man merely wants to
show his friends our beautiful Roussillon, and that makes him suspect!"

"*Ça va, ça va, Monsieur Jean,* if they're your friends———."

"Do you see those seven pine trees up there on the hill?" interjected
the other one, "that's a pretty trail. Spain lies behind it, but you should
go straight ahead, for the path leads to the left where the Spanish border
guards patrol—and you don't want to go there." They both eagerly
described in detail the way to the heights where one could see both
coasts. It was our route, the "F-Route."

"Another thing," said Monsieur Henri. "We would never have
noticed your friends if it hadn't been for this big bundle"—he indicated
the coat. "In the dark we wouldn't otherwise have been able to tell them
from the other people. They can't be experienced smugglers, but it was
our duty to have a look at whatever it was they were carrying."

Hans turned to Dr. Hirschfeld again and glared at him. He swallowed
his anger and said softly, "Give the customs officers the two chocolate
bars you brought along." (Chocolate is now an irreplaceable treasure.)

Dr. Hirschfeld took one of the bars out of his musette and reluctantly
offered it to the customs men. "Isn't one enough?" he whispered to Hans.

But Monsieur Henri had already pushed his hand away. "Keep it for
your own kids—*pour vos gosses.*"

16 February

One saw immediately in the pair who came today that something had
occurred, something which had shaken them to the core. They looked
around continually with an anxious, hunted gaze.

We sat with them on the Grand Hotel terrace. "So you don't know yet," they said, "that Breitscheid and Hilferding have been extradited?"

To us an extradition comes as no surprise, for that's just what we're fleeing from. But why these two? How had they been caught? Had Germany demanded their extradition or did the Pétain government want to show how devoted it was? We knew about the troubles in the Breitscheid-Hilferding case—troubles not only because of their particular danger but also troubles the two themselves caused. We knew that the Centre had tried to get them out of France by a special route because they refused to travel through Spain, either under their own names or under false ones. That was months ago. So until now they'd been sitting here in France, and under their real names. Who knew how many similar cases there were—people for whom it was still possible to flee or to go underground? The dangers of flight frightened them even more than the grip of the gestapo.

The Case of Breitscheid and Hilferding

(From Reports by Varian Fry and Fritz Heine)

Summer 1940

Rudolf Breitscheid, member of the Reichstag and SPD party leader until Hitler's seizure of power, and Rudolf Hilferding, member of the Reichstag and minister of finance, stop in Marseille. Both of them hold visitor's visas for the U.S.A. Czech passports under fictitious names are obtained for them, as well as Spanish and Portuguese transit visas. As neither has a French exit visa, they must cross the French-Spanish border illegally. This they refuse to do.

Reasons: (1) They consider themselves to be persons of international reputation who would be recognized in Spain. (Even if that were so, spectacles, mustaches, and a little hair-dye have already saved many of us.) (2) They consider it incompatible with their position as statesmen to leave by an illegal method. (Haven't they grasped it yet?—that we didn't choose an "illegal" method, it was forced on us by the lawlessness of the National Socialists!) Fry quotes Breitscheid: "Hitler wouldn't dare to request our extradition!" (Can he really believe that, after eight years of Nazi terror?)

Breitscheid persists in his refusal. Hilferding goes along with the opinion of his associate, whose practical sense he seems to trust. So the two continue to sit daily in the same Marseille café, where everyone soon knows who they are.

Early September 1940

Frank Bohn, representative of the American Federation of Labor, buys a ship with which he wants to bring Breitscheid, Hilferding, and others out of France illegally. The two give their consent to this. In a short time the plan is an open secret. The ship is sequestered.

Polish passports with false names are thereupon obtained for them, with all visas; even the French exit visas, so that they needn't cross illegally. At the last moment they refuse.

Late Autumn 1940

Breitscheid, Hilferding, the attorney Arthur Wolff, and the poet Walter Mehring are sent to Arles by the French police and placed under house arrest.

End of 1940

Fry and Heine find a possibility of getting Breitscheid and Hilferding smuggled to North Africa aboard a freighter. The two consent. When the auto to take them to Marseille arrives in Arles, they refuse to go.

Reason: They hope—through government connections in the U.S.A. (with the help of Brüning) and in France (they even appeal personally to Laval and Flandin)—to obtain exit visas.

End of January 1941

On the basis of a telegram from America, Breitscheid and Hilferding inquire at the Arles police prefecture and receive assurance that making application for an exit visa will not put them in jeopardy. Vichy approves the exit visas within a few days, and they are handed over with a notation to take the travel route via Martinique.

Breitscheid, his wife, and Hilferding want to sail on the SS *Wyoming*, which will leave Marseille on 4 February bound for Fort-de-France. The cabins are sold out. Herr and Frau Breitscheid refuse to make the trip in the between-decks dormitory, which they think, due to their physical condition, would be too arduous; they want to take a later ship (18

February), provided that ship traffic to Martinique is not meanwhile discontinued. Hilferding, however, reserves a place for himself for the fourth of February in the SS *Wyoming* dormitory.

30 January 1941
Vichy revokes the exit visas.

8 February 1941
Breitscheid and Hilferding are picked up in Arles by French police, supposedly to protect them from German extradition.

10 February 1941
Transport to Paris pending extradition to Germany.

(Martinique was a French *département*, hence no exit visa was needed to travel there. As Germany had no control over the island, anyone with an American visa could, without more ado, continue on from there to the U.S.A. Indeed, it was this last absurd step, the application for exit visas, which led to the extradition. Hilferding, who had a berth on the SS *Wyoming*, did not sail because the exit visa *which he didn't need* had been rescinded. Walter Mehring sailed in his place.)

End of February
In the evening we sat in our living room. Actually in our *only* room— our apartment on the second floor of Monsieur Ventajou's house consisted of just this single room.

Mademoiselle Rosa called up from below and I opened the door. "*Madame, madame, venez vite!*" she cried. She sounded excited. "You have a visitor!"

Hans and I looked at each other. People never came unannounced. A trap? I started slowly down the stairs. "A friend of your father's!" Rosa called.

A rather corpulent middle-aged man stood in the half-dark of the ground floor. He looks a bit familiar, I thought. He came up to me and embraced me a little too ardently, and said breathlessly in French with the purest *accent boche*:

"Your father sent me, he's in good health, all is well with the family, we haven't heard from you for a long time——."

Mademoiselle Rosa stood unobtrusively in a dark corner, but I saw how attentively she observed the moving scene. The flash in her dark eyes, was that emotion or curiosity? Or both?

I carefully disentangled myself from the embrace, led my guest up the stairs, and closed the door.

The visitor and Hans looked at each other.

"It was recommended that I turn to Jean," the man said in German, and seemed to be waiting for a reply. Then he reached for the dark glasses that covered half his face—he looked like a Sherlock Holmes caricature—and took them off.

"Do you know who I am?"

"Yes," said Hans.

"Oh, so then *you* are Jean!" He sounded relieved. "Before, in Berlin, you were Hans—I see, I understand."

"Now I *am* Jean. At the moment the past doesn't apply."

"Jean, can you help me?" the man broke in. "I was *promised* that you would help if everything else went wrong. So, it *has* gone wrong, and here I am, and I have to get across the border. Will you help me?"

"Now sit down for a minute." Hans said. And to me, "This is Georg Bernhard." (Georg Bernhard was editor-in-chief of the *Vossische Zeitung* in Berlin and, later, publisher of the *Pariser Tageszeitung*, the German-language anti-Fascist newspaper in Paris.)

Georg Bernhard? He was brought across the border weeks ago, I thought. He was Number 3 on the extradition list that the gestapo had presented to the French government.

"First you must describe your situation to us," said Hans. "Then we'll surely find a way to get you out. What's happened? How do you come to be here? What papers do you have for the border crossing?"

To begin with, his wife was also here, explained Bernhard; he'd put her up at the hotel. Then followed a report of the flight as originally planned: A car—a diplomatic limousine!—was to take both of them across the border and then straight through Spain to Portugal.

And what happened? we wanted to know.

Well, the two had waited at the agreed-upon spot, but there wasn't a sign of the diplomatic car (nor of any other). Instead, a guide showed up, who brought them on foot into the mountains and then disappeared during the night. They then found their own way to Spain but ran into all sorts of trouble at the border-crossing; so they fled back to France.

When they'd started off from Marseille, the people at Centre Américain de Secours had given them our address and the name "Jean," as an emergency alternative in case the first plan didn't work out.

Such carelessness! I thought. And a glance at Hans told me that he thought the same. The office in Marseille apparently took that special route to be so secure that they'd given our address to Bernhard without thinking it necessary to inform us. What if Bernhard and Hans hadn't known each other?

"We arrived here in Banyuls this morning," Bernhard continued, "but I waited until it was dark. I've learned the tricks one needs outside the law. Even you, Jean, didn't recognize me immediately with my dark glasses, right? The main thing is not to attract attention. You know, I walked by here five times surreptitiously, to make sure that in the dark I'd be knocking at the right door. One must have a knack for such things."

"You—you walked by here *five times?*" I stammered.

In our little street which led off from the town square this stranger in his city clothes must have really been conspicuous as he walked back and forth staring at the same house on avenue Puig del Mas 16 from behind his dark glasses. Mademoiselle Rosa had doubtless noticed him; she always has one eye glancing out the window. (She told us later, "Your father's friend walked past the house five times before he finally knocked, *le pauvre monsieur*.") And our friends the customs officers below—my God!

But we said nothing. What good would it have done to agitate him now? He'd done his best, after all. A genuine Berlin intellectual naturally couldn't slip into the psyche of a Pyrenees winegrower without ado. It was amazing enough that he still had so much energy after those exhausting and dangerous adventures. Energy to try again, readiness to take on the French police, the customs men, and the *gardes mobiles* once more, then the Spanish authorities, and ultimately the gestapo.

Now he hoped, Bernhard went on, that we could escort him and his wife over the Pyrenees to Spain early tomorrow morning, for they of course had no French exit visas. After what had happened to Breitscheid and Hilferding it was out of the question to apply for *visas de sortie*. Otherwise, he assured us, they had all the necessary papers. "Just look, we have United States visas; here's the Spanish transit visa and here the

Portuguese one. All genuine papers, all in order. We lack only the French exit visas."

Hans studied each document. Then he pushed the papers across the table to me. "Take a look at them."

I leafed through everything several times and then looked at Bernhard. "These are phony papers," I said to him. "The transit visas, the stamps, all of them crude forgeries."

For a moment there was silence. Bernhard stared at me in consternation. "You're mistaken," he said at last, "these are authentic documents. The transit visas were issued by the Marseille consulates themselves. I *know* that, I was assured——."

"Assured?" Hans interrupted. "You were assured? By whom? One of the people from the Centre? Listen: these are not genuine papers. They've been forged—and how! A first-class botched job! They're useless—you can't go to Spain with these scraps, you'd be nabbed immediately. And the gestapo has been waiting for you in Spain for a long time."

Bernhard looked dazed. "You still don't seem to believe us," Hans continued. "Look for yourself. Here. The lower half of the rubber stamp is drawn with a plain blue pencil, but the color is slightly different. Idiots! Irresponsible amateurs! Look at this circle—that's supposed to be a circle? And this letter 'S' is upside-down."

Hans looked up. Georg Bernhard was on his feet, motionless, silent. Then he began to pace back and forth. Now he looks a lot older, I thought, more like my father.

"We'll get you out of the trap," said Hans, and his voice sounded placid again. "We have various facilities for difficult cases. But these papers cannot be used. We'll simply have to wait a few days while another way is contrived."

"Wait? Not tomorrow then?" Bernhard murmured, and continued pacing around the big table in the center of the room. At last he halted. "Jean," he said, "we've known each other for years; back then one often sat together with friends and colleagues. So although you know Georg Bernhard and his work, you surely have no idea that Georg Bernhard is also a gambler—I have been, my whole life long. Not one who just gambles once in a while; I *am* a gambler, understand? The higher the stakes—that astounds you, no?"

"No, I'm not astounded. I knew about it—but why do you bring it up right now?"

"The high stakes! My life, that's my stake now. Will you play along? Let's think it over again calmly. How good are my chances with these papers?"

Hans said nothing, just looked at Bernhard with raised eyebrows, as he always does when he's observing anything intently.

Bernhard continued: "The border inspection is not always thorough, right? Let's assume that tomorrow morning the Spanish guards are sleepy, slipshod fellows. They don't scrutinize the papers so closely, like you and your wife did. Our chances are then at least fifty percent."

Hans kept silent. I interjected: "Even if that were true—think about the rest of the trip! The train inspections in Spain, the Portuguese border. . . ."

"Let it pass," said Hans. "None of this has anything to do with logic. Look at him, he's not even listening to us."

No, Bernhard really didn't seem to be listening. Now, in this cool room, he wiped the sweat from his forehead. "Perhaps my chances aren't fifty percent. But certainly twenty-five percent. Agreed. So, tomorrow morning, what time?" He looked at each of us in turn and resumed his walk around the table. "Jean, you just sit there and shake your head. You have to admit," and now he turned to me, "that it's *possible* we'll get through. Five percent possible, at the very least. I've never been a coward; I'm going, even if I have only the slightest chance. You must help me!"

I was benumbed; it was like a crazy dream. Commonly, many people who came to us were nervous. That was to be expected. But this Georg Bernhard, who wanted to—or compelled himself to—gamble with his life . . . could this be real?

Hans stood up slowly. He placed one hand on Bernhard's shoulder, but carefully, as though with a sleepwalker one doesn't want to wake too suddenly. "We'll help you get across; we'll bring you over the border by a safe route. It's true, one must always be prepared to take a risk; but, indeed, we're sitting here figuring out how to diminish that risk."

Now Bernhard looked at him, but his eyes were glassy.

Hans shook his shoulder. "If you believe that this is a casino, then you've been given the wrong address. You're on the run, we're all in flight, and you know why and from whom."

Now Bernhard seemed to be listening. Hans took his hand away. "Wake up, man!" he thundered unexpectedly, so that Bernhard and I both jumped. "The Nazis haven't made you give in—you haven't been silenced as yet. But now you're surrounded. No, you've never been a coward, but one doesn't play roulette with Fascists. Or do you *want* to give them a chance? You have to decide who you really are: are you a gambler whose time is up, or Georg Bernhard, whose voice cannot be silenced?"

Bernhard wiped the sweat from his face again and sat down. He leaned back heavily and closed his eyes. "I leave everything up to you," he said softly, exhaustedly.

After a short pause I broke the silence. "It's gotten late," I said, in order to direct his attention to something else. "In this town you can't walk around in the middle of the night without looking suspicious. Now we must discuss the most necessary matters."

First of all, the Centre in Marseille must be informed about the bogus documents, because these clumsily made papers had surely been given to other refugees. Then the Bernhards' escape had to be organized, smuggling them over one of the routes that bypassed both the Spanish and Portuguese border posts. Until that was done they had to stay in their hotel room; here in Banyuls, where everyone knew everyone else, they'd immediately attract attention. Never forget, we told him, that this is a border town under strict surveillance; the infamous Armistice Commission is hiding around every corner.

We were friendly with the hotel owner, and he would take care to see that they got their meals without food stamps.

Professor Bernhard seemed to have regained his balance and felt a little more secure; he was optimistic and would make everything easy for us, he said. Hans took him back to the hotel. He was gone a long time.

"*Merde!*" he said when he returned. "That's all we needed. Madame Bernhard would like to *faire de la peinture*. She wants to sit in the marketplace tomorrow and paint the lovely area. It took half an hour of threats and talking-to before she finally promised not to leave the hotel. But she's still sighing, in the midst of all this chaos, '*Je veux faire de la peinture.*'"

"Isn't it unbelievable?" I asked. "Such people—known for their eminent intellects—are found shambling around throughout history with blinders on. Sometimes it seems that the higher the mind, the bigger the blinders."

"It is precisely to them, the exponents of German culture, that the situation is incomprehensible," said Hans. "It's too great a leap. Inconceivable that their homeland has become a barbaric nation and now, with France's help, is searching for them. So they make like ostriches. They're our most difficult cases."

The next morning I took the train to Marseille. When traveling in border areas one must have, besides a *carte d'identité* and a *sauf-conduit*, a special permit, and I didn't even have a valid personal ID. That was no problem at our train station—everyone knew me, I was from the village, and it didn't occur to either the police or the customs men to ask me for papers. Once in the train, I watched to see if gendarmes or policemen boarded so I could speedily make myself scarce, but on this day there was no inspection. In Marseille one had to present one's papers at the platform barrier; anyone suspicious was brought to the men's Camp Les Milles or, in the case of women, the Hôtel Bompard, and reinterned. That was known. Therefore I went into the station toilet, for I knew that it had an unguarded door which opened into the lobby of the Hotel Terminus. Success. But it was already late; the office of the Centre Américain de Secours was closed. I needed a place to stay the night without falling into the hands of the police; in every hotel one had to show valid papers. I called on friends who lived in a small hotel on the boulevard d'Athènes. By chance, Hans Siemsen had a key to the room of an acquaintance who was on a several-days' trip, so I could sleep in his bed.

When the next day I told Varian Fry about the forged papers, at first he didn't want to believe it. His people had assured him that these visas were genuine, issued by the respective consulates—the consular officials had received quite steep bribes for them. I finally convinced him by describing the details of the counterfeiting. "Have other refugees gotten these 'genuine' papers?" I asked him. "Yes," he answered, totally appalled, "a whole series of highly endangered people." They had to be reached before they got to the border. All available Centre personnel went to work on that immediately, and all those who were in danger had been notified by the end of the day.

I assured Fry that we would figure out a border-crossing for the Bernhards where they wouldn't be subject to inspection; by now we had developed sufficient connections to do so.

"Paul went to the border a few days ago," said Fry, "to see whether the Bernhard plan had worked." (Paul was one of his coworkers who often made contact between us and Marseille.) "He's probably with your husband now. Tell him to return immediately; I must talk with him about these consular stamps."

When I got back to Banyuls two days later, the Bernhards were already across the mountains. A *résistance* group whose dependability we'd repeatedly tested had smuggled them across both borders directly into Portugal.

As Fry had assumed, Paul was at our house. He was waiting for me to return, he explained. Was Fry very angry? "He certainly is," I said, "and he expects you back as soon as possible."

When I came into our room I sensed immediately that something was wrong. Hans sat reading at one end of the big, heavy oaken table that almost filled the room; Paul sat at the other end, staring in front of him. When he left the room after a bit I asked Hans what the matter was. "It looks to me like you're not speaking to him."

"Right. I have nothing to talk to him about."

"He's been sitting here for three days and you haven't exchanged a word with him?"

"Correct. I haven't any more words to exchange."

"Is he the one who obtained the 'genuine' visas?"

"Through a gangster he got to know at the *vieux port*; that was his 'connection' with the consulates. He couldn't have examined the visas closely, or he would have seen—that's no longer carelessness, that's irresponsibility. How can one work with adventurers who gamble with the lives of refugees? I don't feel like any light chatter right now."

Next morning Paul rode back to Marseille. A few days later news came that the Bernhards had arrived safely in Lisbon.

Mademoiselle Rosa said how glad she was that I'd heard from my father and that it went well with him. I was quite proud of my acting talent. When I visited her twenty years later, one of her first questions was, "*Et votre ami?* your friend—did he get through Spain and to America all right?"

2 March

Georg Bernhard was indeed a tough case. But what Maurice now dragged over to us. . . !

We knew the attorney Arthur Wolff by name; he'd often defended anti-Fascists in Berlin. Now we have him here, with his wife, Trude. His left leg is completely paralyzed, bound up in a brace; he can hobble short distances with a cane, otherwise he needs crutches. He's a tall, bulky man with snow-white hair and bushy black eyebrows, one can't help but notice him. Here in Banyuls for sure.

Last fall, with Breitscheid and Hilferding, he was placed under house arrest. The day after they were extradited, the Centre had picked up Wolff and his wife and brought them to Marseille. When Maurice arrived here with the two of them in tow, Wolff's hands were shaking and sweat ran down his ruddy face. It is incredible what the two have gone through in recent weeks. In Marseille they were housed in a store-room, concealed behind crates until papers for their escape could be obtained.

The original plan had been to bring the Wolffs and the Bernhards to Portugal by diplomatic limousine over an absolutely sure route. In order to get Wolff and his crippled leg safely to the border, Fry and Maurice had driven him and Trude from Marseille to Les Baux by car and put them on a train to Tarascon, where the Bernhards were already waiting. The four of them waited a week in Tarascon for the car which never came.

New plans, new connections: people who ostensibly worked with the Spanish anti-Fascist underground would carry Wolff over the mountains. Yes, carry.

The Bernhards and the Wolffs went to the meeting-place and waited for the bearers. Nobody came. They didn't wait a whole week this time; a guide made them an offer and they left with him at night. Wolff wanted to try it in spite of his lame leg. They began to climb slowly into the hills, Wolff supporting his left side with a crutch, his wife Trude supporting his right. It didn't work; it was impossible. They had to turn back; the guide returned with them. Now that the Bernhards had gone over—and gotten through—Maurice and another courier had, after several detours, brought the Wolffs here to us.

"Hide them away," said Maurice, "and try to find some kind of route for them. Incidentally, through new connections I have the prospect of getting another diplomatic car."

An argument was unavoidable.

There will be catastrophes if it goes on like this, we said to the two from the Centre. What's the use of your courage and your good intentions if refugees are sacrificed unnecessarily because of careless actions? Difficult cases are difficult to resolve, and rash adventuring hasn't solved anything yet.

We can't help the refugees at all without some occasionally venturesome plans, persisted Fry's coworkers.

Of course one has to enter into ventures and take risks, but not frivolously. Every new method must be thought through and examined in detail, each step accounted for.

We finally agreed that we'd try to find an escape route for the Wolffs from here, while the Centre looked around earnestly for other possibilities.

What should we do with the Wolffs in the meantime?

I remembered that on the way to the Grand Hotel there was a villa for rent. The Wolffs moved in at once—it seemed that money was no problem. Now we can breathe easier, we thought; but the good Herr Wolff had strange ideas about how one "slips through the enemy's nets." When we came to the villa he proudly displayed ten cases of wine he'd had the cooperative deliver.

"They were probably astonished!" he reported. "You have to mislead people if you're outside the law; they'll talk about it in the village and people will think I'm an eccentric millionaire who's settling down here." He'd gotten over his panic for the time being, so pleased was he by his resourcefulness. "I'll live here in great style!"

"If you want to get through, you'll do nothing to attract attention," said Hans. "Luckily, we were able to lodge you here where you won't be so visible. But being conspicuous——."

Wolff cut him short. "No, no, my young friend, as a lawyer I understand rather more about it," he informed Hans. "By appearing to be self-confident I ensure that no one takes us for shady characters. Trude, pour us a little wine."

"Trude," I said, "can't you talk to him? We can't keep him here if he's going to put himself and all of us in danger."

"No one can talk to him, you must have seen that already," said his wife composedly. Wolff drew himself up solemnly, one hand on her shoulder for support, and unctuously began, "I want to prove to you, my dear Jean——."

"Sit down now, and be still," Trude said. "Here we don't have to listen to your summing-up."

6 March

Our friends in Port-Vendres inform us that the route over which the Bernhards were taken through Spain without papers is temporarily suspended.

It surely wouldn't be easy to load Wolff and his leg into a dinghy—that's all the motorboat really is. Still, if the proper papers can be obtained for him, perhaps that's a possibility. Our contact man thinks that if gasoline can be obtained, he can find two people to man the boat and bring the Wolffs around the cape to Spain. Anyway, we spoke to them about this possibility, and Herr Wolff was all for it. Shortly thereafter, he lost his nerve again. Maybe the crew wouldn't be able to find the Spanish coast. Maybe they didn't know how to steer around Cape Cerbère. Would there be room to stretch out his leg? Could the men be trusted?

In his position I can understand his fear, but then he also started to blather, "I have a great idea—I'll tell the two crewmen that I have a million francs hidden in my leg-brace, and that I'll reward them generously if they bring us safely to the other side." Said his wife, "Okay, do it, but without me. First they'll remove your brace and then throw you overboard." Wolff's red face got as white as his hair, and once again his hands started to shake.

A mule was put on the agenda again. Wolff thought he would just have to be tied on securely. But even if a mule was found in the meantime, he wouldn't be able to ride downhill to Port-Bou on the Spanish side without help. Our Greek and the locomotive was also out of the question, for Wolff surely couldn't negotiate the Spanish stretch in the dark tunnel on foot. So first we had to see what the people at the Centre could do; the boat remained as a last resort.

10 March

Meanwhile we have other problem children, and still more to come. They're tall and blond, and don't fit in here at all.

Fry sends us Englishmen, as agreed, two or three at a time. Before we saw them in the flesh we couldn't really imagine how conspicuous they'd be here. The blond hair can disappear under a Basque cap, but what about the water-blue eyes and the pale faces? Even more noticeable, the men are too tall. They must take the train that arrives here in the evening. I pick them up (one can't miss them, unfortunately); they give me half of the torn paper and I show them to their accommodations. We put them up in two different places: with one railroader family the Greek mediated for us, and with a fisherman who rents us rooms without asking many questions. We don't use the hotel in these cases so they have no contact with the refugees. They don't leave their rooms until the morning they meet us in the dark.

The British fliers and soldiers who bailed out or got stuck in France must not be caught here. When they're across the mountains they report to the Spanish border post and state that they're to be classified as "prisoners of war" (which is ostensibly true). They demand to be put in contact with the British legation; usually after a few days, a representative of the consulate in Barcelona comes to pick them up. Then they're dispatched to Gibraltar, and from there back to England. We hear from Marseille that it's working. As Spain wants to avoid friction with England, our lanky lads are in less danger there than are the refugees. We, however, must be doubly cautious with them, for it could easily cost us our necks.

Moreover, we're occupied with still other things. We must not forget who we are and why we're here, doing what we do; it's too easy to get on the wrong track. Of course we want to help the British airmen get back. Of course we consider anyone who stands opposed to today's Germany as allies. And of course we now go for a stretch along the road together. Yet road companions are not always persons of like mind, and working together with someone doesn't mean working *for* them.

Basically it's the same problem as it was a year and a half ago when war broke out, the same points we discussed with political emigrés in Paris. Although France and England are indeed at war with Nazi Germany, it would be simplistic and we would be fooling ourselves if we thought that it's a war against fascism. What's the position of the German left? Some say: No common ground with the powers who had gotten along so well with Hitler when he allowed them to. Others say: We now belong on the side of France and England—anyone is okay who's helping to free Germany from fascism. Many strategists in their enthusiasm go so far as to say that our place is now in the Sahara at the side of the Foreign Legion (where the French government had tried to send our men).

The agreement with Fry is: we help the British who are sent to us by the Centre. We shall assume that these persons have turned to Fry through the intercession of refugees whom the Centre is caring for; we want to know nothing more, and we want to be put in contact with no other agency. It's important for us to protect ourselves; it's just as important that we remain independent. (A bum guess, *monsieur le maire:* we don't work for any government.)

The Toms and Bobs and Charlies (can all of them really be so named?) have their positive sides. They're healthy, strong, and never get upset; and best of all is their self-discipline. Yesterday we dispatched two, this time named Fred and Jack. Not a single superfluous question—of course, Fred couldn't ask very much; he didn't speak a word of French. Jack didn't understand my school English either, but it turned out that he thought he was speaking French, while I thought it was English! That the British had managed to beat their way through so far! It would have been impossible without the help of so many Frenchmen.

We stood up next to the two for comparison; they tried to pull in their heads and make themselves shorter, but they were still more than a head too tall. In the dark the customs men couldn't overlook those heads even if they wanted to. So we had to use the modified method, the "Britannia-Special" method.

We can pretty much depend on the customs officers not being at their posts between three and four in the morning; we discovered that fact a long time ago. Hence, I meet the Englishmen at half-past three and carefully guide them out of the village (by now I'm used to the scary two minutes on the bridge) and up through the houses and trees of Puig del Mas. Then I return, and they follow the path a little farther to where Hans is waiting for them; they can no longer be discerned in the dark among the trees. "It's always a pleasure with them," Hans says, when he returns before noon with a load of firewood on his back.

25 March

Decree of the Pétain government: Border areas are to be cleared of all foreigners within ten days. Of course, Banyuls lies inside the border zone. We thought something was in the wind when, a few weeks ago, we and the few other nonresidents were ordered to the police station for an examination of our papers. Hans had his expired *carte d'identité* at least, but I had no other choice than to produce my old slip, the *refus de séjour*, rejection of residence. After the two gendarmes had formally entered Hans and his ID in the register, the brigadier took my certificate. I was prepared to recite my usual explanation, and opened my mouth to start, when he passed the paper back to me without examining it closely; I swallowed my words. *"Merci, madame,"* he smiled. For a moment I was too astonished to reach for it, so he added, *"C'est tout, madame, c'est tout,"* and pushed the certificate into my hand.

But how will it go this time?

26 March

A telegram from my brother in Marseille, or rather Cassis, where he's now living with Eva and the child: AWAITING YOU IMMEDIATELY STOP BRING SALAMI FOR PANAMA VISA. His telegrams are sometimes baffling even in normal times. At any rate, it must deal with a new flight route that he takes seriously, otherwise he wouldn't be sounding the alarm. We'll soon know what it's about, for we must leave here in a few days.

Fortunately, Maurice has come in the meantime and freed us from the Wolffs. He's succeeded in buying an excellent passport for them—they are no longer Wolffs, they're now named Sanders—and Cuban visas. Now he can have them transported to Cadiz, where they can take a ship, all legal—or almost. What a relief! Lots of luck in Cuba, Señor Sanders.

1 April

One of the gendarmes came to pick us up. The problem has cropped up again: in order to leave here we must have *sauf-conduits*. To get them we need valid identification papers and a permit to stay in the new place of residence. We have to accompany him to the police station to discuss all this.

So, first we drank a glass of wine together and then the three of us started off—with no fuss, we thought. But of course we hadn't figured on Mademoiselle Rosa. As we stepped into the street in dazzling sunlight, she also came out of the house, a shopping bag hanging from her short little arm. Naturally she'd already heard about the new decree. What's going on, where are we off to, she wanted to know from the gendarme. What, *étrangers*? Who are foreigners here? Two other women with shopping nets stopped, and the old man in the blue cap who always stood on our corner limped over. Our gendarme defended himself: "We only want to discuss how they'll get their travel documents—really, this decree! Indeed, it comes from Vichy that no foreigners may remain here."

"You mean *notre maréchal*?" said one of the women, referring to Pétain. "Foreigners? These are our neighbors. Who stood in the chain half the night passing water-buckets during the fire? It was Monsieur Jean of Banyuls-sur-Mer, and now you're calling him an *étranger*?" Others joined in: "She's really right, you know." The woman in the house opposite called from her window, "That's the truth, I saw it myself, *monsieur* helped to put out our fire; therefore he belongs here."

"My ladies," said the gendarme, wiping sweat from his face, "please be reasonable; *monsieur et madame* will return shortly, we only want to talk with them." And so we finally left.

This time all five gendarmes were assembled in the little office to study our papers. Especially mine. We explained to them that my brother had informed us that we had a residence permit for Cassis-sur-Mer, but that the time had become too short for him to send it. The sergeant looked at us; then he said "*Ça va, ça va.* But what should we do with this *refus de séjour*? On the safe-conduct is printed '*Pièce d'Identité,*' with a space after it, and 'No. ———,' likewise with a space. These spaces must be filled in. If we wrote in *refus de séjour*, you would be arrested at the first checkpoint."

There ensued a lively debate—everyone had something to say but none of them had a solution. "The gendarmerie has no jurisdiction over this problem," the sergeant finally decided. "It's an administrative matter and comes under the mayoralty."

So Hans and I went over and explained the case to the Secretary. He was absolutely sure that the whole affair was the responsibility of the gendarmerie, that the mayor had no right to interfere. We went back again; we resolved to stay passive. The gendarmes found City Hall's attitude outrageous. "Those gentlemen only want to shirk their responsibilities, but we'll soon make things clear to them. Let's go!"

Down the street again to the pier. This time all five of the gendarmes came with us. Renewed general deliberations with the Secretary and his adjutant, mainly in Catalan; vehement gesticulations. After a while I said, "Couldn't you just simply write the number of my ID on the blank line after 'No.,' and I'll explain it somehow, if anybody asks?"

"Out of the question!" cried the sergeant, "*Impossible, madame, on va vous coffrer à Narbonne*—there they'd throw you in the clink! No, the line must be filled in."

Then the adjutant said to the sergeant, "If right after the printed '*Pièce d'Identité*' you simply wrote by hand: *Pièce d'Identité*, you'd be sticking to the truth; at the checkpoint they'd surely think you must have made a mistake and really intended to write *Carte d'Identité*—especially since her husband has one."

Everybody found that to be brilliant. So we dragged ourselves back and they issued the *sauf-conduits* to us. Mine stated: *Pièce d'Identité: Pièce d'Identité*. Then we shook hands all around. *Au revoir, bonne chance!*

5 April

The train pulled away from the station and we sat looking out the window. First one rides past *les Elmes*—the cottage on the beach is here. "When all of this is over," said Hans, "and we've grown old and want peace and quiet at last, then we can come back and live there."

Farewell, Roussillon.

10
What's Best? Cassis 1941

The waiting room in the Narbonne train station was large, dark, and dirty. Hans and I could have stretched ourselves out on the empty benches, but this was the locale of the dreaded police raids, each of which had resulted in the arrest of many emigrants. What was it the gendarme in Banyuls had said? *"On va vous coffrer à Narbonne, madame."* The train to Marseille didn't leave until the next morning, and nothing remained except to spend the night here.

First Hans took a good look around. There was a side exit to the toilets and an empty baggage room where one could hide in case of emergency. We stashed our bags behind a counter. Then we took turns keeping watch; while one lay down, the other kept alert so that the cops wouldn't take us by surprise.

It turned out that this was one of the few nights when there was no raid at the station. The next morning we took the train to Marseille, whose station was even more dangerous than the one in Narbonne. For that reason we didn't go through the barrier but took the next train to Cassis, where there had been no inspections up to now. It was only a short ride, not even an hour. We stood at the window, the fabulous Bay of Cassis below us, beyond it the grotesque shape of Cape Canaille with its crooked promontory.

For the first time there was an inspection at the Cassis station on this Sunday noon. The policemen shook their heads when they looked at our papers, and the chief said he'd let us stay overnight with our relatives just this once; we were to report to him Monday morning.

Our niece, Catherine, called Titi by the local people, had meanwhile become two-and-a-half years old. She wouldn't leave her Uncle Hans's side, and next morning, when we set out for the gendarmerie, she took his hand and tripped along too. The grim-faced chief was already waiting for us. He studied the papers once again and itemized: "One

163

carte d'identité, expired a year ago; one residence rejection, likewise unextended for the past year; the *sauf-conduit* I don't even want to look at. You surely know that you can't remain here. You also know that I must turn you over to the Marseille authorities." He hesitated a moment, then continued, "I'll give you until tomorrow to disappear. *Je ne veux plus vous voir ici*—I don't want to see you here again."

We said that our relatives were living here, and where else could we go? The prefecture in Marseille would surely have our papers in order soon, but meanwhile, with the ongoing roundups and street-raids in Marseille. . . .

"Come back, then, when you're *en règle*, in order," the chief roared. "Until that time I don't want to see you here!"

Titi was sitting quietly, well-behaved, on her chair; we'd told her that she must stay still. The chief's bellowing didn't seem to affect her, but I noticed that she was looking intently at his right hand, the one he was waving wildly around in the air as he spoke. She slid from her chair and went over to him. She leaned against him and pointed to his middle finger, which had a thick bandage around it.

"*Tu as bobo, monsieur le gendarme?*—Does it hurt?" Her piping voice was full of sympathy.

The chief broke off in the middle of a word, hand suspended in mid-air. He seemed to see the child now for the first time. He stroked her hair and said, "No, it doesn't really hurt," and lifted her up on his knee. Did I imagine it, or were his eyes actually moist?

He picked up a rubber stamp with his left hand and swatted our papers with it. Titi laughed, the muted thuds amused her. He pushed the papers over to us and said, "Take care—when you register at the *mairie* they won't treat you so gently."

"At City Hall ask for Marie-Ange, the mayor's secretary," my brother had said. "I've already alerted her about you."

The young woman with the tiny gold cross at her throat looked at our papers, shook her dark curly head, and sighed. After giving it some thought, she issued us certificates stating that we had applied for a *permis de séjour*, a residence permit, for Cassis. She then gave us two slips with which we could receive food stamps on the floor below.

"But be careful around the gendarmerie," she warned us. "They could make trouble for you."

Now, what was meant by "Panama visas" in my brother's telegram? And what's this about "salami"—is that a key word?

"We have a connection with the honorary consul of Panama in Marseille," explained my brother. "He's already sold visas to many people, to us too; you must check in with him right away. Of course he's not authorized to issue visas, and the Panamanian government mustn't find out about it. He takes salami in payment instead of money. I've found a shop in the Old Port that carries every kind of delicacy including salami, at outrageous prices, naturally. The whores and pimps who live in that street probably can't afford those prices."

"But what do you do with a Panamanian visa when you can't go to Panama?"

"You can try to get to Portugal with it. Some have already succeeded in doing so."

During this time we'd spent at the Spanish border all our travel documents had of course become invalid. The Czech passports were no longer recognized by Spain; the Spanish and Portuguese transit visas had expired and stipulations had tightened up. But there was also a favorable development; the French authorities issued certificates *au lieu de passeport* on which visas could be stamped. As always, the reasons for such a measure were inexplicable. Perhaps this was one way to get rid of the burdensome foreigners?

So we obtained the *au lieu* certificates and a medium-sized salami and, with them in hand, visited the honorary consul, a fat Frenchman. First off he made us swear an oath that we'd never set foot on Panamanian soil. We swore with a clear conscience. Then he accepted the salami, held it to his nose, and took a few long sniffs. I watched him and asked inquisitively: "*Monsieur le Consul*, do you actually eat all these salami sausages yourself?" Hans stepped on my foot under the table, and I added, "I mean, isn't salami hard to digest?" But the honorary consul wasn't so sensitive. He appeared to be happy to discuss the subject with someone, and he assured us that salami was not at all heavy on the stomach if one ate sufficient garlic with it. While he entered the visas on our papers, I learned from him the subtle distinctions among the various kinds of salami—Hungarian, Italian, fancy donkey-meat, and ordinary horsemeat.

"How about beef?" I inquired.

His double chin quivered with indignation, "No, indeed!"

And now we had visas for Panama.

No ships sailed from Portugal to Panama, so one could only get a transit visa if one had a visa for a country from which Panama could be reached by ship. This country was the U.S.A.

Some possessors of Panamanian visas had already obtained American transit visas; they cost four hundred francs each. That wasn't much, but we had no money. I went to the Centre Américain de Secours and Varian Fry let me have the eight hundred francs. But he was angry that the Panama loophole had become common knowledge. "That's *my* resource," he said. "*We* discovered it. It's always the same—as soon as a new possibility appears, the news gets around and everybody pounces on it!"

"What else can you expect," I asked, "when everybody wants to save his own neck?"

"I still have gravely endangered people here," said Fry. "They must be rescued first."

"You have helped hundreds," I said, "and many more hope for your help. But there are still others, persons who aren't well known and who have no connections. There are too many of them, you cannot help them all. There can be no monopoly on the saving of lives, not even for your committee."

He pushed back his horn-rimmed glasses and regarded me reflectively for a moment. Then he became impatient again. "There's not much time left. If the escape routes aren't kept secret, I won't be able to get my people out—the trap will snap shut."

Certainly he had a point, there was information that must be kept secret. But this whole hush-hush attitude had become a psychosis. There was panicky apprehension everywhere, much of it unfounded, that the lifeboat would be overloaded. "Can you imagine," I asked, "how it feels to keep silent in the presence of a friend about something that could save his life?"

I thought to myself as I left: I wouldn't want to be in his shoes. I wouldn't want to have the power to decide who should be rescued, whose lives should be saved.

The American vice-consul looked at the papers I handed him and said that he had handled many applications for transit visas based on Panamanian visas. "Do you have eight hundred francs?"

I extended my other hand to him, the one in which I'd been holding the money ready. He took the bills and counted them. "New instructions from Washington as of today," he declared. "Transit visas pending departure for Panama may be issued only if the Panamanian government has confirmed permission to enter. A telegram to Panama with prepaid reply costs eight hundred francs. Come back in five days."

My hand twitched; I wanted to take the money back from him. But no, I had to hold myself in check, must even act unconcerned. After all, I couldn't say to him, don't send the telegram, I've just had second thoughts, we don't want to go to Panama, we'd rather stay here. When he received the reply from Panama he could at least assume that we believed the visas to be genuine.

Once again, plans that came to naught. I went back to the Centre to inform Fry. "Now you can see very well what I mean," he said bitterly.

It was a long summer in the delightful fishing village of Cassis. We lay on the beach in the sun or we went to the *roches blanches*, the white cliffs, where it was peaceful and solitary. I lay on my back in the water for hours; I'd found that in salt water the emptiness in my stomach and the weakness in my head and legs felt less intense. So I looked up into the blue sky and thought: If we only had some money for bogus bread-cards.

One day my bathing suit was stolen. It was a catastrophe, for there were none to buy. However, I had a large Provençal head-kerchief, and under Hans's mistrustful gaze I cut something out of it which fifteen years later would be called a bikini.

In Cassis there were now dozens of emigrants who had fled here to escape the constant street roundups and arrests in Marseille. Indeed, here the *mairie* and the *gendarmerie* grumbled, but at the same time kept one eye closed. Edmund was here, and Heinrich, who still hadn't found his family. The no-longer-young man with the stubbly beard whom one saw roaming about in a greasy soldier's uniform was, if one looked closely, the Berlin art critic Paul Westheim; he had forged papers, and in that getup was scarcely recognizable.

Around noon, when hunger was greatest, Claire began, "Now I'd like to have a Wiener schnitzel that hangs over the rim of the plate, juicy and—." That was as far as she ever got, because we held her mouth shut or angrily tossed her into the water.

Most evenings we went to the Bar de la Marine. There were about a dozen of us who sat in the back room, including three young Britons who lived on the hill above the town. The innkeeper's wife, the heaviest woman in Cassis, brought us wine from her secret stores. We switched on the radio a couple of minutes early in order not to miss the news from London and heard the end of the German-language broadcast that preceded the French one. If the landlady returned with her wineglasses at that moment, her face got deep red and she cried, "*Arrêtez! je n'aime guère cette langue!*—I don't have a special love for that language!" She evinced no interest in our assurances that it was part of the same broadcast from London.

The Centre, Varian Fry's committee, made efforts to keep its promise and help us get out of France, but escape routes were steadily becoming scarcer. A letter came from Fritz Heine in Lisbon: "Unfortunately, news received today from New York says that Emerescue cannot obtain United States visas for you." (Emerescue—Emergency Rescue Committee—was the organization that had sent Varian Fry to France.) "They will try to get Cuban visas for you and are prepared to put up the deposit. You can be sure that I will do everything I can to help you."

Another letter from American friends: "Perhaps we can help you get to the Jewish farmer-colony in San Domingo . . . in the meantime we're sending you some articles of clothing."

Less and less often did anyone succeed in getting out of France. Escape was considered and reconsidered from every angle: If the Germans occupied the south of France, one could perhaps try to escape over the Alps to Switzerland, even though their borders had been almost completely sealed off to emigrants since the outbreak of war. But one would not be safe even there—well before the war, if they caught us, we were generally deported to France. Perhaps it would be easier to hide out here in France, to go underground with forged papers, to find lodgings with sympathetic French people? Maybe even in a town like Cassis?

In May my brother, Hans, received a United States visa. In spite of opposition by Congress and President Roosevelt, his wife, Eleanor, by exerting pressure—if the truth be told, by blackmail—had effected the issuance of several hundred "Emergency" visas; they were also called "Danger" visas. Those who received them were principally well-known artists, writers, and scientists. My brother, a physicist, was one who was delivered in this way. Fry's Centre arranged and paid for the crossing, mainly by ships that called at the French island of Martinique. My brother and his family sailed on the SS *Winnipeg*.

It was almost a fitting interlude that the *Winnipeg* never reached Martinique. It was seized on the high seas by a ship sailing under a Dutch flag; no one aboard the *Winnipeg* knew who had concealed themselves behind this "neutral" banner; in panic, many of the emigrants threw their papers, books, and manuscripts overboard. It wasn't a German ship, though, but a British one. The *Winnipeg* was rerouted to Trinidad, where the emigrants—men, women, and children—were once again placed behind barbed wire. After a time, those who possessed American visas were allowed to proceed.

Hans and I were in Marseille on the very day the news came, and we walked down the Canebière, the famous principal street that led to the Old Port. Hans always walked along the outer edge of the sidewalk; he'd gotten used to doing so since 1933 when he was an outlaw in Berlin, and it had become instinctive. One had a better overall view, he said, and could get away faster in case of a street roundup. Often I thought: One day, when we live in some country as law-abiding citizens, will he stop walking along the curbstones, keeping everything in sight?

We always ran into friends on the Canebière. Today they stopped to ask: Do you know? Have you already heard? Germany has invaded the Soviet Union.

This time it was not a rumor.

Those strategists among the emigrants who were still around sat in their regularly patronized café. Today things were different; people at the various tables were no longer segregated according to party, group, or political leaning. Persons who up till now had never said hello to each other were debating the Theme of the Day from every angle. Although it seemed to me that each of them was listening only to himself.

"This is the beginning of the end for the German Wehrmacht. I give Hitler two months." This well-known strategist, author of numerous articles, had unfortunately guessed wrong most of the time.

Maxim, the Russian emigrant, known to be a rabid enemy of communism, announced: "Now's the time to use my South American visa. I must go someplace where I can register to volunteer."

"As a volunteer?" I asked. "For what?"

"To join the Red Army, naturally."

"You? But you hate the Soviet Union!"

"That has nothing to do with it. You're confused about the basics! Mother Russia is being attacked and I, Maxim, should stand aside? We Russians——."

A gray-haired journalist whom everyone knew interrupted: "You fools! Can't you see—the advance of the barbarians is unstoppable. Adolf Hitler, Imperator Rex of Europe and Asia!"

"He's off his rocker," from a voice in the corner.

From another table: "The working people of every country will rise up to defend the Soviet Union."

"Oh, so now it's no longer an imperialistic war?" The two disputants had jumped to their feet.

"Come on, let's go," said Hans, urging me toward the door, "before the police get here."

More and more friends came to Cassis. We were able to put some of them up in our house in the rue du Jeune Anacharsis. (We tried to find out who the young Anacharsis was, but when we asked people in our street, they just looked at us and shook their heads, as if to say, "How can anyone be so uneducated?")

I was glad when Erna and her little daughter came and I was able to get a room for her in our building. We'd been friends for so long; in Berlin when we were quite young, then in Paris, and now on the Mediterranean.

Arthur Koestler's first wife, Dörte, came too. When Koestler finally succeeded in obtaining a visa for her, she fell downstairs, broke several bones, and couldn't make use of the visa for some time.

What did we live on back then? I think on a miniscule allowance which the Centre gave to their wards. Rent was cheap, and with the best intentions it was hard to spend much on food.

It must have been midsummer when suddenly there were no more sardines. Cassis lived mainly from the sardine catch. In the morning one bought freshly caught fish on the quay, and if there was enough I'd broil sardines for breakfast for the whole house. They were so fat that one could broil them without oil.

But one day there were none. It was inexplicable. The boats went out every night, using up valuable gasoline, and returned every morning empty. They started to search for the cause; there was much discussion and excitement, and a variety of opinions. It must be the weather. No, it's the moon. Or the Germans are behind it. As nothing helped, it was decided to make a pilgrimage. They must start on Saturday evening in order to reach the chapel on the mountain exactly at midnight, the chapel where the guardian angel of sardines was ensconced. The entire town turned out, and Erna and I went along just out of curiosity. I remember that I was quite weak with hunger.

The next morning the boats returned empty, and on the next, and the next.

A thirteen-year-old boy thought: I'm going to make a stab at finding out what's wrong. He took a boat while his father was asleep and snooped all over; he went out through the mouth of the bay, farther than was allowed, and cruised back and forth.

We were lying on the beach when the boat returned. In the distance we saw the youth, his pant-legs rolled up, jump out and run to the quay, shouting something. They clustered around him, a crowd gathered, some ran to their boats. We walked over to the quay.

" I saw it myself!" The boy had to keep repeating to new arrivals what he'd discovered.

"*Une dauphine!*—a dolphin, big and fat, and a young one, too. They wait outside the bay and eat all the sardines!"

They succeeded in bringing in the giant fish the next day. The young one escaped. There was an unforgettable triumphal procession led by the thirteen-year-old hero, and the festivities lasted for several days. The fishmongers, with their big aprons, spent a day and a night butchering the dolphin, and we lined up with the others to buy a piece. The dolphin's head was hung above the shop door. The whole village ate to repletion.

And the sardines came back to Cassis.

Erna and I often rode the bus to Marseille to check up on our various concerns with committees and officers. Sometimes we met with Paulette, who had finally been released from the Hôtel Bompard after intervention by Varian Fry. They had arrested her months earlier during a raid.

The presence of Germans in Marseille was ever more obvious, almost as if the south were already occupied. The Armistice Commission occupied the big hotel at the end of the Canebière; we noticed how many people spat on the street as they went by. When, on our way to the Old Port, we had to pass the hotel, we linked arms and crossed to the other side of the street.

Erna and I had run around for the entire day, and as usual hadn't accomplished much. We trod wearily up the wide outside staircase of the St. Charles railway station. It was a sunny day, but the treacherous mistral was ice-cold and blew right through a person's clothing.

We walked along the platform. The Cassis train was overcrowded as never before. Passengers hung from the windows and stood jammed against the doors. They wouldn't let us board anywhere. The train started off slowly and we began to run, trying to find a compartment where we could squeeze ourselves in. A door in front of us flew open, arms stretched out to us, and both of us were pulled up onto the step. "*Merci, merci!*" we said breathlessly as the train picked up speed, and we collapsed in a heap on a vacant bench. At that moment we noticed that the compartment was full of German uniforms.

The only other civilian was a young Frenchwoman in a corner next to us who had turned away to face the window. An officer bowed, smiled at her, and asked her permission to smoke. His stilted French reminded me of the hated Ploetz Historical Atlas of my schooldays. The young woman threw her head back and regarded him with icy eyes. She said, "*Je vous en prie, monsieur,*" and it sounded colder than the mistral. After a bit the same officer spoke to us, but Erna and I paid no attention; we began a lively conversation about household affairs, naturally in French. Apparently offended, he went into the corridor. He'd surely hoped to impress the soldiers with his linguistic proficiency and his worldly manner.

Now we sat on our bench, across from and next to us German soldiers speaking German.

"Take a look at the dark little devil," said one soldier. That was me. "A purebred exotic French," said his neighbor.

The soldier opposite us put in, "I like the blond better, the one with the long legs." That was Erna.

The situation was critical. A dozen German eyes were focused on us and we could not, must not, make a grimace. Also, we must not say anything wrong, in case one of them understood French. How does one suppress laughter? I thought of a joke and hastily told it, and we laughed and laughed until tears came. The soldiers watched us with surprise.

We've never forgotten the next forty minutes. The soldiers discussed our anatomies, as soldiers will, and dissected us with their eyes. We told jokes and laughed. And when we ran out, we started over again with the first one and laughed even more.

Finally. Cassis.

I got out first, Erna behind me. As she stepped down to the first step she caught her heel and stumbled. The soldier at the door grabbed her arm. "Stay on your feet, little one," he said. Erna regained her balance and stepped down. The stationmaster whistled, the train gave a jerk. Before Erna closed the door, she called back: "*Keine Angst, ich schaff's schon!*—Don't worry, I'll manage!"

Which was better at this time? To be a Jewish emigré or an "Aryan" German? What should one profess to be? How should one register?

Hans and I found one answer as unsuitable as another. The best solution was not to profess anything and not to register. When we submitted the *au lieu de passeport* certificates for Panamanian visas, mine was immediately processed, but Hans had trouble. "Are you a Jewess?" I was asked.

"Yes." On mine she wrote: *Réfugiée provenant d'Allemagne.*

"Religion?" Hans was asked.

"Protestant."

The girl behind the counter said curtly, "Then you cannot retain the certificate."

"Why not?"

"These travel certificates are only for refugees."

"I am a refugee from Germany."

"No," said the girl authoritatively. "You aren't a refugee; Protestants are not persecuted in Germany."

"How's that again?"

But she cut off debate. Apparently, Vichy had issued guidelines in accord with German instructions, and it was in order at this moment to let the Jews leave. Other refugees must be held at the disposal of the German authorities. Hans was able to get his certificate only through the intervention of someone he knew who had connections.

Then from the Pétain government came a decree for Jewish registration. We saw that this was a first step toward Jewish persecution in the unoccupied zone on the German model. What to do? Many Jewish emigrés asked themselves: Which is better, to register or not to register? Wouldn't it be better to stay within the law? If one didn't register and was caught. . . .

I didn't register. We were of one mind that it couldn't be "favorable" to register for persecution. Should it be possible to get away, it could only be by not complying with such laws.

At about the same time the Third Reich requested all Aryan Germans in France to return to their homeland. Transportation free of charge. Whoever went back willingly need fear no reprisals. Even political refugees could again, unmolested, lead peaceful lives in the company of their loved ones.

"They're crazy," said Edmund, "if they think anybody will fall for that."

"Maybe they think that anyone who returns willingly is no longer dangerous," Heinrich said. "Whoever turns himself in, they think, is sick and tired of it all."

Scarcely two weeks later Edmund returned from Marseille with the news that Heinrich had registered for transport home.

Heinrich? *Our* Heinrich? Impossible!

We slowly pieced it together from conversations he'd had with friends.

The wife and child he had had to leave behind in Paris were untraceable. There could be only one explanation—they must have returned to the Rhineland after Paris was occupied. Then why wait, why sit here on the Mediterranean? No papers. No money. When the Germans occupied the south, the gestapo would find him here. So perhaps it was more advantageous to go back willingly. The hiding, the eternal flight since 1933 when he'd come out of the concentration camp—he'd had enough.

They'd finally softened him up. Was he still alive?

We found out later that at the very time we were talking about him he was no longer among the living. He had never seen his wife and little daughter again.

Indeed, there weren't many who applied to go "home to the Reich," but Heinrich wasn't the only one. And it was reported that those who were not executed immediately were sent back to the concentration camp.

One would assume that Hans, with his *carte d'identité*, even though it had expired, was in a better position than I with my residence rejection. But nothing was the way one thought.

We had, of course, the provisional certificates from the mayor's office, but the police had to go by the extension of the *carte d'identité*. Applications for such were routinely rejected and applying emigrants sent to concentration camps in accordance with government regulations. The single exception was made for persons who were due to depart within three weeks. My papers were in such miserable shape that the Cassis gendarmerie chose simply to ignore my existence. Hans, on the other hand, had to apply for the limited extension, and received it on the basis of the unusable Panama visa, which served at least that one purpose.

"The three weeks are up and you still haven't left," said the police sergeant when he saw Hans on the street. His face started turning red. "It's against regulations, I have to——." He choked on the rest. "I don't want to see you again!"

All summer Hans first looked carefully around the corner before leaving our house to walk down the steep rue du Jeune Anacharsis, and if the sergeant was in sight on the quay, he quickly retreated. But if the gendarme came out of a bar or the tobacco shop unexpectedly and an encounter was unavoidable, he turned his head and didn't look at Hans. As the town was so small, it also sometimes happened that the two suddenly met face to face, and then Hans would placate him: "In three weeks for sure."

We sat with a few other emigrants around a table in the Bar de la Marine and waited until time to listen to the BBC broadcast in the back room. We drank "coffee," and I had a plateful of *oursins*, sea-urchins, in front of me. *Oursins* are prickly little spheres one must break open skillfully in order to reach the tiny edible center. The others laughed at me and my endless sea-urchins, but I found that for an empty stomach they were better than nothing at all.

Suddenly all was silent. Five policemen came in, accompanied by our sergeant. They were Marseille police carrying out one of their raids in our area. Too stupid, that at this very moment we had to be sitting here where there was no other exit! If we tried to slink into the back room now we'd only be leading the police to the radio apparatus.

The police went from table to table in the semidark room, checking papers. Finally they came to us. Luckily, the other two couples sitting with us had valid papers. "Report to the prefecture in Marseille tomorrow morning," they were told. Now there were just Hans and me

left. I squeezed into the corner and made myself real small. The
policeman held a hand out to Hans. *"Vos papiers, monsieur."*

Hans pointed at our gendarme, who was leaning on the bar at the
other end of the room with his back to us. "The *brigadier* is familiar with
my case," he said with calm assurance.

"Eh, brigadier!" the policeman called across the room, "this *monsieur*
says you know about his case. Is that correct?"

Our gendarme turned around and asked, "Which *monsieur*——?" He
spotted Hans and his mouth fell open.

"Is that right?" called the policeman impatiently.

"Yes," said the sergeant hesitantly. "Yes, I know about his case, and
yes, I know him. And how."

The policeman was pressed for time. *"Merci, monsieur,"* he said to
Hans. "Pardon the intrusion. *Bon soir."*

Lucky once again!—but how long could this game be played, this
"within three weeks"? Things were getting too hot for Hans. Fritz Heine
had mentioned Cuban visas. Herr R., who lived in Cassis with his family,
had bought Cuban visas and was to sail shortly. When we said that Emerescue was trying to get them for us, he laughed. "Do you know what the
visas cost? No committee can afford to pay that much. Five hundred
dollars' fee per visa, a two-thousand-dollar deposit per person, and the boat
fare five hundred dollars each." He was right indeed, nothing was going to
come of it.

Paul Westheim came trotting up a little later, wearing his old uniform,
and showed us a paper: a visa for Mexico. For him, the well-known critic,
the polemicist against the *"Kunstpolitik"* of the Nazis, it had surely been
easy to procure an entry permit. Another person rescued! We celebrated
with one of the last bottles of wine, and Westheim, who usually held
himself aloof, talked a lot and grew livelier. He spoke of the future—
perhaps his outpouring remains in my memory because in those days one
sometimes forgot that there was a future. He spoke of the cadres, which
must be preserved for the culture of the Germany of tomorrow.

As for us, my brother in New York was making strenuous efforts to
get us out; some of the friends we'd guided across the Pyrenees were
also helping. Ecuador was mentioned, Peru, Argentina. But nothing
worked out.

Autumn had arrived, the year 1941 was drawing to a close. We just
had to try something else. Then another telegram came.

11

Twenty-Two Elderly Jews

The telegram was sent from New York and arrived in the Marseille office of the Centre Américain de Secours in mid-October 1941. It read: CUBAN VISAS FOR F OBTAINED STOP UTMOST URGENCY. It had been exactly one year since the committee had given us its assurance that it would help us in our own flight when the time came. We had always considered this promise to be a dim glimmer of hope; the more time that passed, the nearer it got to cutoff time, the dimmer it seemed to be. It wasn't as in a dream, where one chases after something without ever catching up with it: for in a dream, until one wakes, one believes in realization. But here there was nothing to believe in.

"Our assorted transit visas must be renewed," said Hans, "and we need travel IDs for the Cuban visas. Then we must see about boat tickets, but for them we have first to get an exchange permit, so you'll have to——."

I interrupted him. "Where is Cuba, anyway?"

"I don't know exactly, somewhere between North and Central America. Why do you have to know that now?"

"Because it doesn't sound to me like a real country: Cuba. Just like those visas for China or Panama, pieces of paper—but no *place* one can go to. Do you know what kind of language they speak there?"

"It doesn't matter—Spanish probably. First of all we have to get your parents out of the occupied zone; that won't be easy. Do you think that now they'll finally agree to come?"

"Edmund is convinced of it. Father told him last time that he had definitely decided, after that incident on the street."

A German military unit was now stationed in the garden city la Butte Rouge south of Paris, where we had lived and where my parents had been left behind. (It was now well over a year since I had fled from Gurs.) When the north was occupied, not many people stayed in the

town. The young men had all been drafted, and most of the remaining
populace had joined the millions who—by car, train, and on foot—were
trying to flee south. A few hours before the Germans arrived, those
people who still remained began an exodus southward on foot. They
were mainly elderly persons and women with small children. As all other
residents in the rue Robert Hertz pulled out, my parents threw a few
possessions in a baby carriage and headed south too, as fast as their feet
could carry them. After some two hours they were overtaken by German
troops and turned around, back to the rue Robert Hertz.

Thus people continued to live in the now-occupied garden city. To a
certain extent the German soldiers behaved politely to the inhabitants, as
if they wanted to demonstrate: see, we aren't savages, we're not wild,
we're civilized. That had its effect. At the start of the occupation, *"Ils
sont corrects, ils sont polis, quand même"* was often heard. Clinging to such
a belief helped to reconcile one to living under enemy occupation. But
the fear and terror were only temporarily subdued—they quickly reap-
peared when one learned that André, who worked at the nearby military
airfield in Villacoublay, had been arrested and shot as a spy. One
couldn't pretend to be deaf and blind, one was forced to think about it
when one saw his widow and her two-year-old Nicole in the marketplace. And Jeannot, who worked in Paris, was arrested in a street raid,
held as a hostage, and shot; there were hundreds of such cases.

Still, my parents found that the environment in la Butte Rouge,
which they'd become familiar with in past years, was no more dangerous
than in any other place in France. Here they were known and people
helped them. Father could give German lessons—now much in
demand—and Mother sewed intermittently for the neighbors in
exchange for provisions. They wanted no more helter-skelter; they were
older, their health had suffered, they had no money—and they were
tired.

One morning Father went for his daily walk. He left the house at
10:30 as always, his *béret basque* on his head and cane in hand. As
always, he walked up the slightly inclined rue Robert Hertz toward the
woods at its end, with erect carriage and steady pace. As always. The
street was empty except for two German officers approaching on the
other side. One of them was the garrison commander, and Father heard
him say: "See that old French Jew over there? He's the one I'm getting
next."

Father thought: Now just keep walking calmly, don't let on that I understand; at least they think I'm French. When he got home, at 11:15 as always, he said to Mother, "Perhaps we should think it over again, about going south to join the children."

"My brother has written from New York," I said to Hans. "Here, read his letter."

"I had two job offers," wrote my brother Hans, "and have accepted the one from the University of Kansas, although it's less tempting to me. But they're prepared to advance me enough money to buy Peruvian visas for our parents."

" 'Peruvian visas for our parents,' " my husband read aloud. "Should that be possible, then we have to bring them here; they can only obtain those visas here in the unoccupied zone. There isn't much time left, we'll have to organize the crossing for them right away. I mean today."

"Maybe I should go and get them?"

Hans shook his head. "Not you. You can't go to the house where the gestapo searched for us the day Paris was occupied. And with your papers, the expired *refus de séjour!*"

"Edmund, perhaps?"

Since the occupation Edmund had gone across the demarcation line to Paris many times in order to take care of vital affairs for other emigrants, and while there he had always visited our parents. He and a few other friends were the only contacts we had with them, for correspondence between the zones was limited to an exchange of postcards—cards of a very special kind; they had preprinted sentences, for example: "It goes well with us"—"Greetings from grandmother"—"The weather is nice"—"The children are well." One could place a checkmark next to a sentence and append only one's name and address.

"Edmund?" said Hans, and thought for a moment. "No, that's not right either. I know, he'd want to go immediately, and he has the necessary experience—but it would be irresponsible, for we emigrants are doubly endangered."

We were still sitting in the office of the Centre Américain de Secours. "We'll miss the bus home," I said. Home was still Cassis-sur-Mer.

"Maybe you ought to talk to Mademoiselle Bertrand first," Hans suggested. "Ask her whether she would bring your parents here and how much it would cost. Surely we'd find help getting the money together somehow."

I walked over to the old house not far from the office, where she lived in a room on the fourth floor. She was home.

Mademoiselle Bertrand was a Frenchwoman in her mid-thirties, a small but sturdy, energetic person. She had friends among the emigrants: she understood their position and had sympathy for them. As she was familiar with many areas along the demarcation line, she brought people across the line into the unoccupied zone. It was an increase in income for her, and she was happy to help. I explained to her why it was so urgent in my parents' case and asked when she could leave for Paris.

She was awfully sorry that she couldn't help, she said, but she had just now decided that she wouldn't be bringing anyone else across the line. Surely we knew that now the surveillance was twice as strict; there was frequent firing—firing at people who were trying to cross illegally. And did we actually want to subject our parents to that danger? No, it wasn't worth it, to risk one's life for a little money.

Yes, we knew it had become much more dangerous, I said. But there was nothing else for it, the old folks would hardly survive the occupation, and now there was still a possibility of getting them out of France. Indeed, how could I sail for Cuba when my parents were stuck fast in the occupied zone?

I saw the distress and sympathy in her eyes, but she kept shaking her head regretfully.

We talked for a long time. We considered what other possibilities there were but hit on no solution. "It's true, I know the entire area," she said after a while, "I have helpers among the residents on both sides of the line." She reflected a bit longer. "If I used some other crossing point—let me think it over, perhaps farther west—but this would be the last time, and then never again."

We were of one mind that this time she should bring only Father and Mother across, not a group of four or five as she had been doing. Now that would be too dangerous. And she would have to ask for more. Certainly, I said, of course I understand, we'll set about raising the money. Today was Thursday. Maybe Monday she could leave.

Mademoiselle Bertrand was on her way to Paris by Monday afternoon; she'd ride to la Butte Rouge early the following morning. Meanwhile, through an acquaintance who had a business associate in Paris, we'd been able to inform Father and Mother. They could bring no baggage with them. Mademoiselle Bertrand had assured us that the spot she'd chosen to cross the line this time wasn't too arduous, but with my aged parents. . . . So once again they must leave everything behind—how many times during the past eight years? I thought: That won't be the worst for them, for with each move there's less to lose.

We figured that Mademoiselle Bertrand would be back with them on Tuesday, or perhaps Wednesday. After the crossing they would stay overnight in a hotel in the "free"—or, more accurately, the unoccupied—zone. (How could one speak of "free" when the Pétain government attempted to outdo the Germans in persecuting Jews and anti-Fascists?) On Thursday at the latest they would take the train to Marseille, and on the same evening Mademoiselle Bertrand would bring them directly to us in Cassis.

But they didn't come on Thursday either.

On Friday Hans said: "You know that we can only figure the time approximately. Both of us know very well that there are always unforeseen delays."

Saturday we went to the station to meet every train that arrived, and morning and evening to the bus depot. There had been no gasoline for a long time, but the bus ran on gas produced by burning charcoal. It ran and stopped, and then slowly wheezed ahead along the glorious coast; but going uphill it ran out of breath every time. Everybody got out, the driver poked around in the charcoal, the passengers shoved and complained, and someone usually said, "*Voilà l'essence de notre maréchal*—There's the gasoline our Marshal (Pétain) gives us!"

But my parents didn't come. Hans said again, surely their departure had to be postponed for some reason or other, and they have no way of notifying us. We must simply be patient. But I could see that now he was nervous too.

On Sunday I saw a small item in the newspaper: SHOOTING ON THE DEMARCATION LINE. Four people had tried to cross to the unoccupied zone; one was killed. The location was not given.

"These incidents happen all the time," said Hans. "Mademoiselle Bertrand is a clever, experienced guide." All that was true. "No reason to assume that the shooting had anything to do with your parents." Maybe not, but maybe yes.

Monday I rode to Marseille. There didn't seem to be much point, but I went to Mademoiselle Bertrand's apartment anyway. No one answered when I knocked, so I shoved a note under her door with the phone number of Mademoiselle Jeanne in Cassis, through whom she could reach us.

She didn't come on Monday, she didn't come on Tuesday. I called on acquaintances who might perhaps know something. Anything new on the *ligne*? Had anyone heard from Mademoiselle Bertrand? No one could help me.

Tuesday evening, on the way to the bus, I saw Franz, a young Austrian emigrant. We stood on the street and I told him the story about my parents, that we'd been waiting since Thursday and hadn't heard a word from them. And that Mademoiselle Bertrand had vanished.

"Vanished?" said Franz. "She's right here in Marseille."

"Impossible. She was to come directly to Cassis with my parents. And that was almost a week ago!"

"But I'm telling you," Franz repeated, "she's sitting in her apartment, I just came from there."

A few minutes later I was in her building and up on the fourth floor. The door to her room was ajar. I pushed it open.

After the sunlight outside on the street my eyes had to adjust to the semidark room. First I saw her pale face and the dark hair falling over her forehead. She was sitting at a little antique desk, and when she raised her eyes she opened them wide and looked at me, appalled. Then she covered her face with her hands and started to weep. I walked the few steps over to her, shook her by the shoulders and asked, "What happened? Tell me, say something! What happened?"

"I could do nothing—I couldn't help them," she sobbed.

"Are my parents alive? Tell me whether they're alive."

"Yes, they're alive. But——."

"Where? Tell me where they are."

"In Mâcon—in jail."

I got a little dizzy and had to sit down. She wept.

"When were they arrested?" I asked after a moment.

"Thursday."

"And since when are you back?"

"Since Saturday."

"And why didn't you——?"

"I couldn't," she broke in. "I just wasn't strong enough to tell you."

My God! and we had had such trust in this woman, I thought; we still have two weeks and then we must leave.

I held myself back and kept silent for a while—I had to give her time to pull herself together if I wanted to learn anything. She gradually quieted down and began to relate.

"All went well on the ride to Paris; I went to your parents and we agreed to leave the next day, Wednesday. They were all prepared and quite calm. On Tuesday I spoke to several friends in Paris. Among them was an old couple who had planned for a year to get across the line into the unoccupied zone but had kept putting it off. The usual doubts: Where can we go? How shall we live? Won't the south be occupied soon anyway? They were dismayed when they learned that this would be my last trip to Paris. An hour later they appeared at my hotel; they had decided—would I take them along? I hesitated, for I had promised to take only your parents because of the danger with larger groups. But I simply couldn't say no to these friends, for I knew indeed that this was their last opportunity.

"That afternoon they came twice more to my hotel room; each time they spoke of other people who were desperate to get out. Could I help them too? They even brought money with them, and kept saying: 'Help us, do help us!' I don't myself know how I finally came to assent, why I put aside my own strict security rules. It certainly wasn't the money. It was a sort of panic which affected me too—yes, that was it, last-minute panic. First I agreed to take four people, then six, then—it didn't seem to matter any more. When we met on Wednesday morning to make final preparations, there were twenty-two.

"Yes, naturally you're shocked," she continued. "I know it was a terrible mistake. Twenty-two, all elderly people; I believe all of them were Jews. And all women except for your father and one other man. I explained to them that all of us would take the same train but that we must disperse ourselves in different compartments, never more than two together. That they must not be identified as a group, and that they must behave so as not to attract attention.

"On the train ride everything went well. We got out not far from the demarcation line. Besides us, only two women left the train; obviously local residents, they stared at us but then went their way. My people stood all huddled together on the platform and whispered excitedly to one another.

" 'Don't stand together, move away from each other,' I said softly. Then I led them out of the station, sat them down in small groups in various bistros, and said, 'I'll come back to get you soon.' I went to an acquaintance who had been working with me for months. 'The situation has changed drastically during the last few days,' she said, 'surveillance has been increased and there have been repeated shootings.' I would have to guide the group over a roundabout way, not the one I'd planned to take. It was longer and more difficult, however.

"I went back to the various bistros and directed the people to a meeting place outside the town. It had rained and the way to the *ligne* was soggy. In places we had to crawl through mud on our knees, sometimes through underbrush. The old people followed me silently, and we crossed the line unnoticed.

"When we reached Mâcon in the unoccupied zone it was starting to get dark. The people were bunching together again. I couldn't keep them apart, and I thought, it will be a miracle if the police don't notice us. I took them to a hotel where I always stayed with people I brought across; the owner was trustworthy and she didn't ask for papers. She wasn't prepared for so many, but we laid mattresses on the floor and were able to put all of them up in vacant rooms.

"About three o'clock in the morning there was loud knocking on the door of the room where I was sleeping with three other women.

"Police. 'Take your things and come downstairs.' More police were waiting for us in the dimly lit lobby. My people came slowly down the steep, dark stairs. The policeman in charge informed them that they were all under arrest for crossing the demarcation line illegally.

"I went to him and said I'd like to speak to him a moment alone. In the little adjoining room I explained to him that all these people had been separated from their children during the German advance, and that I was only helping them to get to their families in the unoccupied zone.

" 'How did they come over? Do they have papers?' he asked.

"I said, yes, their papers were in order. I'd taken everybody's papers with me.

" 'Show them to me,' he said, holding out his hand. I opened my purse and pawed through it for a few seconds, finally taking out a handful of bills and offering them to him. He slowly pushed my hand away and went back into the lobby. 'The people's papers are *en règle*—in order,' he said to the other policemen. As they left he turned to me and said softly, 'You should be more careful, Mademoiselle.'

"When we set out for the train station the next morning, I admonished my people once again not to cluster together. The train to the south was late and I went to find out when it was expected. When I returned to the concourse I saw the group standing huddled together in a corner—twenty-two elderly, rather strange-looking, frightened people. At the same time I saw several policemen advancing toward them; they weren't the same ones who'd come to the hotel during the night. The chief was a brutal-looking type—it turned out later that he was the Mâcon *commissaire de police* in person—who roared at my folks, 'You are all under arrest!' I stood to the side, and as they were led away I followed them at a distance, so as not to be arrested myself."

Mademoiselle Bertrand fell silent. There were tears in her eyes again. As I looked at her it struck me how different she looked today. Never before had I seen her without makeup.

"Please continue," I said. "They were put in jail—do you know where? Did you try to establish contact with them?"

She paced back and forth agitatedly in the little room. "No," she said in a tremulous voice, "no, right then they were not jailed." She sat down again and stared in front of her. Finally she continued:

"First they were locked in a hall at the station. The commissioner left and his underlings guarded the prisoners. I walked slowly past the glass door of the hall a few times; some of the prisoners saw me but none gave a sign of recognition. After a while the commissioner returned and the group was herded outside onto another platform where an engine with one car was standing. The question darted through my head: What was he intending to do with them?

"I had followed them without being observed. Now I started running until I caught up with the commissioner, and called out, *'Monsieur, attendez monsieur!* The people you've arrested, they're friends of mine; I take responsibility for them. Where are you taking them—surely not back to the occupied zone? You wouldn't do that, you can't deliver them to the Germans?'

" *'Mais oui, madame,'* he answered, 'that's exactly what we are going to do. They are foreign Jews. You say that they're friends of yours? You'd do better to keep away from them.'

"Meanwhile they had loaded all the people into the car; the train started up slowly. I ran alongside and kept talking to the commissioner; he grabbed me and yelled, 'Get away, or I'll arrest you too!' Then he jumped aboard the train.

"I went to the waiting room; I was so jittery that I had to sit down. I thought it over: What could I do now? Perhaps I should return to the occupied zone—I'm French after all, and have travel permits for both zones. I could try to speak with one of the German officers; when it comes to that, the military isn't the gestapo.

"A train pulled in. It was a locomotive with a single car. Wasn't it——? The commissioner got out, he gave an order, the doors were opened. My people began to come slowly down the car steps. I counted: twenty-two.

"I have no idea what happened. Your parents will know. But now they're locked up."

"In Mâcon?"

"There was no room for them in the Mâcon jail. The women were put in the attic of a Catholic hospice. Your father was locked in a wooden shack on the station platform. It's an equipment storeroom adjoining the station toilet. The shack has no window, and of course no water or heat. I don't know where the other man is."

She gave me the address of the hospice and the name of the Mâcon *commissaire spécial de police*. "It is hoped that these are only rumors," she added, "but it is said that now people are being deported to the east." (As we later learned, the first deportations actually occurred that very week.)

"Have you informed the families of the other people?" No. "Do you have the addresses of their relatives? Please do that right away. You must pull yourself together—perhaps these people can still be saved."

I hurried down the stairs. We had to leave for Portugal in two weeks in order to make our ship connection; perhaps that was the last ship.

I went directly to the office of the Centre Américain de Secours. Because of the increasing obstructionism of the authorities, the work of the committee had been sharply curtailed during recent months. A succession of coworkers had been arrested, and some, among them Varian Fry, had had to leave France.

"Can you help us, do you know of any way at all that I can get my parents out?"

No one could advise us. Every connection the committee had to higher agencies had dried up. All agreed that on no account must we miss our ship after the efforts it had cost to obtain visas for us. Someone suggested that we should leave at once, that in Portugal we would surely have a better chance, through connections, to free my parents. "You don't believe that yourself!" I said angrily. "Are you trying to kid us?"

In the evening we sat together with friends in Cassis and considered what we could do. Edmund was there too.

Organizing an escape attempt was out of the question—on that point we were unanimous. With the exception of Edmund. He told us that he would ride to Mâcon tomorrow and scout around for escape possibilities.

"No," said Hans, "give up that idea; under these conditions planning an escape would be irresponsible." Without contacts among local residents such an undertaking would end in catastrophe, for my parents and for Edmund himself. Even if it were possible to spring Father from the shack—maybe with the help of railroad men—what would happen to my mother? No, it was impossible.

Edmund remained stubborn in his intention. Everyone tried to dissuade him; there was a heated discussion. I remember how Hans pounded his fist on the table when argument didn't help. And finally Edmund gave in, "for the time being," as he said.

The only way was to coerce the *commissaire* into releasing them. How could that be managed? Whom would he listen to? Who could put pressure on him, and how?

Everything had to be tried. Tomorrow in Marseille I would go to every organization that had anything at all to do with aiding emigrants. Hans still had to deal with several time-consuming formalities concerning our departure; he would also get in contact with influential persons he knew. The others would speak with friends who perhaps knew a way out.

There were about fifteen aid organizations for emigrants in Marseille. There was HICEM, which cared for Jewish refugees; Dr. Joy of the American Unitarian Church; the Field couple, who represented the Quakers, and whose chief activity was providing food for emigrants in French concentration camps; a Protestant group that had its own assistants in several of those camps—I can't remember the names of all the aid organizations, but I spoke with all of them. They all showed interest in the tragic situation, but none could offer a solution. And there were so many other urgent cases to which they had to devote themselves.

I told the story to everyone and anyone who would listen. Maybe someone would have an idea, or knew somebody who could help. One morning on the way to the bus stop I saw Marie-Ange, the secretary to the mayor of Cassis, and I even told her about it; she had always proven herself helpful to us emigrants, she had become a friend. Of course she couldn't help me, but I simply had to tell her what had happened to my parents.

When, after two days, we hadn't accomplished anything, we debated whether I should ride to Mâcon and try to speak with the commissioner, although he was obviously a Nazi friend and collaborator. I phoned him first to see how he reacted. I was the daughter of Monsieur and Madame Ekstein, and would come there tomorrow to visit my parents, if he would be so kind as to arrange for me to see them. He began shouting into the telephone, and I heard something like *ces juifs-là*. I could *not* see them, and if I came to Mâcon I would be immediately arrested.

So there was no point in that. I rode back to Marseille to talk with other people.

In the bus I ran everything through my head again; it all went around and around. We *must* find a solution. I simply couldn't leave France— and Europe—while my parents were being held prisoner by these Fascists. On the other hand, my husband *must* get out of the trap. I couldn't leave him, nor could I leave my parents: there was no way to choose between them—so there had to be another way out.

At the end of the day, with nothing accomplished, I ran into Fritz, a young emigrant we'd become friends with in Marseille.

"Have you tried the Swedish Consulate?" he asked, after he had listened to my story.

"The Swedish Consulate? No. I went to the American, but they wouldn't let me in. Why do you suggest Sweden?"

"Listen a minute," said Fritz. "It's only an idea of mine and maybe nothing will come of it, but it can do no harm. I was told that Herr Berglund, the consul, has a brother who is a Socialist journalist. That's all I know, and even that's just hearsay. You can't refer to me; he doesn't know me from Adam."

That didn't sound very hopeful. But I really didn't know anyone else to whom I could turn. Sweden, it occurred to me, had taken over diplomatic representation of Germany in the Pétain government of unoccupied France. Who knows, maybe that would be a help?

It was already late afternoon, and the Swedish consul sat alone in his small office. Mr. Berglund was a tall, slim man, reservedly polite. He listened as I related what had happened to my parents and he said, "I'm sincerely sorry, but what led you to come to me? It surely must be evident to you that my consulate can offer you no help."

"Somehow I had the feeling," I said, "that you, as Sweden's representative, would have understanding for my dilemma."

"A feeling?" he asked, surprised, though it seemed to me as if his eyes smiled a little, so I continued: "I thought perhaps you could give me some advice. We have to leave, you see, and there's not much time left."

He grew formal. "You can expect no help from me. I very much deplore the circumstances, but as the representative of my government I cannot intervene."

"I naturally don't know my way around on the diplomatic level," I said cautiously, "and certainly you're following the established rules, all of which I'm sure are justified. But the times in which we live are out of joint, and what has happened to my parents is altogether abnormal. Can't it be that those established rules have lost their significance in a world where all values are topsy-turvy?"

"You're speaking of moral values, if I understand you correctly," said the consul. "My role here is limited to consular duties, and unfortunately there is no correlation between those duties and your case."

"But," I tried to remonstrate, "your government represents Germany's interests in France."

"Perhaps you refer to the fact that the Kingdom of Sweden has taken over *consular* representation of the German Reich," he corrected me.

"Oh—yes, that's what I meant. In any case, I believe the Mâcon commissioner would consider you as Germany's representative, and for him that's the highest authority."

"Are you implying that I should misuse my position?"

"Misuse?—*abuser?*—I've come to you with a plea to help counteract a shameful abuse—*pour arrêter un abus honteux!*"

I'm doing this all wrong, I said to myself at the same moment. I shouldn't challenge him; I should try to humor him instead of provoking him—well, it doesn't matter, there's no trace of a reaction anyway.

After a brief pause this idea occurred to me: "Perhaps you could summon my parents to your consulate? *Une convocation?* Simply a request to call on you. The commissioner would surely let them come to Marseille; he wouldn't ignore a letter from you."

"Madame, I don't know your parents at all, and I can have nothing to do with them. I'm afraid there's no purpose in further discussion of this matter."

So once again, nothing. Now I should stand up and take my leave. But I hesitated a moment and thought: This man can help me. I don't know anyone else I can turn to. And I became determined not to leave but to just sit there until he did help me. For where else could I go?

I wondered why he didn't stand up. He simply sat there at his desk, silently, motionless. I could think of nothing else to say, I'd said everything. So we sat there across from each other, wordlessly, for what seemed to be a long time. There was nothing to talk about, no more to say.

But then at last he spoke again. "Is your father a Jew?"

"Yes."

"Where do your parents come from?"

"From Vienna."

"What did your father do there?"

"He published a journal."

"What sort of journal?"

"A literary journal. Pacifist."

Again there was silence for a while. Then he said: "I can give you a *convocation* for your parents only if you swear to me that they will never appear here at the consulate. I must have your promise that the letter will be used solely for presentation to the commissioner of Mâcon."

I promised and I swore.

He went into another room and I heard a typewriter clatter. I saw some consular envelopes on his desk, and I let one disappear into my purse. One never knew, perhaps I'd need it.

I remember the wording of the letter he gave me not only because of its content but also because of its style:

"*Nous, Consul Général du Royaume de Suède, représentant le Deutsches Reich en France, convoquons M. et Mme. I. Ekstein à se présenter sans défaut au consulat* . . . (We, General Consul of the Kingdom of Sweden, Representing the German Reich in France, hereby convey to Mr. and Mrs. I. Ekstein a summons to appear forthwith in our consulate . . .)."

Consul Berglund had thought of everything; the letter was backdated a week, and he gave me the original and a copy, both bearing his signature and the consular stamp.

I was at the main post office ten minutes later; I put the copy in the consular envelope, addressed it to the *Commissaire Spécial de Police de la Ville de Mâcon*, and threw it in the mailbox.

"Monsieur Ekstein," said the commissioner, "I wanted to see you because I have received a summons for you and your wife from the Swedish consulate in Marseille. It seems that some matters there need to be attended to."

"That is true. It is with reference to an affair of great importance," said my father. His reflexes had always been astoundingly rapid.

"I wish you had informed me of that immediately."

"I hardly had an opportunity to do so."

"On no account do I want to delay you in complying with the summons," said the commissioner. He was polite now, almost charming. "But we have a problem here. In order to allow you and your wife to ride to Marseille, I must issue a *sauf-conduit*—a travel permit. As you know, for that you must have a *permis de séjour* for the place of destination."

"Well, that presents no problem," said my father without hesitation. "We've been issued a residence permit for the Municipality of Cassis-sur-Mer."

"Do you have that in writing?"

"It wasn't possible due to the irregular mail service between the two zones. Our children in Cassis have the permit. Please do get in contact with them."

The mayor of Cassis sat in his office conversing with a visitor. His secretary, Marie-Ange, was working at her desk in the next room. The telephone rang.

"This is the police commissioner of Mâcon speaking," said the voice at the other end. "I'd like to talk to the mayor."

After a second or two Marie-Ange said, "Unfortunately, *Monsieur le maire* is not here. He had to leave for a few days. Can I help you, perhaps?"

"That's hardly possible. It's about a couple named Ekstein who are here in Mâcon; they say that they have a residence permit for Cassis. I can't give them a *sauf-conduit*, however, without confirmation from your mayor."

"Monsieur and Madame Ekstein?" asked Marie-Ange haltingly. "Yes, now I remember. Just a moment . . . here, I've found it. *Monsieur le maire* gave me the *permis de séjour* before he left, in case it was required."

"That should do very well," said the voice from Mâcon. "On the strength of it I'll issue the *sauf-conduit* to them immediately. *Merci, Mademoiselle.*"

"*Il n'y pas de quoi, monsieur,*" answered Marie-Ange. "No thanks necessary, it was my pleasure."

That was in the morning. My mother and father arrived in Cassis on the evening train.

Five days remained for us to be together in Cassis. We had so much to relate, to discuss, to ask, to arrange. And what could be done for the other people being held in Mâcon? Two of them were also released through intervention by their families, but the rest were still being held. They had also heard the rumors about deportation to the east. Mother had the names and addresses of relatives of the women; they had to be contacted.

It was late, we had to sleep. But we hadn't heard yet about the train they'd been put aboard in Mâcon, and what happened when they were transported to the occupied zone. "Okay," Father said, "let me tell you about it quickly."

"There we all were in the train. We knew, of course, that we were being brought back to the occupied zone. We'd only gone a short distance when the train stopped again. I stood at the window and saw that the station was full of German uniforms. I slowly let the window down so I could hear. The commissioner got off and went over to someone in a black uniform—it must have been a high-ranking SS officer. The commissioner clicked his heels together; if he hadn't been wearing a French police uniform, I would have sworn he was a German Nazi. He spoke to the SS man in a mixture of French and German. He reported that he had arrested *vingt-deux juifs allemands*—twenty-two old Jews, he repeated in German—who had crossed the demarcation line illegally; he had brought them back to hand them over to the German authorities. He clicked his heels again.

"The Nazi officer stared at the Frenchman, and I heard him say: 'You're bringing us what? Twenty-two old Jews? The man is no doubt crazy! As if we didn't have enough Jews here already!' Then he roared, 'Away with you and your Jews, idiot!'

"The train ran back to Mâcon and we were locked up."

(Twenty years later I heard a radio report about the Eichmann trial in Jerusalem. It said that Eichmann had tried to show that he had even aided Jews occasionally. He stated, among other things, that once he had been offered a group of German Jews who had crossed the demarcation line illegally. He, Eichmann, had ordered the French officer to send the people back to the unoccupied zone. Reason: Germany wanted to be rid of Jews.)

After five days we took the bus to Marseille for the last time.

I looked back; my parents stood there waving to us and we waved in return. How often in the past eight years had we waved goodbye to each other?

We sat down, and I felt the strain of recent weeks draining away, leaving me limp. And I wondered: We're traveling to an island named Cuba. Father and Mother are free, although they can't come with us. I'm sitting here and nothing touches me. I have no fear, I'm not happy, nor am I sad. I feel nothing, nothing at all.

12

Travel Preparations

Autumn 1941

We still had to have our visa applications for the United States transferred to Cuba before our departure. Indeed, word had spread that in
the new place of residence a person seeking entry to the U.S.A. was
given preference in processing if there was a previous application on file.
But we weren't sure that the transfer of a previous application played a
role in the issuing of visas. Then, too, we really had no idea at all
whether we wanted to go to the States from Cuba. It would depend on
how we got along in Cuba, and how long the war lasted, and when we
could return to our homeland, and . . . and. . . . But just for the very
reasons that we couldn't plan, we wanted to leave nothing undone, no
avenue unexplored.

As I was in Marseille every day trying to arrange things for my
parents, I went to the American consulate too. By now there were no
long lines of people; the hopeful crowds had dwindled away.

I explained the reason for my visit and was admitted after a short wait.
The consular official already had our dossiers on the desk in front of him
and was leafing through them.

"You say it deals with an entry visa, an immigration visa?" I nodded.

"They've mistakenly brought me the wrong dossier," he said, and
stood up. "Excuse me a moment, I'll go and look myself."

His steps grew fainter. I leaned over the desk and opened the file
folder. A telegram lay on top. It read: ENTRY PERMISSION FITTKO
APPROVED FOREIGN OFFICE PANAMA.

I closed the folder and fell back in my chair. Had I read it right? I
stood up quickly and read the telegram again, carefully. There was no
mistake, the word was plain: APPROVED.

The official's steps approached, and I sat up straight and tried to look composed. He had another sheaf of papers under his arm. "Here are the documents with the applications for entry visas," he said. "We'll have them transferred to Havana." He looked at the dossier on the desk again. "These are requests for transit visas for emigration to Panama. No doubt you've decided in the meantime to change your plans. Have a nice trip."

So—we could have sailed for Panama in May! Now it was November and we were off to Cuba.

There were still several preliminaries to our journey that had to be seen to. We had already taken the precaution of obtaining statements from the Ministry of Justice that we were not criminals. Now we had to present exchange permits.

The exchange value of the French franc had meanwhile fallen so low that francs were practically valueless abroad. Atlantic ship passage and certain visas had to be paid for in dollars. The Pétain government allowed Jewish emigrants a one-time purchase of five hundred dollars per person at the official rate. One became accustomed to inconsistent actions; and basically this one was not so strange, as Darlan had recently let it be known that Vichy's aim was to allow—even encourage—Jews to emigrate.

Hans had to explain to me several times what this exchange permit was really all about. How could dollars be bought when there was no money to buy them with? That was just it, he said, it was the difference between the official and the black market rate; if one first bought dollars at the former rate and then sold them at the latter, which was of course forbidden, one had about six times the amount of francs as he'd paid for the dollars. I said it sounded pretty complicated to me.

There must have been other emigrants who didn't understand the rules of currency speculation, otherwise the business of the speculators wouldn't have gone so well. They had sprung up suddenly everywhere, everyone talked about them, but only a few knew what the money manipulators actually did. They applied for and procured the exchange permit, bought dollars, sold them again, and then handed over whatever money was left after subtracting their fee plus expenses. The speculators could be recognized by their highly elegant clothes, clothes they must have bought on the black market.

"You're entitled to the exchange permit," I pointed out. "You don't need a wire-puller at all." But some replied that it was all too complicated, and others objected that the permit wasn't issued to ordinary private persons: the application must be submitted by a *macher*. Cases were reported where a *macher* manipulated the circumstances in such a way that the "customer" ended up with almost nothing.

"No *macher* is going to pull a fast one on us," Hans decided brusquely. "We're going to handle it ourselves."

I looked at him. We? Hans the non-Jew, with his Berlin *accent boche*, wanted to parley with Vichy to obtain a permit intended solely for Jews?

He noticed my expression. "Women get by better here." He added, "You can do it."

Exchange permits were issued by the Banque de Change in Châtel-Guyon, close to Vichy. But first I had to have a *sauf-conduit* for the trip, which fell under the jurisdiction of the Marseille *préfecture*. However, the time was too short to wait for it, and one risked arrest by going there; so I went to the subprefecture in Aubagne. The service office was empty, the boss no doubt taking his afternoon nap. A tiny girl came crawling in. I sat down on the floor with her and we played with the doll she'd dragged in behind her. Our giggling woke her papa, and he came in, buttoning his uniform; he saw us and started to laugh too. "I've come," I said, "to pick up a *sauf-conduit*."

"You've come to the wrong place," he said. "Unfortunately I cannot help you; you must go to the *préfecture* in Marseille."

I looked very disconsolate. How could I have made such a mistake? I had to catch the train in two hours, now I wouldn't be able to manage it.

The child was crawling all over me and plucking at my hair. We all laughed, and the boss gave me the *sauf-conduit*, saying, "I really shouldn't do this, I'm just making an exception."

The train went only as far as Clermont-Ferrand; from there one had to take a bus. Among the passengers, in addition to local residents, were several easily recognizable emigrants. Some looked like the *machers* I'd seen in Marseille.

The bus rode through the dark landscape and no one spoke. In the middle of the night we halted at a little dump somewhere outside Châtel-Guyon. "End of the line, everybody out!" said the driver. There was a solitary building near the bus stop, a small inn; we eight or ten emigrants walked over.

The innkeeper came out and said that she didn't have rooms enough for all of us and we'd have to double up. As I started to go through the door with the others, a tall, chunky man shoved me to one side. It was G., the Hungarian journalist we knew from Paris, where he'd written for anti-Fascist newspapers. How is it possible? I thought. Now he's behaving just like a Fascist!

The innkeeper took me by the arm. "There's no more space in the rooms. Come with me—I'll push two tables together in the dining room, there you can at least stretch out."

I came to the square where the building housing the Banque de Change was located. I started to walk up the wide front staircase. No other person anywhere; I was entirely alone. My heels echoed on the marble steps. I looked up at the building and saw, at one of the windows, two gray-haired men in black suits staring down at me. Then other men appeared at other windows and also stared down. They all seemed to look alike. From way up there, I thought, I certainly must look small on these broad stairs.

A gray-haired man opened the door and looked at me curiously. He pushed a dusty chair over to me and had me fill out a form; he took it and vanished. Returning, he sent me to an office where another gray-haired man—or was it the same one?—received me.

"So you want an exchange permit," said the official. "Perhaps you are not aware that there are agents for such matters. How did you arrive at the idea of coming here all by yourself? We don't handle individual applications—everything is done through the agents."

I asked whether it wasn't allowed to apply for the license oneself. "It's not exactly forbidden," he replied. "Only there would be enormous confusion if all applicants came themselves. One needs an expert because of the complicated instructions," he added. "So, much as I'd like to help you. . . ."

"That's nice, that you'd like to help me," I said. "Could you please tell me how to go about submitting the application?"

"Well, first of all," he said, "it can be done only through a bank, for only banks have the authority to possess dollars." At which bank did we have an account?

The Crédit Lyonnais flashed through my mind; it was a large bank in Marseille.

"The Crédit Lyonnais," I said.

If I really wanted to try it, the gray-haired man said, I could call at the local branch of that bank; perhaps someone there would check by phone with Marseille and submit the application for me.

At the Crédit Lyonnais I was received by Monsieur Duval, a young man who acted surprised but seemed to be obliging. He couldn't promise, but he'd try——. "Perhaps if we sit down in a café," he said, "we can discuss the matter further."

Duval was new to this branch office. He was a Parisian and had wanted the transfer, he told me, on account of the change of air. As he spoke he threw me a searching glance, as if to ask, Do we understand each other? As I wasn't sure what he meant, I smiled understandingly and murmured, "*Ah, oui.*"

He wanted to know when I'd left Paris. "Before the occupation? You can't possibly imagine how changed everything is." He talked about life under an occupying power, about fear and anger, and of the growing resistance. Here in the unoccupied zone one was in another world.

"It's to be hoped that the south will remain unoccupied for a while," I said.

The young man shook his head. "On the other side we have an opposite point of view. I'm here for only a short time; I'll be returning in a couple of months. There are a few things here I must attend to." He contemplated me.

Would he explain to me what he meant by an opposite point of view? He surely wouldn't want the Germans to occupy all of France?

He fiddled around with his teaspoon for a moment. Then he looked at me again. "The sooner the better."

"Better—for whom? For what?"

"A divided France is also split internally," he said. "The people here try to adjust—life is still bearable. But when the south is occupied, when everyone here feels the terror too, when hostages are shot, that will unite France. Over there we're waiting for that day."

I examined Monsieur Duval more closely. Half an hour earlier I had thought I saw a nice, rather shy young man before me. Now I saw cold eyes set in a hard countenance.

"Doesn't the unoccupied zone have advantages?" I asked. "Wouldn't it be easier to organize resistance from this side?" I wondered at myself, at my abandoning all caution; instinctively I trusted this man.

"The people here aren't ready to sacrifice," he replied. "When one day the first boys are caught here and sent to Germany for labor service, that will change. But let's return to your affair. You have an account at our bank in Marseille?"

"Yes."

He studied me again. "Do you know *monsieur le directeur* Marius there?"

"Yes, a good old friend," I said without thinking. Well, why not? Every other man in Marseille is named Marius.

"That could make issuing your authorization easier. I can telephone *monsieur le directeur* from the office."

How could I talk my way out of this? I could just say it was a case of mistaken identity. Instead I said, "Good, let's go."

"One moment more," said Duval. "I'd like to ask you something. Perhaps you can help me, too, in a matter of great importance. You're a friend of my friend Marius—a reason for me to trust you implicitly."

Good God! I thought.

"It couldn't have happened better than this," he continued. "It concerns a message containing information—encrypted information for which he's waiting. On no account can I entrust it to the mail service. Would you——?"

"Gladly. I'm happy to be able to help you."

I don't know whether he actually telephoned. Anyway, our application was approved on the same day, and I rode back the next morning with a large envelope and one of Monsieur Duval's calling cards, on the back of which was written something about *notre chère amie, Mme. Fittko.*

Groups of emigrants were standing around in the large foyer of the Crédit Lyonnais in Marseille, waiting to change their francs to dollars. There were Machers, currency manipulators among them, recognizable by their attire. "We've been coming here for days," one man told us, "and every time the bank runs out of dollars." Most of those waiting were people the Jewish committee HICEM was helping to depart. At least there were still people who could leave France.

The official rate was thirty-two francs to the dollar. That morning the Centre had lent us thirty-two thousand francs, with which we could buy a thousand dollars. We wanted to make the exchange at once, so that we could return the borrowed money as soon as possible. Then I would call on Director Marius and hand the envelope over to him. We waited. Intermittently someone's name was called. After several hours the feared announcement came: "The dollar reserve has run out for today. Come back early tomorrow morning." The emigrants crowded around the announcer, begging him to make an exception; they would miss their ships. He merely shrugged his shoulders.

I said to Hans, "Wait here for me, I have to deliver this envelope before they close. And perhaps *monsieur le directeur* has a few dollars hidden away somewhere, who knows?"

"Take care when you talk to him," said Hans. "How did it ever occur to you to pass yourself off as one of his friends?"

"I just had to answer 'yes' when asked—I didn't stop to think about it."

I walked over to a uniformed official; he turned away when he saw me coming. His back seemed to say, don't come to me, I can't help you. I walked up close to him and said loudly, so that he couldn't help but hear, "Please take me to *monsieur le directeur Marius*."

He turned his head and looked me up and down. I thought, I can be just as arrogant as you can, Buster. "*Monsieur le directeur* is expecting me," I said. "Present this card to him."

It was a joy to see the man's consternation. He hesitated for a moment and then disappeared. He returned with hasty steps a half-minute later, bowed, and begged me to follow him; *monsieur le directeur* wished to see me. Indeed, my heart pounded a bit. What would I do if he called me to account?

The door of the sumptuous office opened. Monsieur Marius came toward me with arms outstretched.

"I have just telephoned Monsieur Duval—he has told me about you. How happy it makes me to become acquainted with you! Monsieur Duval's friends are also my friends."

I hope he doesn't notice my confusion, I thought, and said, "The happiness is all on my side, and of course Monsieur Duval's friends are also mine." Then I handed him the big envelope.

He said something about the inestimable service I had rendered France and asked whether there was anything on earth that he could do for me. I mentioned the dollar trouble, and that because of it we might miss our boat. He made a few telephone calls, then said that the bank really didn't have a single dollar left but that an armored car was leaving immediately for the *fort* to fetch the thousand dollars for us—we would be able to make the exchange within half an hour.

Thus we got our thousand dollars on the very same day.

I said to Hans, "I'm honestly embarrassed; we always grouse about how the emigrants push past people, and now we're doing exactly the same thing."

"We haven't taken anything from anyone," he reassured me, "nor have we cheated anybody."

On the black market the dollar was worth some hundred and eighty francs. We went to old Claude, who Hans thought was the least unscrupulous of the manipulators, and sold him half of our dollars. For the first time I actually began to believe in this currency wizardry, now that I'd seen a transaction with my own eyes. Yesterday we had had nothing—today Hans had stashed five hundred dollars for Border Control in his wallet and we'd gotten ninety thousand francs for the other five hundred. We gave the thirty-two thousand francs we'd borrowed back to the Centre and gave my parents forty thousand francs to help them through the period before their departure. The rest we distributed among several friends. There would certainly be trouble at the border when we could show only half of the dollars we'd exchanged, but we'd talk our way out of it somehow.

Friends gave us two old suitcases for the trip. Packing went fast, but there were still many matters to take care of in these final days. Hans acquired a notebook, a tiny one that could easily be destroyed, and entered in shorthand the things we could do in Cuba for our friends still here. They came and we sat together and talked until late into the night, and they were glad that, again, some of us would succeed in escaping. I wondered at myself, for I felt no common gladness with them; it was as if all of this had nothing to do with me. What had happened to me? Finally, at long last, we were escaping from the trap, taking a sea voyage to an island named Cuba—and it was all the same to me. As if I were hollow inside. Pumped dry.

We picked up our exit visas. In line with new regulations, applications were no longer made through the Vichy government; permits were issued directly by the responsible prefecture. Now we, who had smuggled people over the mountains a whole winter long, could cross the border with a genuine *visa de sortie*.

With that our travel preparations were complete. There was still one item, however—a decision we had to make. And it wouldn't be an easy one.

Since we'd gotten the Cuban visas, we had been approached by various people who wanted us to carry certain materials through Spain to Portugal. Not much was said about this "hot" stuff, but it was evident from the places in Lisbon where the things were to be delivered that it had something to do with the British. It was also intimated that people who helped with this work could, if necessary, count on reciprocal help. Hans said no. Links with espionage were out of the question; our work lay elsewhere.

They didn't give up. It was a case of assisting the Allies against the Nazis, and the type of assistance shouldn't make any difference to us.

Hans was unwavering. We were not the right people for this type of work, it wasn't within our competence. He repeated to me what he'd often said before: "Once you make first contact with them, you're sitting in a trap, they have you in the palm of their hand. You slither easily into something, and suddenly you pull a blooper and find yourself on the wrong track. Right now spying is aimed at enemies, but next time . . . ? Better to stay away from it altogether."

Leoni the Greek, whom we'd known for a long time, also approached us. We'd heard rumors that he had connections with the English. "I can speak openly to you," he said. "It has to do with information that must be transmitted to the Allies—urgent information. You take the stuff with you and in Lisbon make connections with——."

"No," said Hans. "You'll have to find somebody else."

"Leoni," I said, "it's a mystery to me how someone like you can switch polarities this way. You're a political opponent of the Nazis— don't you see the difference between resistance efforts and working for an intelligence service?"

"Just because we're politicals we cannot stand aside. In battling the Nazis any and every path is the right one."

"It's not our path."

Leoni came back the next day. "I have to talk to you about something else, about the leadership of the Spanish Republicans who are in hiding in France. Perhaps they can be helped to get out—lists of names and other data must be taken to Lisbon."

"And we should travel through Spain with them?" I asked.

They had experts, said Leoni, who wrote the encoded lists on tissue-thin paper which was then rolled up tightly, put into capsules, and inserted in toothpaste or skin-cream tubes. In Lisbon we would not come in contact with the English at all, only make delivery to Spanish connections.

That sounded mysterious. Who would help to bring these people out? The English?—why should they suddenly concern themselves with Spanish Republicans?

"It has nothing to do with political sympathies," declared Leoni, "but rather with expediency. Sometimes mutual interests play a part. These Spaniards in France have connections with frontier guides. The English want their help in establishing an escape route for their downed fliers; on their part, they've promised to help these persons, who of course cannot travel through Spain, to get out some other way. Here in France they would be goners if they were spotted—the Pétain government would turn them over to Franco." He paused. "Won't you think it over? Will you risk it, taking the lists through Spain?"

Hans looked at me. "Give us the tubes," he said.

"Not too much toothpaste," said I. "That would atract attention; take some shaving cream too."

I woke up when the train stopped and saw the little border post and the mountains surrounding us. "You were asleep all the way," Hans said. "I wish I could relax. I'm too nervous."

I laughed. "Now when everything is legal, when we're traveling with genuine papers, with valid overseas visas and the whole shebang, now of all times, when we're practically standing with one foot in Spain, you're nervous."

Spain—the tubes came to mind again, the quantities of toothpaste and shaving cream we'd strewn around under other things in our two bags. I also had a tube of beauty cream in my purse.

Several emigrants were already standing at a long table in the bare room, being processed by border-control officials behind the table.

Through the open door across the room one saw a railway platform. On the tracks stood a train with a panel on its side: ZARAGOSA. Spain was there outside—Franco Spain—and that was our train.

Hans took our papers and the American dollars out of the briefcase. Now it hit me again that we had only five hundred dollars of the thousand needed to exit, the thousand entered on our travel papers. How could I have forgotten that?—I'd relaxed much too soon.

French and Spanish customs officers stood behind the table. A French one was rummaging around in our suitcases. Now I was nervous, too—those cursed tubes! Many too many! Five toothpastes, three shaving creams. They were sure to be noticed.

But customs appeared to be looking for other things; the officer's hands emerged from the disarray of our clothing and linen. In each one he held—a pack of cigarettes. Wordlessly, he let them vanish under the table. They were the packs we'd bought for the trip at unbelievable prices from colonial soldiers in Cassis. A great loss. But the tubes were safe for now.

The open bags were pushed over to the Spanish customs men. The burrowing started again. The Spaniard fished out my perfume bottle—Chanel No. 5, a good-bye gift from a dear friend. Under the table it went. Then he took the chunk of bread Edmund had managed to get for us, because there was no bread in Spain. We stuffed the rest, including tubes, back into the bags.

"Empty your purse!"

My temperature rose. Maybe the Spaniard, the perfume-lover, was going to take the tube of skin cream for his wife. She would surely discover the list—I began to perspire. Now he was holding the cream in his hand; he considered it, then put it down on the table in front of him. His other hand held *my* cigarettes; they disappeared under the table lightning-fast.

I had to divert him. "Keep the cigarettes, but give me back my case!" I cried, and held out my hand; while doing so, as if by chance, I pushed the tube of cream closer to my purse. "My beautiful leather case—my husband gave it to me for my brithday." I started to sob softly.

"You must be mistaken, *señora*, I saw no case," said the man, and looked past me. "Move on!" He shoved the purse over to me with all its emptied contents. With my forearm I swept them all together and into the purse. The tube was there.

Meanwhile Hans was at the French passport control window, and I
overheard him with one ear. The official said, "That's five hundred
dollars. Where is the other five hundred? Your papers say that you
obtained a thousand dollars for export. What did you do with half of the
money?"

"I can explain it to you. We had expenses for the trip——."

"That's unlawful!" the official yelled at him. "I'll have you arrested!
What did you do with it? Probably sold it. Or gave it away. To whom?
To whom did you give the money?" He leafed through the travel docu-
ments. "Here it is: 'Nationalité: provenant d'Allemagne.' You're a
German—no doubt you gave the five hundred dollars to your friend,
Herr Hitler?"

Hans turned red. I grabbed my purse and ran over. "That's indeed
absurd!" I interrupted the official's tirade: "Can't you see what's
stamped there? 'Réfugié provenant d'Allemagne'—réfugié—do you understand?"

"Herr Hitler?" said Hans slowly. "Monsieur Hitler? Who is Herr
Hitler's friend?" The official goggled at him. "I'll tell you who's a friend
of Hitler!"

I took his arm. "Be careful what you say," I whispered.

Hans spoke louder, "Who spent seven years courting Hitler's friendship? While we fought against the murder-gang, who drew up——" I
grasped his arm. He shook me off.

"Ça va, ça va," said the dumbfounded official, patting Hans on the
shoulder.

"——contracts with the murderers? La France glorieuse!"

He's never spoken French so fluently before, I thought.

"And now, now again you stand obediently at Herr Hitler's beck and
call——"

People were standing around us: both French and Spanish customs
officials, railroad men, travelers. They tried to pacify Hans: "Ça va, ça
va!"

"——and we have to keep on fleeing. Do you want to hear why? Do
you want to know who gives Monsieur Hitler presents?"

The Frenchman extended a hand to him holding our documents. I
quickly grabbed them. "Vous êtes en règle," he said to Hans. "Your
papers are in order!"

But Hans didn't hear him. He'd started a counteroffensive to save the situation, and now the floodgates were open, the torrent unstoppable.

"It's France who gives presents to Hitler. The gifts are refugees like us who have to keep on the run. Otherwise *la France généreuse* will turn us over to the wild beasts."

"You can go through," cried the French official agitatedly, waving his arms and pointing to the portal to the Spanish train, "go, *tout va bien!*"

"Your Marshal Pétain has sold us——."

"Come along!" I yelled, and shook his arm again, as I sometimes did to wake him from a nightmare. Here we stood with one foot—almost—outside. Here was the experienced resistance fighter, trained to keep silent, a man who hadn't known release from tension for years. Right here, right now, the bottled-up words had to come out.

A piercing whistle came from the Spanish train. The locomotive emitted a hellish clatter. Hans tried to drown out the uproar, but I could hardly hear him.

"——yes, I'm a *boche*, but one of those who fights against the Nazis—do you understand that?"

"The train is leaving!" someone cried. The engineer jumped down from his locomotive, grabbed Hans by one arm and pulled him, Spanish customs pulled his other arm, the French official kept clapping him on the shoulder, which also helped a bit to push him forward. Another step—Hans was actually standing with one foot on Spanish soil. He yelled back, "A pair of buddies, *c'est le führer et votre maréchal!*"

We climbed aboard and the train chugged through the rugged landscape. We were in Franco Spain.

Children begged for bread at every station. We had none for them, as the customs official had stolen ours. There was a broken windowpane in the compartment and the door wouldn't close. I squeezed myself into a corner. Hans threw his light coat over me, but it didn't help much, and I complained off and on, "I've never frozen like this before."

A little later I said to Hans, "We're on ground where so much blood has flowed for freedom."

13

The Next Forty Years

(From Various Notes)

Spain

Three uneasy days. The toothpaste and shaving-cream tubes with the lists in them seem to weigh a ton here. Even so, in Madrid we went to the Prado for a couple of hours.

In our *pension* there is a group of Jewish youths who come directly from Berlin. We wanted to talk with them to hear how things are going there. They were excited and a bit confused, and they told us of a rumor: Jews were put aboard a train, ostensibly for resettlement in Poland, but then gas was pumped into the cars. Afterward I said to Hans, "Did you hear that? Terrible, how the Nazis frighten the Jews—these youngsters seemed really to believe that such a thing is possible."

Portuguese Border

Our compartment is full of emigrants. The train stops, we are at the border, now we're actually in Portugal. Representatives of the Jewish refugee committee HICEM stand on the platform and wait for us. Someone is waiting for us! Someone is concerned about us.

We get off and stand on neutral ground. A fellow passenger says to me, "There's a piece of real soap in the toilet." I walk faster, and then I feel the smooth soap in my hands, and let it glide back and forth, over my face and arms, too. I feel the foam between my fingers—how good it is! Soft, white soap—not a gray sticky, gravelly mass that abrades your skin.

Lisbon

Maurice and his wife picked us up at the railway station and dragged us straight to the Swiss bakery; I ate chocolate cake with whipped cream and I'm still sick.

The tubes and their lists delivered without a hitch, to a Spaniard in a private residence.

We meet acquaintances, among them Spanish fighters, who are waiting for ships to Mexico. Our ship has left without us, no more empty berths. The committee promises to put us aboard the next one. Paul Westheim is still here, he too is waiting for a berth to Mexico. Meanwhile we ramble through the city with him and he shows us the secret wonders of Lisbon, the nooks and crannies, and little churches and old buildings, and mosaics usually invisible to visitors.

Berthold Jacob, Berthold Jacob once again! He was abducted by gestapo agents from the office entrance of the Unitarians, right here in neutral Portugal. Just like back in 1936, when we were together in Basel and he was kidnapped out of neutral Switzerland. The Nazis will never let him escape another time.

Aboard the SS Colonial

A little ship, doesn't even look like an ocean steamer. It allegedly once belonged to Kaiser Wilhelm. Incredibly crowded. We're still in the bay, but the throwing-up is starting already.

So many people one can hardly move. Among them many old people and small children. Most of them are Jewish, only a few "Aryans" in between. We sleep way below decks in a dark, enormous room without hatches, normally used to stow baggage. Men on one side of the ship, women and children on the other. Almost all are seasick; we others are nauseated by the stench.

When I wake up I see a fat rat running back and forth on the girder directly above my head. The blond Russian next to me reaches for my hand and presses it, whispering, "Don't move, *ne bougez pas.*"

Many emigrants in first and second class don't want to let us third-class passengers on "their" deck or in the salons, as they paid more for passage. Hans made a sort of bed out of a second-class sofa for an elderly lady with a *scheitel*—the wig that Orthodox Jewish women wear. A passenger—he said he was the chairman of the Jewish Committee in a southern German city—came racing up in a fury. "That's *my* berth!" he yelled at the woman. "Get off, or I'll throw you off!" He started to tug at her arm, and she opened her mouth wide in fright and began to weep softly. Her youngest son, about ten years old, stood next to her saying,

"Mammele mammele———." Hans went over and held the man's hand fast. "There'll be no throwing off here, my friend," he said. "If I catch you once more———." The chairman tore loose and ran away. At the door he turned around and shouted at Hans, "You eastern Jews, I know you!"

A group of young people have ganged up together and, under the leadership of Aga Khan, as they call fat Hansel Kohn, pass the time playing silly practical jokes. They often make me laugh, but sometimes I get mad when they confuse the already intimidated people even more with their ridiculous *bobards*. A loud whisper, "The Captain says the danger is temporarily over," generates panic. Yesterday they passed the word, "We all have to change to another boat at midnight." A few people actually started dragging their luggage up the steep ladders.

Several of the worst smart-asses came, one after the other, and wanted to speak to us in confidence.

It must have gotten around that Hans and I know all about documents. One senses their fear as they show us their visas. "Does it look genuine enough? Can I get by in Cuba with it?" They're very good forgeries, quite skillfully made, and with a little luck all will be well.

That's the reason for all those stupid pranks. They're just trying to drive away their own anxiety.

We conversed with Frau Levy, who often comes to sit with us. Herr Levy is a wholesale merchant from Bremen—they came straight from there. His business was, of course, taken away from him. Their children are all married and in America. "For years they've been pressuring us to come," she tells us.

"Why did you wait until now?"

"My husband always said, 'Nothing will happen to him who does no wrong.'"

For ten days we've been floating on the Atlantic Ocean. A woman has died. The old Orthodox Jew Hans has become friendly with asks him whether he will sit *shiva*. "But I'm a Goy!" says Hans. "*Macht nischt*, you're a good Goy," says the old man, and pulls Hans along with him.

I've been sleeping on deck since it's gotten warmer.

On the fourteenth day a cry awakens us: "The coast! Cuba!"

Havana on the blue-green sea. The morning sun pours bright gold on the white buildings; brown children on the pier beg for pennies and dive into the water to fish them out. People stand on the quay and peer at the SS *Colonial*, looking for relatives. Many laugh and wave, throw their straw hats into the air, and shout things to their folks on board, although in this hubbub they can hardly be heard. I also see people weeping; how often have they come here to the harbor in vain?

After many hours of waiting in the now incandescent sun, we're all debarked, conveyed, and locked up in Camp Tiscornia.

Cuba (From the first pages of the Cuban diary)

Friends who have gotten here before us connect with us in the camp and give us some orientation. The president is named Fulgencio Batista; he's a bandit. The government, the entire country, is corrupt. You can't even get a death certificate without a bribe.

There are hundreds of emigrants in Camp Tiscornia. A second ship arrives—perhaps the last?—into the camp with all the passengers. They're trying extortion; we should pay them more money. As we don't have any, they let us out after about ten days. Over time, most of the others are also released—the genuineness of their visas doesn't play a great part, bribery is more important.

We're lodged in Máximo's Hotel, a curious big building of three stories; the interior is like a penitentiary, with open walkways around and around, and innumerable doors to the rooms. Tiny, graying Máximo is one of the many Jews who immigrated here from Poland many years ago. His hotel houses hundreds of emigrants at inexpensive rates. Hans talks with him often. It's the end of November 1941.

Early December. Japan bombs Pearl Harbor. America enters the war. Finally! Cuba sides with the United States.

My parents. Now they're stuck in France, they and all the others. Connections are broken off.

In Cuba non-Jewish Germans are declared to be enemy aliens and are arrested. A German has been caught who was allegedly carrying on radio espionage from a small boat off the coast. No further details are given in newspaper reports, but as a precautionary measure he was beheaded, and the hunt for enemy aliens goes into full swing.

Police come to the hotel. Máximo, who's on a good footing with the cops, swears that Hans Fittko is a Jew; what's in his papers is false. "I know who's a Yid, *claro que sí es hebreo*," he says in his Yiddish-Cuban jargon, and presses something into the policeman's hand. Hans is released.

With the help of the Emerescue committee in New York, and because of the solidarity among us politicals, numbers of other "Aryan" political refugees are protected from internment. But not all. Those arrested, together with Nazis living in Cuba, are taken to the Isla de Pinos and imprisoned on the island. The Cuban authorities turn camp administration over to the Nazis.

The year 1941 is coming to an end. On Christmas it's 32°C (89.6°F) in the shade.

1942 (From the Cuban diary)

". . . announced the extermination of all European Jews," the newspapers write, the radio says.

Extermination? No, that can't be true.

Certainly the Nazis are capable of every crime. But this monstrosity is inconceivable—no.

I know that the pictures I paint to myself are only feverish fantasies. The black uniforms with the death's-heads exterminating millions of humans, just as I exterminate the *cucarachas*, the cockroaches in our kitchen. I spray insecticide on them and watch how they writhe grotesquely and then collapse—oh, this is insane, I must think of something else. But I can't. I have to pull myself together; I try, but it doesn't work.

The Jewish organizations have called for a protest demonstration. A procession of thousands whose families are to be exterminated streams through the broad, sunny *avenidas* of Havana.

Who is listening to us?

1943 (From the diary)

Since Hans has been working on his book he doesn't seem to notice the activity around us. Friends come and go, Cubans and Germans; our little room is always full. There are heated debates, but now without

him. He sits at the table in the corner with his back to us and writes,
filling one notebook after another, as if he were in a soundproof room.
In the evening he hands me the manuscript and says, "If there's anything
in there you don't like, change it."

From the manuscript:

> ... for one day the Nazis will be repaid a thousandfold. Not by their own
> methods. We will never sink low enough to torture others. But the guilty
> ones must be destroyed root and branch. If the opportunity is missed
> once again, then everything will have been for naught.
>
> Was it humane in 1918 to go easy on the German Reaction—the
> warmongers, the leaders of the right-wing terror units, the "Free Corps"?
> Today they are exterminating entire nations.
>
> The Nazi murderers must be convicted by Germany itself. They are
> known in every town, in every city . . . the best of the German people, the
> Resistance fighters, must sit as judges.

In matters of birth and death the Red Cross mediates to arrange telegrams to and replies from occupied Europe. In November of 1943 my
brother could wire our parents about the birth of a daughter. An answer
finally came in February of 1944:

CASSIS, FRANCE

CONGRATULATIONS ON THE BIRTH OF LILI STOP
OUR IMMINENT DEPORTATION PROBABLE

FATHER MOTHER

Can no one in the world do anything? Father is now well over
seventy-four, and mother is sixty-eight.

Summer 1944 (From the diary)

The new government here has offered us Cuban citizenship. With it
we'd have regular passports! How long have we been stateless now?
Eleven years. Hans has said it so often: "If one only had a passport."

Now it's possible at last, and now he suddenly says, "No, it won't
work." That I fail to understand.

"Maybe you want to believe that you'll finally be able to see your
family again?" he asks me.

"And you? The war's coming to an end and you want to go back.
That would be easier and faster with a passport."

"Return, naturally, but not as a Cuban," says Hans.

"A passport is merely a piece of paper which makes life easier," I say. "It hasn't anything to do with the fact that you're now, as ever, a German anti-Fascist."

"It's a piece of paper which gives me protection that the German people don't have. In the future development of Germany we anti-Fascists can play a part only as Germans among Germans. Not with the passport of one of the victorious powers."

September 1944 (Diary)

News leaks out slowly about family members in Europe. Dispatched—deported—last report from a transport—missing. Acquaintances from Hungary and Yugoslavia learn that *all* Jews in their homeland were deported, therefore their families too. Very seldom does one hear that someone survived: "My daughter came through!" "My uncle is still in Theresienstadt."

End of September 1944

We've been sent a small notice that appeared under *Gesucht wird* in a Jewish-American newspaper: COUPLE I. EKSTEIN SEEKS CHILDREN IN USA AND CUBA.

Our parents are alive! They've survived the German occupation in Cassis. (As we learn later, the gendarmes, the town administration, and the *résistance* of Cassis had protected several hundred refugees from deportation.) They were not gassed.

1945

First contact with the Fittko family in Berlin—excerpt of a letter to Hans from his sister Marta.

". . . if only Mother had still been alive. A day before she died we showed her a photo of you that we'd hidden. 'Yes, yes, that's him, my Hans,' she said, and added, 'he was always a good boy, and he still is.'

"We haven't had it easy either. The children weren't allowed on the Buddelplatz, the playground, because their uncle was a 'criminal.' In mid-June 1940 the gestapo picked me up again. Right off: 'Where is your brother?' I answered, 'You already know we haven't heard a word

from him since 1933.' One of the bullies shouted, 'He was in Paris, the
devil! but he got away from us again!' I stood up and said, 'Gentlemen, I
thank you from the bottom of my heart. Now I know that my brother is
still alive.' Then they let me go."

From a letter from my brother in Kansas City:

". . . at last a response from our parents. They're waiting for our
return . . . it should be possible soon.

"*A bientôt, au revoir à Paris.*"

End of 1945 (From a letter from Franz Pfemfert in Mexico):

"Your last letter especially delighted us. Mainly because your intention to return to the land of the mass murderers has not yet been realized. . . ."

Hans Fittko to Franz Pfemfert: "Any talk about returning is pointless,
as the American State Department will not issue transit visas to us political refugees, and from here no other travel possibilities exist."

In the evening there's always a light ocean breeze on the terrace of the
Café Aire Libre at the corner of the boulevard, and there we cool
ourselves off after the heat of the day and before the muggy night. Hans
has learned diamond-cutting, as have many emigrants, and I've found a
job in an office. Thus life has become a little easier for us, and in the
evenings we can afford a Cuba Libre or a sherbet. It's the same with
these tropical fruits as with everything else here; in the beginning the
taste is strange, not like fruit at all—why can't they taste like strawber-
ries, or cherries? But comes a day when we notice that mangoes and
fruta bombas are part of our daily lives; we can't imagine how we ever
got along without them, and I can't even manage to recall the taste of
plums or pears. And it's the same, as I say, with all else. In the beginning
it is difficult to comprehend the people—not only do we hardly understand the language (the fourth one since we emigrated) but *how* they
mean what they say. Indeed, like everyone else, we now say *mañana*
when we mean "maybe soon."

We were sitting one evening with friends in the Aire Libre. Herr
Gruber, who has a business in the city, came and wanted to talk to Hans
about something. We moved to another table with him.

"I had a strange visitor today," he said, "and I'd like to get your advice, because there's something very fishy about his story. In this case I don't know my way around, and I'm not sure what's behind it all. I thought, you have experience. . . .

"So—early today, just after I opened the store, a man came in and asked for Herr Gruber. In German. He looked exhausted, as if he hadn't slept for a long time. His suit was filthy, and everything about him seemed to be in disorder. He wore European clothes like you don't see here; I noticed that immediately.

"He said he'd just arrived in Cuba; he didn't explain how, and I asked no questions, for I didn't want to get involved in a matter that doesn't concern me. The man—he calls himself Herr Schuster—knows no one here. He explained that he saw the name Gruber on my sign and came in in order to speak with a countryman; he needs help, and so he turned to the first German name he saw.

"He's run out of money and urgently needs to borrow some. Right away I said that unfortunately I couldn't help him. But the affair didn't end there. He pulled a little bag out of an inside pocket of his coat, took things out of it, and laid them on the table in front of me. They were diamonds. Of course I haven't a clue as to whether or not they're genuine–I thought first of you. Anyway, Herr Schuster wants to hock or sell the diamonds, and I should find someone to help him do so. He can't simply go to a pawnshop, he says, because he has to be careful. I think he's landed here without any papers—he behaves like a hunted man. There must be Germans here, he thinks, who will help him with the diamonds, and anyhow, only Germans would have understanding for his predicament.

"As I said, it all seems weird to me. What do you think, Herr Fittko? The man is coming back tomorrow. Shall I throw him out? Or call the police? Or . . . will you talk with him?"

Hans thought it over. "The fellow interests me," he said. "I'd like to have a look at him." He would meet with him the next evening, under another name naturally, in an out-of-the-way café where he wouldn't immediately run into acquaintances. "I'll go alone," he said to me. "The fewer people he gets to know, the better."

Hans took a streetcar to the suburb Marianao, and Gruber and I waited for him at the Aire Libre. It was after midnight when he returned.

"One could recognize him without a description, this German," said Hans, "sitting there stiff and alone at a table, a dark suit among all the white, beige, and pink linen shirts, the *guayaberas*. Unmoving, except for his eyes flitting back and forth. He flinched slightly when I stepped up to his table. I spoke to him in German and his rigid face relaxed. He said, 'Ah, a Berliner!' and suddenly the rest of him relaxed from head to toe. To my surprise he was immediately trusting, and became even more so.

"Herr Schuster started telling about the end of the war: fear of the Russians, preparing for the flight, the diamonds—exhaustively, with all the details. He said, 'It all went well that far, I got to the Balearic islands with my family. But then the trouble started. We naturally couldn't stay there indefinitely. The big wheels were all speedily transported farther, but they didn't give a shit for people like us—you can't picture our predicament, how everyone tried to trip up the others, these national comrades, these heroes. . . .' He asked me whether I could imagine his terrible situation, always on the run and in constant danger, and I said, 'Yes, I can well imagine it.' Then he went on with the recital, how in desperation he had made his way alone to Spain; in Cadiz he stowed away on a freighter. Now he had to travel through the States, for that was the only way out of Cuba. I asked, 'Isn't that rather precarious? Couldn't things easily go wrong in America?' The man hesitated for the first time, and stuttered something about 'connections . . . I mean friends in the U.S.A. with whom I can stay . . . they'll help me to go on.' Then he added, 'When at last I reach my destination I can arrange to bring my family there.' I asked, 'There? Where?' and he said, 'Well, you know—somewhere in South America.' But first it's urgent that he get hold of some money. With that, and with trembling fingers, he pushed a little gray bag across the table to me. I took out my loupe and examined the diamonds. They're genuine, very good stones, slightly blue, as well as I could see in that light. The man said: 'I have still more, larger ones too. Whatever you can get for them.'

"I promised to look around for a buyer. He'll be waiting for me at nine o'clock tomorrow evening in the same café."

Gruber needed a moment to take it all in. "So, he's a boss Nazi," he said at last, and gasped for breath. "Indeed, I had such a strange feeling right away. What do we do now?"

"He's not one of the better-known Nazis, this man who calls himself Schuster," said Hans, "but he must have been in some leading position, otherwise they wouldn't have shipped him off to the Baleares with the others."

"Now the authorities must be informed immediately," Gruber said. "Is that the purpose of the rendezvous tomorrow evening?"

"Yes, that's the purpose," Hans replied. "But I'm not so sure how it will turn out. Sure, I'd like to pass along everything I've gotten out of the bastard. But to whom? The Cuban police? Ridiculous!—corrupt as they are, the Nazi would easily buy himself out with his diamonds. The Americans? They don't trust us emigrants at the embassy; the military authorities even less. The Secret Service? They don't have anything more important to do than infiltrate the emigrant clubs with informers."

"But one can't just simply let him go!" cried Gruber excitedly, constantly fiddling with his eyeglasses.

"That's so. But I myself can do nothing more," said Hans. "From now on I have to keep out of it."

"But why?" Gruber wanted to know. "How come?"

"I'm a German, a non-Jew, a political emigrant, a refugee actually. If I were to become involved in any business with a Nazi boss who's landed here illegally—diamond smuggling, all highly suspicious. No, I can't afford that."

To Gruber, Hans's misgivings seemed overcautious—now that he himself was a Cuban citizen. The next morning he went to the Interior Ministry, reported the case, and told where the man could be found that evening. A few hours later Gruber was arrested at his place of business. He was cross-examined for several days, then freed, then interrogated once again. He was told that "Herr Schuster" had meanwhile disappeared.

From an article by Hans in a German-language emigrant newspaper (published by Fritz Lamm and Hans Fittko):

> Many of our friends here ask us, "How can you possibly want to return to Germany? After all that they've done to us?"
>
> What they—the Nazis—have done to us obliges us to return. During all the years of exile we have waited for this moment. Together with the Resistance fighters we must expunge the roots of fascism and punish the guilty ones.

The Allies have conquered Germany. But only we can free Germany
from fascism.

Marlene asks: "Then you wanted to return to Europe? You had no
intention at all of coming to the U.S.A.?"

Marlene, my youngest niece, has many questions. She's now studying
the history of the Nazi period; she's looking for answers that she hasn't
found in books. She wants to hear from me: Were you there when they
became jubilant over Hitler? The Resistance you speak of, what did it
do? Why doesn't anyone know about that? If Grandfather dropped
everything and left right at the very beginning, why did most of the
others remain? What did you live on during the emigration? How did
they treat you—the Czechs, the Swiss, the Dutch, the French? How was
it—the persecution, the exile, the camp—*Tell me what it felt like.*

We're sitting in the living room and looking out over Lake Michigan
with its invisible far shore, and I think: How long has it been? I've lived
here in Chicago's Hyde Park for more than thirty years. Marlene turns
her head toward me, and in her eyes I see many impatient questions. She
has my frizzy hair.

No, I say, during the war it never occurred to us at all to immigrate
here. We had fled only in order to survive the Nazi period and then
return home again.

Then how does the story continue?

It was already two years after the end of the war. The political
emigrants still sat in Cuba hoping for an opportunity to sail to Europe.
They waited and debated: about the atom bomb and Hiroshima; about
the future of Germany, now divided; about the politics of the Allies in
Europe and the new roles of the old political parties. Over there,
Western Europe was being "de-Nazified." An international tribunal sat
in judgment in Nuremberg; after a ten-month trial, sentence was
pronounced and ten Nazi leaders were hanged to appease the world's
conscience. But the court did not sit in judgment on fascism.

"I don't understand you," said Marlene, surprised. "Wasn't the
Nuremberg War Crimes Trial a lesson for the Germans?"

"What should the Germans learn from it? They learned that the victorious can hang the defeated. How one frees a country from the spirit of

fascism, how one creates peace and freedom and democracy in one's own land, those things they couldn't learn."

"But you and Hans, when did you decide to come here?"

Hans asked himself back then: Is there still a place for me over there in occupied Germany? Is there still a homeland to whose future the years of exile give meaning? Hasn't Germany passed up the opportunity once again?

Because of his sudden illness we never reached an ultimate decision. In Cuba a diagnosis couldn't even be made; they attributed his condition to the years of persecution, living conditions, climate. We came to the United States to get competent treatment, but in his case medical science could not help.

"Can it happen again?" asks Marlene.

"The same as before? Hardly. Although the breeding grounds of fascism have neither temporal nor geographical borders."

She questions further, "You don't consider the Nazi episode to be typically German?"

Inhumanity is typical of fascism, not characteristic of a nation, I try to explain. Only the structures change. One would so like to believe that the character of the German people was responsible. For then one could also believe that it could never happen here. Those who so believe have not learned anything.

"And you," asks Marlene. "Where is your homeland now?"

Now—now my home is here. Although the dream of peace and freedom lives everywhere.